THE FUTURE OF THE
Southern Plains

THE FUTURE OF THE
Southern Plains

Edited by Sherry L. Smith

Published by the University of Oklahoma Press, Norman,
in Cooperation with the William P. Clements Center for
Southwest Studies, Southern Methodist University

ALSO BY SHERRY L. SMITH

Sagebrush Soldier: Private William Earl Smith's View of the Sioux War of 1876
(Norman, 1989)
The View from Officers' Row: Army Perceptions of Western Indians (Tucson, 1990)
Reimagining Indians: Native Americans through Anglo Eyes, 1880–1940 (New
York, 2000)

LIBRARY OF CONGRESS CATALOGING-IN-PUBLICATION DATA

The future of the Southern Plains / edited by Sherry L. Smith.
    p. cm.
    Papers based on a joint William P. Clements Center for Southwest
Studies and Dept. of History Sharpe Symposium held at Southern
Methodist University, Dallas, Tex., in spring 2001.
    Includes bibliographical references and index.
    ISBN 0-8061-3553-0 (alk. paper)
        1. Southwest, New—History—Congresses. 2. Great Plains—History—
Congresses. 3. Southwest, New—Environmental conditions—Congresses.
4. Great Plains—Environmental conditions—Congresses. 5. Human
ecology—Southwest, New—Congresses. 6. Human ecology—Great
Plains—Congresses. 7. Ethnicity—Southwest, New—Congresses.
8. Ethnicity—Great Plains—Congresses. 9. Southwest, New—Economic
conditions—Congresses. 10. Great Plains—Economic conditions—
Congresses.
    I. Smith, Sherry Lynn.

F786.F88 2003
979'.034—dc21

                                                      2003047399

1   2   3   4   5   6   7   8   9   10

In memory of Cetan Luta and Senga Pineleaf

Contents

Illustrations

Figures

Maps

Acknowledgments

This book evolved from a joint William P. Clements Center for Southwest Studies and Department of History Sharpe Symposium that took place at Southern Methodist University (SMU) in the spring of 2001. David Weber, director of the Clements Center, and Jane Elder, then assistant director, initially conceived the project. Andrea Boardman, current executive director of the Clements Center, and I carried it forth. David, of course, maintained a constant interest in the project and, time and again, provided support and wise counsel. Andrea bore the greatest burden of organizing the symposium at a time when she was just learning the ropes at the center. She managed beautifully, and I am grateful for her enthusiasm, professionalism, and patience. As for the history department, James Breeden, then chair, was a pleasure to work with as we managed the financial and academic angles. I am especially appreciative of his well-known commitment to students, allowing both undergraduate and graduate students access to all aspects of this event—at no personal expense to themselves. The history department's Mildred Pinkston and Julie Stewart answered many questions and provided advice to Andrea and me. SMU history department graduate students helped out enormously. Beverly Baker, Dionne Procell, Bonnie Martin, and Clive Siegel, in particular, took on many tasks ranging from publicizing the symposium to taping the participants' seminar. Camille Sharp, former history student, and Meredith Dickenson, of SMU's Public Affairs office, also pitched in. History department colleagues Edward Countryman, Kenneth Hamilton, John Mears, Alexis McCrossen, and Robert W. Righter participated formally in the symposium program. Hermann Michaeli helped out in so many ways; the Clements Center is fortunate to have him as a friend and supporter.

This book differs from many other collections of essays, I believe, because the individual chapters speak directly to one another. From the beginning, that was our intention. To encourage this, we asked the contributors to participate in a seminar and discuss one another's essays as well as larger issues regarding the Southern Plains. Before congregating, the participants agreed to read one another's essays so that our discussion could have a starting point. And it worked. The time people put into reading one another's essays and the energy and dedication they brought to this seminar was impressive. In revising their work for publication, the participants also bore in mind one another's essays, providing a cohesion that would be missing otherwise. I am very appreciative of all contributors' efforts to build consciously upon one another's work. Thanks to all of them.

Finally, the book stage: first, thank you to Chuck Rankin, editor-in-chief at the University of Oklahoma Press, who understood the value of this project from the outset, and to the anonymous readers whose suggestions for improvement were most helpful. Arnoldo DeLeon deserves special recognition for his tremendous help in editing portions of this manuscript. Dionne Procell pitched in, helping with endnotes, and Julie Stewart prepared several versions of the manuscript for the publisher. Andrea Boardman and Ruth Ann Elmore took on the huge responsibility of acquiring illustrations, maps, and permissions. Sam Ratcliffe and Ellen Niewyk, head and curator respectively of the Jerry Bywaters Collection at SMU, tracked down jacket art possibilities. Ruth Ann's artistic eye aided the process. Last, my husband and fellow historian, Robert W. Righter, went well beyond the call of duty here: accompanying me to Archer City, helping me clear up computer glitches, giving guidance and advice based on his own editing experience, and encouraging me with humor, patience, and love.

THE FUTURE OF THE
Southern Plains

Introduction

SHERRY L. SMITH

Archer City, Texas, rests on the cusp of the Southern Plains. Recently, my husband and I drove west and north from Dallas, in the direction of this tiny town. As we proceeded, trees became scarcer, rock outcrop-pings increased among the vegetation, and the wind became constant. Our purpose was twofold. We had just heard a collection of distin-guished scholars—people whose essays make up this book—speak about the future of the Southern Plains, and we wanted a taste of that country. We also wanted to visit the little town that Pulitzer prize–winning author Larry McMurtry had turned into a book-buyer's mecca by transform-ing abandoned storefronts into satellites of Booked Up, his secondhand book business.[1]

As we entered the town, the first thing that caught my eye was the marquee of the movie theater. I was impressed and surprised that the marquee was there, although the letters and words on it have slipped from my memory. I found this a hopeful sign—assuming it was the very same theater immortalized in McMurtry's novel *The Last Picture Show* and featured in the Peter Bogdanovich film of the same name. If the movie theater was still standing, then perhaps the doleful predictions about life in the Plains small towns had been overstated. Only as we slowed down to take a closer look, did I realize that merely the facade of the building still stood. Only the section of the theater that met the street, the most public and visible part, was intact. The remainder of the structure was now brick rubble. Beyond the deceptive outer appearance lay little but sad remnants.

As we turned the corner onto the main street, however, we saw more promising evidence of livelihoods, and even of life itself. We could discern, in about five or six different storefronts, McMurtry's book business. A café located across from the courthouse was open for business, and down the highway a bit we could see the famous Dairy Queen immortalized in *Walter Benjamin at the Dairy Queen*, a reminiscence of McMurtry's beginnings as a reader and writer. The fast-food eatery has the framed covers of McMurtry's novels as wall decorations. Not far away, visitors to the town can stay at The Lonesome Dove Inn, a bed-and-breakfast named after the local author's prize-winning novel, where guests can choose among suites named for McMurtry's other works. In short, Archer City has become, as writer Susan Sontag once told him, a Larry McMurtry theme park.[2]

But what would Archer City be without McMurtry? Even if he is able to revitalize this town, how many other Southern Plains towns can claim Pulitzer-prize winners? Is Archer City an anomaly on the Plains? Does the crumbling picture show, in the end, better symbolize the region's future than the bookshops and the bed-and-breakfast do? Judging from journalists' takes on such matters, the picture show wins this contest, hands down. *The New York Times* recently noted the dramatic dwindling of the Plains population—from the Dakotas to the semiarid sections of Kansas, Oklahoma, and West Texas. The newspaper cites the 2000 census, which demonstrates only the latest phase of this decades-long shrinkage, and points out that some counties' population loss is so significant that "the terrain is essentially vacant."[3] In West Texas, twelve counties have lost more than 50 percent of their population since 1950, prompting a columnist from *The Dallas Morning News* to suggest that a list of endangered communities should accompany the endangered species list. "A Dallas apartment complex can house more people than a 900-square-mile, rural West Texas county," he claimed. While Austin's population has expanded by 30 percent over the last decade, towns such as Haskell, Muleshoe, Snyder, Post, and Paducah can do little to stop the out-migration. According to a writer from the Oklahoma City *Daily Oklahoman*, southwestern Oklahoma's situation seems similarly "bleak." There a thirteen-county region has lost 32 percent of its population since 1940.[4] It appears that historian Frederick Jackson Turner "overstated and over-anticipated the closing of the American Frontier."[5] According to Turner, the frontier is an area that consists of two people per square mile, and if we use his definition, then every census since 1890 reveals places where the frontier is actually *returning* to the Plains. Kansas now has more "frontier" counties than it did one hundred years ago.[6] A number of factors explain the waves of economic and social collapse that have affected populations on the Plains. These include the unrealistic federal land policies that, starting in the 1880s, lured farmers west with inadequate one-hundred-and-sixty-acre homesteads; the periodic droughts and depressions, including the famous 1930s Dust Bowl; various agricultural downturns, particularly in wheat and cattle prices; and the oil busts of the last two decades that lowered commodity prices to the breaking point for many families and corporations.

Demographers, geographers, and historians, among others, have long pondered these events, and some have even offered suggestions for coping with them. It has been more than a dozen years since Frank and Deborah Popper, a geographer and a land use planner from Rutgers University, first came on the scene, predicting further population decline and offering their Buffalo Commons idea. They suggested that part of the Plains should be transformed into a space for bison and prairie restoration, ecotourism, and the marketing of buffalo products. Initially, the men and women of the Plains found such notions offensive, even threatening. When the Poppers made speaking appearances in the region in the early 1990s, they sometimes required police protection. Now some communities welcome the New Jersey–based couple, as their vision seems to be turning into reality. While human populations decline, buffalo numbers increase. Not only are bison recolonizing, but North Dakota's state bank now even makes loans for buffalo ranching. Approximately 300,000 bison currently inhabit North America, mostly on the Northern Plains. *The New York Times* stops short of endorsing the Poppers' plan, calling it "a dream," but it does, rather remarkably, conclude that modern, machine-driven farming is not suited to the terrain and sees reversion to native grassland as more appropriate than conventional farming.[7]

Few people on the Southern Plains, however, are talking about a Buffalo Commons, and the Poppers, apparently, have never been invited to speak in Texas.[8] In fact, few commentators have turned their attention to the Southern Plains dimension of this phenomenon at all. Easterners and other outsiders seem more drawn to the plains of Montana, Wyoming, and the Dakotas than those of Texas, Oklahoma, and New Mexico. Perhaps the relative indifference toward the Southern

Plains stems from the contemporary absence of buffalo, animals whose presence often invokes a romantic reaction to the northern region. Perhaps the lack of historical battles such as the Little Bighorn, with its powerful hold on the American imagination and consequent imprint on American popular culture, has something to do with it. To be sure, the U.S. Army wrested the Southern Plains from its American Indian occupants by force, but the battles that ensued never ended with dramatic American Indian victories. The Battle of Palo Duro Canyon, for instance, concluded not only with an army victory but also with the slaughter of Comanche, Kiowa, and Cheyenne ponies—an image Americans find less appealing, stirring, and inspirational than that of Custer's Last Stand. Or perhaps commentators have shied away from the Southern Plains because so much of the region is Texas.[9] Texas, by virtue of its history and its nature, seems a place apart from much of the rest of the West. Generalizations that work elsewhere and pronouncements that apply to public lands in other sections of the country do not apply so readily in the Lone Star State.

Whatever the reason for journalists' slights, this book demonstrates that scholars have not ignored the Southern Plains. It brings together the insights and informed judgments of historians, a geographer, and a paleoclimatologist—who have dedicated significant portions of their intellectual lives to examining and understanding the Southern Plains. Some of these scholars grew up in the heart of the region; one on its edge. Others came to it through an interest in the Ogalalla Aquifer, its petrochemical resources, or its unique aesthetic. Together they provide a view of the Southern Plains, past and future, notable for its depth, both intellectual and emotional. The cumulative effect of their work reveals that the region's story is as compelling and complex as its northern neighbor's.

Where, exactly, is the Southern Plains? The answer is a bit slippery, for the definition depends on *who* answers the question and on *when* one asks the question. In other words, the answer is partially contingent upon history and context. To a Mexicano of the nineteenth century, this region would be considered part of El Norte. To a Comanche, it would be home. To an Anglo-American, it would be the Southern Plains. For the purposes of this book, however, the contributors agree that the contemporary Southern Plains corresponds to the one defined by geographer Robert Bailey.[10] Bailey based the boundaries of the region, at least in part, on vegetation, and the Bailey-defined parameters of the Southern

Plains look something like this: begin around Abilene, Texas, for the eastern boundary; arc up through Oklahoma to the Arkansas River for the northern rim; move west along the Arkansas to take in southeastern Colorado and eastern New Mexico west of the Pecos River; and swing around to the south to incorporate the Monahan Sand Dunes. Precision is counterproductive, and some would urge stretching the eastern boundary to Texas's Edwards Plateau and going as far south as Interstate 10. But the heartlands of the Southern Plains are indisputable; they include the Texas Panhandle, eastern New Mexico, and corners of Colorado, Kansas, and Oklahoma.

The Southern Plains. Courtesy of Dan Flores, from his book Caprock Canyonlands: Journeys into the Heart of the Southern Plains *(Austin: University of Texas Press, 1990).*

There are many characteristics that define the Southern Plains apart from the Central and Northern Plains. Contributors to this volume emphasize the Southern Plains as a place of pulsating drought and aridity, a region with ties to southern political traditions, and a place with a longstanding, unique settlement presence of Mexicans and Mexican Americans. What became Texas and New Mexico were Hispanic homelands before Anglo occupation. New Mexico, in particular, sent families and colonies, radiating eastward and outward across the Southern Plains, where they encountered Anglo-American settlers moving to the west from the Red River Valley. When these cultural shock waves washed over one another, the Anglos eventually prevailed, chasing Hispanic sheepherders away—though not entirely. The bicultural, bilingual heritage of the Southern Plains not only remains but, in recent decades, has strengthened as migrants from South Texas and immigrants from Mexico increase the Hispanic presence in the twenty-first century.

On the other hand, American Indian occupants have largely disappeared from the heart of the region, at least as any kind of viable, visible presence on the landscape. Texas was particularly effective in purging itself of most American Indian occupants. Today the few tiny reservations that exist rest on the periphery of the Southern Plains and include the Tiguas in El Paso and the Kickapoo in Eagle Pass. By the close of the nineteenth century, all the Southern Plains tribes had experienced conquest and had been consolidated on reservations, mostly in Oklahoma. Southwestern Oklahoma remains the home of a number of American Indian agencies and tribal governments as well as the site of Comanche, Kiowa, Wichita, and other allotted reservations. Still, American Indian occupation is not especially pronounced, and reoccupation of this region's core lands does not seem likely. While some observers see the depopulation of Anglos on the Northern Plains as an opportunity for American Indians to repopulate their prior lands, gain "cultural importance in this socially emaciated region," increase their political power, and create "a new coherence in Native American life where coherence was so brutally fractured long ago," few predict similar prospects for American Indians of the Southern Plains.[11] Without reservation land bases to build upon, a resurgence of Native population seems unlikely.

The Southern Plains shares some characteristics with the rest of the Plains and offers others that are unique, but why does this area merit special attention? What can this place teach us? Why should anybody—

particularly those who do not live there and perhaps have never even traveled across its highways on their way to other, presumably more appealing places—care about the future of this region? For environmental historian Dan Flores, the explanation is simple and straightforward. He sees the Southern Plains as "the cutting edge of the modernist experiment with the exploitation of North America. This is the place that is going to show us the outcome first."[12] This is a story about limits, about moving up against limits in a place that has never been easy. It speaks to themes of depleting resources, failing communities, scarce water, swept away species, and disappearing ways of life. Moreover, it foreshadows what can happen—what is *going* to happen—in a lot of other places on the globe, as the region is in the midst of debate over exploitation-conservation dialectics and the implications reverberate worldwide. Because the Southern Plains is such an extreme land, a place so clearly defined by finite resources and where the powerful forces of an industrial, even postindustrial, nation have been brought to bear on it for over a century now, it will show the direction that the economics, politics, and demographics of other places will go as well.

What pertains to water and agriculture is also true of oil. Historian Diana Davids Olien believes that the oil industry, as it is practiced on the Southern Plains today, represents the future of domestic production throughout the lower forty-eight states. Dwindling resources, increased litigation, and environmental concerns add up to disincentives to explore or exploit on the domestic scene and thus encourage offshore exploration and development. Unless the United States decides to tap the resources of Alaska's National Wildlife Refuge, the future of Southern Plains oil production represents the future of national onshore production. The region's representativeness goes on from there. Historian Jeff Roche argues that the political problems of the Southern Plains are the problems of rural America, writ large. Yolanda Romero's description of Mexican and Mexican American migrations speaks to major demographic trends that not only typify other sections of the nation but also reverberate across international boundaries. The story of the Southern Plains, then, is a lens through which one can examine a host of developments and problems that transcend section, state, and even nation. Far from being a provincial account, this book demonstrates how one can simultaneously go west and go global.[13]

Yet this is also very much a story about America. Or perhaps, more accurately, it is a counternarrative to the one Americans most like to tell about themselves.[14] The accounts of the Southern Plains in the pages that follow are not trumpeting tales of unlimited opportunities and qualified successes, but they are stories about failing as well as succeeding. They tell of species disappearing, drought inevitably returning, people leaving the land rather than settling it, corporations ruling rather than intrepid pioneers controlling their own livelihoods, and communities refusing opportunities to put aside immediate economic interests for future generations' recreational needs. Yet, the picture that emerges is more nuanced and complicated than a simple tragedy of hopes gone awry, of environmental constraints forcing people to come to terms with climatic limitations, or of selfish people unresponsive to future generations' needs for parklands. Geographer John Miller Morris, a great-grandson of Southern Plains pioneers, takes issue with the more baleful views of journalists and some of his fellow essayists. He does not see the glass as half empty. Even as he acknowledges the inevitability of change and the probable demise of the family farm, he believes in alternatives to the gloom-and-doom scenarios. Morris is enchanted with the inherent beauty of the escarpment country, for example, and believes that if people will only get off the interstates—"those corridors of perceptual death"—they will discover the inherent beauty in the Southern Plains landscape. The opportunities for ecotourism and heritage tourism remain untapped.[15] Moreover, the region produces an enormous amount of the world's food and will continue to do so—as long as the water lasts. Historian John Opie presents case studies of Plains water districts struggling to achieve a measure of sustainability regarding the critically important Ogalalla Acquifer. He does not know if they will succeed, but at least they are trying.

What these essayists do in the chapters that follow, then, is offer some reasonable predictions about the future of the Southern Plains that are based on a deep understanding of the region's past. And that past is long one. Historian Elliott West and paleoclimatologist Connie Woodhouse provide hundreds, even thousands, of years' worth of perspective, on both climatic change—particularly the frequency and severity of drought over the millennia—and human adaptation to those changes. There is something comforting in these essays. Change is inevitable. Humans have survived. New innovations, such as horses or technologies that made tapping aquifers more efficient, have opened new possibilities for exploiting resources. But there is also something disquieting in these accounts. For all the devastation the Dust Bowl years wreaked on the Southern Plains, Woodhouse explains that the region has experienced even worse droughts—and probably will again. For all the centuries of human exploitation, West argues, the last century's pressures far exceeded anything the region witnessed up to that point. How quickly the bison vanished once the forces of "voracious capitalism" and international industrialism hit. In fact, the pace of change and the complexities of the last one hundred years presented the Southern Plains occupants with a breathtaking swirl of opportunities, challenges, and new problems.

The essays of Morris, Opie, and Olien close in on that last century of human occupation, focusing particularly on events since the end of World War II, when technological change made pumping the Ogalalla Aquifer more efficient, and oil and gas exploitation boomed before it busted. Farming, livestock raising, and oil production typified the most significant economic activities of the Southern Plains, and these chapters explain what drew and sometimes sustained people, which resources lasted and which dwindled, and what forces—corporate, capitalist, and climatic—complicated their lives.

As the essayists investigate the past, they also speak to the present and the future. What measures are the men and women of the Plains taking to provide a sustainable future? How much control do these people actually have over their fates? To what extent do corporate bottom lines, global markets, finite aquifers, and unpredictable weather patterns determine economic outcomes? To what extent do Americans have a moral obligation to perpetuate ways of life that do not necessarily make economic or environmental sense? No one disputes the crucial role government has played in propping up this region, whether in the form of agricultural subsidies, military bases, or prisons. Should such support continue?

The last question moves into the realm of politics. Farming, stock raising, and oil interests have prevailed politically in the Southern Plains over the last century. Will that remain the same? Will the "cowboy conservatism" Roche outlines in his essay maintain its political force, as the population ebbs from rural to urban areas? What political consequences can one expect as the Hispanic population increases in numbers and influence in the coming decades? Yolanda Romero details the gradual process by which Mexicans and Mexican Americans found their voice and demanded change in the 1960s and 1970s. How will this expanding demographic group's economic, political, and social needs cohere with future political power structures?

And what are the prospects for a renewed Southern Plains aesthetic? As Flores explains, in the nineteenth century, before the agrarian "assault," visitors marveled at the abundant wildlife on the Plains. Early twentieth century observers, such as Georgia O'Keeffe, appreciated the openness, the sky, and the space. But opportunities to set aside particularly lovely stretches of Southern Plains canyon lands as a national park failed, in part, because of greed as well as indifference, both locally and nationally, to preservation of the Plains ecology. Now, in the twenty-first century, environmentalists and urban-based outdoor recreationists are demanding more access to and preservation of these canyons and grasslands. Elsewhere on the Plains, these political interest groups are already having an effect. A senior policy advisor to the U.S. Forest Service acknowledged that "the cattle and oil industries no longer have the grasslands to themselves. They must share with wildlife watchers, hunters, hikers and mountains bikers, all eager to indulge in the last remnants of the American prairie."[16] When this led to reductions in grazing lands and tighter restrictions on oil and gas drilling in McKenzie County, North Dakota, for instance, ranchers and oil and gas interests balked, setting off debates about public lands that had never before reached such a fevered pitch in that country. Given the political inclinations of most Southern Plains people, one should expect similar reactions there.

The fact that much of this region is private and not public land was a major obstacle to conservationists in the 1930s and remains one today. Moreover, the water laws of Texas underscore how deeply rooted the tradition of private property rights remains in this section of the Southern Plains. Texas allows landowners the right to pump underground aquifers to their hearts' content—even to the point of pumping it dry and with no regard for their neighbors' well-being. In other words, groundwater is private property, and private property trumps everything else. Match that legal right with thirsty urban areas such as El Paso and its growing neighbor across the Rio Grande, Juarez, Mexico, or the Dallas/Fort Worth metropolitan area, and you have the latest potential boom for the Southern Plains: water drilling. Texas oilman T. Boone Pickens, for instance, is buying up West Texas ranches for the purpose of pumping the water beneath them. His plan is to pipe and sell it to parched urban consumers. Water mining, as this latest development is called, poses serious threats to the Ogalalla Aquifer and to the farmers whose irrigated fields depend upon it. The Texas Supreme Court recently ruled, however, that the rule of capture (which permits unregulated water pumping) prevails in groundwater districts like those described in Opie's essay. Quite simply, this situation adds up to a potentially explosive political conflict with ranchers battling oilmen-turned-water-miners and urban water users challenging rural users' assumptions that the water's highest and best use remains agricultural. The economic and environmental ramifications are enormous. Some West Texans seem resigned to their fate, arguing that the region's best hope is to harvest and ship the water, thus providing a livelihood for at least one more generation or two. Others prefer a variation of the rule of capture, which permits pumping groundwater as long as it does not impair one's neighbor's water right. This would presumably protect irrigated farming while simultaneously fending off what Texans continue to see as anathema: any state or government attempt to regulate water and property. The ultimate outcome of all this will be determined in the courts and state legislatures. But as the population and consequent political power of the rural Southern Plains counties dwindle, the long-term odds appear to favor urban interests.[17]

In the end, most people neither want Southern Plains water nor intend to recreate on its grasslands or in its canyons. Instead, if they experience the place at all, it will be as passers-through. Ironically, the ribbons of highway they navigate represent an indisputable economic shot in the arm to those communities lucky enough to line the interstates. Although Morris notes their cultural limitations, there is no denying that Interstates 40 and 10, which intersect the Southern Plains, generate life and commerce along their shoulders. In some cases, these highways have stopped rural depopulation as companies have installed plants by the roadways and found workers in what were nearly abandoned towns. They have birthed new jobs and businesses as they have spawned supermarket-sized gas and food stations, chain motels, and even casinos. Sayre, Oklahoma, situated on Interstate 40 and fifteen minutes from the Washita Battlefield National Historic Site in Cheyenne, takes advantage of its tourism potential. The battlefield marks the spot where, in 1868, the Seventh Cavalry led by Lieutenant George Armstrong Custer attacked a Cheyenne village, killing more than one hundred people. The Custer name is gold, bringing in over twelve thousand visitors to the town in 2001. In other places, new factories, meatpacking plants, and warehouses crop up. In fact, in contrast to the rest of the region, the two counties that include Amarillo, Texas, in the heart of the Southern Plains, grew 16 percent in the 1990s. Interstate 40 played a key role in maintaining this city's role as a major commercial center, with the freeway serving as the primary artery of its economic lifeblood. In other words, the infusion comes from elsewhere. It is transitory and dependent on a healthy national and global economy. And its reach is very limited. The interstates' magical flow of money and economic power fades for communities located more than four or five miles away.[18]

In fact, the interstate comes nowhere near Archer City, Texas—Larry McMurtry's hometown. He probably prefers it that way. As he exchanges his father's cattle ranching for "book herding," McMurtry is one Southern Plainsman who seems to have made his peace with the changing world. One might even argue that he has built a career on it. Admitting that he has always been fascinated with vanishing breeds, McMurtry has devoted much of his writing to the death of the cowboy. He understands that the entire range-cattle industry was probably a mistake that was "based on a superficial understanding of plains environment" that mismatched "beast and place." Men like his father cut a tragic figure as they toiled and struggled, lived off credit, studied range science, and still failed to thrive. His father had "attached his heart to a hopeless ideal, a nineteenth-century vision of cowboying and family pastoralism," an ideal not completely false, just only briefly realizable. For his part, McMurtry chose another life—one of literature, of herding "words into novel-size ranches," that provides him tremendous freedom to think, write, read, and make a good living—even in Archer City.[19]

But what will be the fate of other sons and daughters of the Southern Plains? What will be the prospects for *their* children and grandchildren? This book encourages you to exit the interstate and travel into the heart of the region, explore its small towns, oil patches, water districts, family and corporate farms, canyons and escarpments, in search of some answers.

Notes

1. John Schwartz, "Pulitzer Prize Winner Also a Profitable Bookseller," *New York Times*, 23 July 2001.

2. Schwartz, "Pulitzer Prize Winner"; Larry McMurtry, *Walter Benjamin at the Dairy Queen: Reflections on Sixty and Beyond* (New York: Simon and Schuster, 1999), 77.

3. "Unsettled Plains," *New York Times* 3 June 2001.

4. Scott Parks, "Vanishing Way of Life," *Dallas Morning News*, 6 March 2000; Ron Jackson, "Conditions Bleak for Great Plains," *Sunday Oklahoman*, 5 May 2000. See also Parks, "My Little Dying Town," *Dallas Morning News*, 8 July 2001.

5. Florence Williams, "Plains Sense: Frank and Deborah Popper's 'Buffalo Commons' Is Creeping Toward Reality," *High Country News*, 15 January 2001.

6. Williams, "Plains Sense."

7. "Unsettled Plains."

8. "Unsettled Plains." For information on buffalo ranching see Florence Williams, "Making Buffalo Pay," *High Country News*, 15 January 2001. For an early article on Buffalo Commons see Deborah E. Popper and Frank Popper, "The Great Plains: From Dust to Dust," *Planning* (December 1987): 12–18. The information that the Poppers have never received an invitation to speak in Texas came from Dan Flores, "Future of the Southern Plains" participants seminar, Southern Methodist University, Dallas, Texas, 6 April 2001.

9. I owe this insight to John Opie. In response to my question about why the Southern Plains hasn't attracted as much attention as the Northern Plains, Opie suggested that "people don't know what to make of Texas." "Future of the Southern Plains" participants seminar.

10. Robert G. Bailey, *Ecoregions: The Ecosystem Geography of the Oceans and Continents* (New York: Springer-Verlag, 1998).

11. "Unsettled Plains."

12. "Future of the Southern Plains" participants seminar.

13. Patricia Nelson Limerick, "Going West and Ending Up Global," *Western Historical Quarterly* 32 (Spring 2001): 5–23.

14. This point was made by Jeff Roche, "Future of the Southern Plains" participants seminar.

15. John Miller Morris offered this comment, "Future of the Southern Plains" participants seminar.

16. Michael Milstein, "Change on the Plains," *High Country News*, 5 June 2000.

17. For information on water mining see Joe Nick Patoski, "Boone Pickens Wants To Sell You His Water," *Texas Monthly*, (August 2001), 118–21, 185–89; Jim Yardley, "For Texas Now, Water and Not Oil is Liquid Gold," *New York Times*, 16 April 2001; Steven H. Lee, "Who Gets to Drink?" *Dallas Morning News*, 4 March 2001; Jim Yardley, "In a Changed Texas, Ranchers Battle Oilmen," *New York Times*, 29 May 2000; Parks, "Water Investors Eye Liquid Assets," *Dallas Morning News*, 21 May 2000; and Kay Yung, "Back in the Saddle: Boone Pickens is Dealing Again," *Dallas Morning News*, 3 November 2002. For information on the national dimension of water shortages see Timothy Egan, "Near Vast Bodies of Water, the Nation Still Thirsts," *New York Times*, 12 August 2001.

18. Peter Kilborn, "Interstates Giving Boost to Rural Economies," *New York Times,* 14 July 2001.

19. McMurtry, *Walter Benjamin at the Dairy Queen,* 184–204; Ron Jackson, "Spaceport Promises to Revitalize Western Oklahoma," *Daily Oklahoman,* 6 May 2002. In a variation on this theme, western Oklahoma hopes to snare a spaceport capable of launching, and landing, commercial shuttle-like spacecraft. The region's sparse population, isolation, and the presence of a 13,500-foot runway at the abandoned Clinton-Sherman Air Force Base in Burns Flat are among the "assets" it hopes will sell its location for this twenty-first-century style of transport.

Trails and Footprints

The Past of the Future Southern Plains

ELLIOTT WEST

In Charles Kuralt's popular bicentennial tour of states, "On the Road," he called early Wyoming "a place of passage, a kind of alkali hell to be got through."[1] Although it is terribly unfair to both places, the same might be said of the popular impression of the Southern Plains. Truckers roar back and forth along interstates and other main arteries. Summer vacationers zip along in their vans, windows rolled against the heat, parents staring grimly at the horizon as children behind them fight over comic books and Game Boys and smear one another with grape jelly. When the inevitable question comes from the back seat—"Are we there yet?"—and it comes in Garza or Yoakum or Dickens or some other West Texas county, we can be almost utterly certain that the answer will be "no." Thousands of feet above, others pass through. From a window seat they might glance down briefly in daylight at what seems empty and timeless, and at night they might wonder idly about some town that shows up as a cluster of lights with tendrils reaching into the darkness, reminding travelers perhaps of an enlarged photo of nerve ganglia they saw years ago in a biology text. Even if these birds of passage knew a town's name, it would probably mean nothing: Justiceburg, Gomez, or

Close City; Seminole, Polar, or Peacock; Halfway, Midway, or Circle Back.

Those who live on the Southern Plains and watch their towns over time might feel they are seeing a slow-motion version of human passage. People have been leaving most of the region over the past several decades. Today, Comanche County has about fourteen thousand persons. In 1910, it had more than twenty-seven thousand. Shackleford County's population has declined by half since 1930, Fisher and Throckmorton Counties by two thirds. Knox County is down 77 percent. Every county that has gained population is along an interstate or a major U.S. highway. Each has held its own, that is, by feeding from those who flow through.

Even positive population figures can be deceiving. Snyder, about eighty-fives miles southeast of Lubbock, has held steady in numbers over the last thirty years, but, as the young have left and the less affluent have moved to the area, and as the region has suffered from sagging oil prices and a stubborn drought, the economic underpinnings have shrunk alarmingly. The tax base of Scurry County in 1990 was $1.6 billion; today it is estimated at $600 million, a decline of 62 percent in only a decade. Shops line the streets at the center of Snyder, but the town is fraying at the edges. Driving west on U.S. 180 on a cool, cloudy June day, I counted four consecutive boarded-up businesses. There was a rusting oil tank with Magnolia's old flying red horse up top, a few ranch-style residences with gardens, and a ghost sign for the defunct Ponderosa Motel. The one surviving business admits to the area's transience—the Trailertopia mobile home park. Passing me in the other direction were four ramshackle trucks hauling tinny rides and facades advertising a midway and games of chance, a gimcrack carnival, one more bunch that would light briefly before passing through. And then on the edge of town a fading sign: "Snyder! Hurry Back!"

Snyder is going through some tough times, as are Lamesa, Crosbyton, Kermit, and dozens of other towns on the Texas Southern Plains, and it is easy to feel pretty discouraged for the fine people who live in and love that country. But as is often the case, discouragement is deepest when our view is the narrowest. Looking only at the current situation, or looking back only a few decades, the trajectory of events seems more desperate, more headed-for-hell, than when we pull back to view a longer perspective. Granted, a broader look sometimes makes a situation seem *really* bleak, not just troubling but hopeless. Still, in the case of the

Southern Plains there is some solace in the deep past, if for no other reason than that it is a story of persistence in a place of both hard limits
and continuing opportunities.

Sending out Needful Things

One historical pattern, for instance, almost jumps from the record. For
as far back as we can see in this area's human story, the Southern Plains
has been a source of materials others have needed and have been willing
to pay for—in one way or another. A bit north and east of Amarillo is
the Alibates Flint Quarries National Monument. It preserves a distinctive outcropping about ten miles square. Just below its surface is a layer
of flint about six feet thick. This stone is splendidly suited for knapping
into various tools. It also has a beautifully distinctive texture, with rich
swirls of bright color found in no other quarries in North America. This
unique patterning makes Alibates flint highly traceable, so we know that
it was first taken from the earth, probably hacked out with wooden mal-
lets, at least twelve thousand years ago. In fact, it was the favored material at the site of Blackwater Draw, the dig that first revealed the earliest
culture of North America, the one that took its name from the nearby
town of Clovis, New Mexico.

Early Americans traded Alibates flint over huge distances, and it
shows up throughout most of the Southwest and Great Plains. It became
the raw stuff of a technology that sustained changing cultures from the
Pleistocene until the eve of the present day. Artisans fashioned it into
virtually every stone tool imaginable—spear points, awls, hide scrapers,
buttons, fishhooks, knives, drills, axes, chisels, hoes, darts, arrowheads,
and choppers swung by gravediggers. In exchange Alibates quarriers
received pottery, obsidian, pipestone, and seashells. During a tiny portion of this operation, a mere four hundred years between the twelfth
and sixteenth centuries, a society of farmers flourished beside the quarries. They cultivated maize, squash, and beans in nearby fields and lived
in houses made from stone slabs. Soon after these farmers left, the flint
trade picked up, jolted by an infusion of new goods brought by the first
European contact. Production continued for three centuries more, until
the digging finally stopped around 1870.

The Alibates quarries, that is, provided thousands of persons with an
essential raw material from the time of the earliest human presence in
what is now the United States until the Grant administration. This is a

record. Nowhere else in North America, perhaps in the western hemisphere, did people use the same piece of land for the same purpose longer than on this plot of the Southern Plains.

Alibates obviously reveals only so much about the region. It is a tiny spot in a vast country, and, while it points deeply into the past, it doesn't have much directly to say about the present and future. Let's face it: the flint business is not what it used to be. But this ancient workplace does stand as a dramatic illustration of a far broader pattern. Particulars change, but ever since people first left their marks on our land, they apparently have looked to the Southern Plains for needful things. That other more obvious feature mentioned earlier—people passing through in the short and long term—ought to be seen in balance with this one. Something similar can be said about anywhere else, of course. Pennsylvania and Alabama and Oregon also have had plenty of human traffic and have resources that others have sought, but, when we look back on the long history of the Southern Plains, there is a strong impression that these two traits stand out more starkly than elsewhere. Just as striking as the traits themselves—a land of transience, and land of resources sent elsewhere—has been the interaction between the two.

Take, for instance, a resource taken from this area for almost as long as flint—bison. The two, of course, literally ran together. The first proof of the existence of ancient culture in America came from two sites, both on the Southern Plains: an arroyo of the Cimarron River near Folsom, New Mexico, in 1925, and two years earlier (and much less known) on Lone Wolf Creek, near Colorado City in Mitchell County, Texas.[2] Both discoveries were of ancient flint spearpoints embedded in bison skeletons from a long-extinct species. Whether bison were hunted continuously from then until now is a matter of argument. There may have been two long stretches when the weather warmed and rains slackened, the first from about 5000–6000 B.C. until about 2500 B.C. and the other from around 500 A.D. until 1300 A.D.[3] Virtually no bison bones can be found in sites from those times, and there is good reason to think that many or most people also left during those years—an early coordinated coming and going, perhaps, of humans and resources. By 1300, bison and people were back, plenty of them in fact. Like the period immediately before it, this too might have been a shifting of people and what people needed. The previous century had seen a calamitous southwestern drought, a disaster that seems to have triggered the collapse of the famous Anasazi culture of the Four Corners region. In a social unraveling that apparently included brutal warfare and cannibalism, these desert dwellers dispersed, many of them moving east to become the Pueblo peoples of the upper Rio Grande and Pecos River valleys.[4] Bison, too, may have been driven eastward by the drought and also drawn by wetter and greener times on the Southern Plains.

Where, how, and why people and animals moved, one thing is clear. About six or seven hundred years ago, people and bison fell into a pattern that would help set the rhythm of life in this region until near the end of the nineteenth century. Behind this pattern was a simple match between needs and opportunities of two areas—the Southern Plains, on the one hand, and the settlements of the Pecos and the upper Rio Grande valleys on the other. The river peoples were corn farmers who lived clustered in villages, some quite sizeable. With such numbers they put a strain on the game populations around them. This left them in need of an element essential for human nutrition—protein. People on the Plains had plenty of protein—it ran around in great chunks of up to two thousand pounds—but as nomads they did not cultivate crops like corn that provided carbohydrates, another basic human need. Village farmers, that is, were short on meat and protein and long on corn and carbohydrates. Plains hunters had exactly the opposite problem.

It was a match made in Adam Smith heaven. Its earlier history is naturally fuzzier in the record, but the archaeologist Katherine Spielmann has used computer modeling on what we know from the ruins of the Pecos pueblo to estimate how much corn was grown and stored and how much local game was hunted.[5] The villagers often would have run out of deer and other game, she suggests. Somehow they would have to make up the difference. But how? Their large underground bins, she calculates, would have stored a lot more corn than they needed for themselves, even if they held onto some extra for emergencies. The likely explanation, she writes, was that the villagers engaged in a vigorous exchange. From the country around what are today Las Vegas, Santa Fe, and Taos, they sent corn onto the Plains to the east. In return, bison meat and skins (and perhaps prairie turnips, a rare instance of a protein-rich plant gathered by American Indian women) moved east-to-west out of a huge swath of the Southern Plains, from the Oklahoma and Texas panhandles, down nearly to the Big Bend.

Again the Southern Plains were sending out from their abundance something that others needed badly, and those doing the swapping were making a living from it, as with the flint trade. Thinking this trade back to its fundamentals, we should recall that those hunters were not so much bartering meat as they were a vital human need—protein. Taking another step back, we see that protein was being produced by an animal that could do something people could not—eat the grasses that grew abundantly on the Plains and convert the energy stored there into what the animals needed, including these crucial amino acids. People of the Plains essentially were waiting for this animal to draw from the country's reservoir of energy and to transform it into something they could use. Then they would step in and grab it. Next they took part of what they seized, sent it out into a land of needful neighbors, and swapped it for something else they had to have.

Nothing in these basics made the Plains different from any other human homeland. Wherever they have lived, people have drawn directly and indirectly on nature's energy and have used it, directly and indirectly, to satisfy their wants. What did set the Southern Plains apart was the jarring contrast between appearance and reality. The Plains would seem sparse and stingy, and in one sense they were. Other restraints kept the human population thin, well below what was on either side, and required those scattered people to keep always on the move to find what they needed. And yet these inhabitants also were dealers in abundance. The grasslands they roamed over were one of the continent's greatest reservoirs of energy only once removed from a human grip. That gap was bridged by a mechanism, the bison, that tapped into that energy with remarkable efficiency and as a result was available in mind-reeling numbers, about eight million on the Southern Plains according to a recent estimate. Finally, there was a bonus: a bison was a unique concentration of energy converted for human use, the largest land animal in the western hemisphere. A bull could weigh as much as a well-loaded nineteenth-century farm wagon. With one kill a plains hunter captured the power of grass transformed into the stuff for many meals, for part of his family's clothing and housing, for weapons and tools, for toys, and for the trappings for his worship of a generous god. And the hunter could also use this abundance to reach outward for what the bison could not provide.

A slim population in an apparently empty land, a shrewd understanding of possibilities that met immediate needs and that pulled more from a wider world—it was an old pattern on the Plains, and one that would unfold again.

What Coronado Did Not See

Turning again to the exchange of bison for corn, we cannot know for sure that it went just as Spielmann suggests. Most of the products in question would have lasted only a season of good meals, so reconstructing this scene six or seven hundred years later is informed guesswork. But there is another strong point in favor of her argument. When Europeans first saw this region, they described a pattern much like this. On the Southern Plains, Coronado's men found people, almost certainly Apachean, they called the Querechos. Then, and on later expeditions, the Spanish were fascinated. These American Indians painted themselves bright red; they drifted over the land followed by packs of skinny dogs; they lived in small conical tents—mini-tepees—that one writer thought were "built as skillfully as those of Italy." As for subsistence, "they neither plant nor harvest maize," wrote Coronado's scribe, but "subsist entirely on cattle [bison]." As many would remark later about Plains American Indians, they consumed or used virtually every part of these animals. They clothed and housed themselves with the skins; from the sinews they made thread and from the bones, awls. Bladders became water jugs. They ate the fat raw, and as for the meat, "taking it in their teeth, they pull with one hand; with the other they hold a large flint knife and cut off mouthfuls, swallowing it half-chewed, like birds." [6]

Besides consuming such things themselves, they also traded bison meat and other animal products with Pueblo peoples, part of a network stretching far to the west and south. New Mexico and Arizona produced turquoise, cotton blankets, pottery, and corn. From the Gulf of California and the Pacific Coast came coral and a variety of shells. Central Mexico sent the bright feathers of parrots and macaws. [7]

So if we imagine our way five-and-a-half centuries into the past, and if we stand on the Southern Plains and look west and south into this network, we can begin to get a feel for where this country stood in a much larger scheme. People of the Plains, like the "Vaquero Indians" Vicente Zalvidar saw along the Canadian River in 1598, journeyed to New Mexico, where "they sold meat, skins, fat, tallow, and salt in exchange for cotton blankets, pottery, maize and some green turquoises which they use." [8] All those goods, plus shells and feathers, have been found scattered in sites up to central Kansas, down to south Texas, and east through Oklahoma. Digs along the Canadian River have unearthed piñon nuts, obsidian from the Jemez Mountains, and turquoise from around Cerrillos. In the Pecos pueblo there were shells from California and the Gulf of Mexico. Entertainments there included music from flutes fashioned from the ulnae of whooping cranes from the Texas coast.[9]

Plains traders looked also toward the more humid East. On the eastern fringe of the Southern Plains were settlements that played the same role of the Pecos pueblo. The Spiro Mounds in eastern Oklahoma, just over the state border from Fort Smith, Arkansas, apparently were the ceremonial center of a trade entrepôt funneling goods to and from both the Plains to the northwest and the permanent towns and villages down the Arkansas valley toward the Mississippi. The mounds contained magnificent prestige goods—cups of engraved marine shells, a many-colored cloak with embroidered falcon feathers, ceremonial axe heads, copper headdress ornaments, human effigy pipes of Alabama red pipestone, shell gorgets in motifs of severed heads and fabulous spiders. This was presumably the rich harvest of the middlemen of a vigorous exchange. Spiro was apparently an important waystation within a great braiding of trade routes that stretched across twenty meridians.[10] At the center of this system, both a provider of resources and a passway of commerce, was the Southern Plains.

The Spanish stumbled into this sprawling network. Eavesdrop briefly on two moments during the first conquistador expeditions into this region. It is the late summer of 1540. Coronado, in the Zuni settlement of Cibola, meets a delegation from the Pecos pueblo. The men greet him with gifts of dressed bison hides, shields covered with bison skin, and headpieces, probably also made from the animals.[11] This encounter begins the allurement of Coronado toward his ultimately disappointing trek to Quivira. Now, eleven months later, stand in the swamplands of far northeastern Arkansas along the Mississippi River, just under a thousand crow-flying miles to the east. Hernando de Soto has just seized the town of Capaha, and with it eight American Indians "who were not natives of this place but strangers and merchants who in their trading passed through many provinces." De Soto presses them for salt, which they trade "among other things."[12] What else they carried is unknown, but as the Spanish moved through this area they saw the heads of bison bulls displayed over the door of a cacique; cured bison tails; bison-hide shields, which they confiscated as armor for their horses; and on several occasions dressed bison robes, which were brought in great numbers as tribute from American Indians from near present Fort Smith and close to the old trading entrepôt of the Spiro Mounds.[13] The latter two items—bison robes and shields—were identical to what was given Coronado far to the west. And all these bison products apparently were imported, for de Soto's men saw no actual bison, which were said to flourish in a spare and sparsely populated land to the west.[14]

With only the vaguest awareness, the Spanish were touching and moving through a system of commerce in which vital Plains products flowed across the continent. The system was so efficient, in fact, that before the Spanish realized it, their own goods were sucked into it. The first Spanish entering northern Mexico from the south sometimes found metal buckles, files and rasps, horseshoe nails, and other items already in circulation. The earliest in Sonora arrived to find that their own chickens had beaten them there.[15]

One other valuable trade item coursed through this system—people. The Spanish described, and soon took part in, a considerable commerce in slaves. In northern Mexico desert towns they saw slaves in wooden stocks being bartered for the usual products and reported others taken in fights with the bison-hunting Querechos to the north.[16] In Pecos, Coronado described slaves from the Plains. The status of these men and women was surely quite different from how the Spanish understood the term *slave*, and, as in American Indian societies throughout the continent, they likely played some role of social and economic liaison among cultures.

It is in that context that some students of the period, including the eminent Plains archeologist Mildred Wedel, suggest a new look at one of the most famous figures of the Coronado expedition: the Turk.[17] In the chronicles, he first appears in Pecos, that funnel of traffic from the Plains. It was he who led Coronado on his odyssey across the Southern Plains in search of Quivira, first well to the south and then north all the way to the great bend of the Arkansas River. There Coronado became frustrated and convinced his guide was lying and had him garrotted. Wedel and others suggest that the Turk, called a slave, is in fact better understood as a trader, probably subservient to those men from Pecos whom Coronado met in Cibola or others like them. If so, he might well have been a veteran traveler on those arteries stretching far to the south, west, and east. Interestingly, he knew some Nahuatl, the language spoken most widely in central and northern Mexico, and his beguiling word portraits of lands to the east included towns, great rivers, and long, canopied canoes strikingly similar to what de Soto's chroniclers were simultaneously describing in that country where they had their own encounter with traders from distant lands.[18] Perhaps what usually have been taken as his tall tales were reasonably honest descriptions of what the Turk knew, with copper, likely the only yellowish metal he had seen, substituting as gold. As to his origins, most agree that the Turk was a Wichita Indian from what now is southern Kansas, and so had been centrally placed to travel to both fringes of a commercial network.

Seen this way, the famous episode of Coronado's foray to Quivira becomes tantalizingly fuzzy. Is it best understood as a vile plot meant to lure the Spanish to destruction or as the invaders' failure to see truly what was before them? Was the Turk a sly deceiver or an opportunist who ended up literally choking on his own misinterpreted words? Was this a missed chance by the Spanish to link, at least in understanding the basic mechanisms at work, the two parts of America they were probing simultaneously for the first time?

For those of us interested in the Southern Plains, this new perspective suddenly makes this old story seem startlingly familiar. Coronado, the first tourist to complain about the area's emptiness and sterility, was also the first to miss its crucial contribution to economic meshings that reached ultimately across the continent. De Soto, even as he was being given great numbers of bison robes as tribute, also brushed aside the implications, partly because of what he heard. Standing on his closest approach to the Plains, he was told that out there "were many cattle [bison]," but "the land was poorly settled . . . and had little maize." Learning that "there was a scattering of population toward the west and large towns toward the southeast," he reversed his course, "fearing . . . they could not feed themselves [to the west] . . . because of its scattered population."[19] And the Turk? Without pushing it too hard, his unfortunate end also might be seen as an early instance of a certain underappreciation of country that, however empty it might look, is in fact full of possibilities.

The Spanish and the Spark of Change

The Turk's encounter marks as well a transition to an era of rapid change, with the same resources now sought more eagerly, put to more uses, and sent out even more distantly than before. The Spanish, mostly without realizing it, would set loose spectacular changes by introducing horses to the Plains and the mountainous West. Essentially, this single addition realigned Plains peoples with their environment by permitting them to tap more immediately into the grasslands' vast stores of energy. For centuries, it had been the bison and other grazers that had exploited the grass directly. The people who hunted and consumed and traded those animals had the disadvantage of working once removed from the energy growing around their feet. Now people controlled and spent that energy directly, or nearly so, by riding atop swift and powerful animals that turned grass into power. Horseback hunters suddenly were on a kind of par with their prey. The same advantage increased hugely people's ability to fight, to move about in pursuit of other resources, and to connect with distant markets.[20]

The Southern Plains essentially became a new place—and a much more desirable one. The result was a dramatic shuffling of populations. In the late seventeenth century, roughly coincident with the first great dispersal of horses out of northern New Mexico, Shoshonean-speaking immigrants arrived from the northern Rockies and eastern Great Basin. They called themselves Numinu; others used a name given by their Ute relatives and allies: Comanches. These newcomers acquired horses and during the first half of the next century shaped their culture around the potential of a fusion of human and animal power. This, in fact, marks the birth of the Comanches as a people. Only with their expansion onto the Southern Plains and their adoption of the horse did the many related bands among the Numinu conceive a common identity. It was a cultural union of people, their new home, and the heady sense of command that came with the mastery of horses.

From the northern Rockies and Plains came the Kiowas, and, along the way to establishing themselves in alliance with the Comanches south of the Arkansas River, they too acquired horses and developed a vision of themselves, to use the phrase of one of their descendants, the novelist and essayist N. Scott Momaday, as "centaurs of the spirit." Cheyennes moved onto the Plains from the Missouri River Valley, and, after living for a while around the Dakota Black Hills, shifted farther south with some of their bands, the Southern Cheyennes, gravitating with the Southern Arapahoes to the Arkansas River on the northern edge of the Southern Plains. The Apachean groups met by Coronado were driven off the Plains entirely or to the western fringes near the Pueblos, where they took up residence with their sedentary relatives.

Measured merely by this simple tracking of peoples' movements, these were some of the most turbulent years in the history of the

Southern Plains—rising and falling of fortunes, peoples born and peoples banished, and political and social restructuring. Few places in North America witnessed anything comparable. And yet, when we set this period in the larger context of what came before, we see that older patterns persisted. The new Plains people continued to send out their abundant resources to meet a hungry demand elsewhere. They continued a vigorous interaction with those on their fringes, and they tapped into systems of trade reaching much farther beyond. With their heightened mobility, they took part with an unprecedented vigor in the old motif of constant movement over large areas.

The trade in humans gathered momentum. Father Anastasio Dominguez in 1776 described Comanches bringing for sale in Taos "pagan Indians, of both sexes, whom they capture from other nations." They were bought by locals, including high officials, who, another priest complained in 1761, "gorge themselves" on the young women and men offered in the markets. In the eyes of the law the transfer was often that of ransom, although these ransomed American Indians *(indios de rescate)* were bound to their ransomers for ten to twenty years, much like indentures in the English colonies. Also classified as slaves, servants, and orphans, these purchased captives composed 10 to 15 percent of the New Mexican colonial population by some estimates. In settlements closest to the Plains the figure was as high as 40 percent. The "other nations" raided by the Comanches were those around the other edges of their orbit, in the Central and Eastern Plains and in southern and central Texas.[21] The easternmost New Mexican settlements also were alternately patronized and terrorized by the Comanches. One month the people of the Plains would come into the fairs to trade slaves, robes, other bison products, and sometimes goods, such as firearms, from the far side of the Plains. The next month they might raid the same area, killing residents and seizing more captives.

Whichever way the traffic moved, most captives were under fifteen or so, and most were female. Girls "of serviceable age" brought usually a couple of horses. Boys came cheaper—a horse or mule, plus a few extras. Besides what might seem the obvious reason, sexual use, the price disparity reflected the slave trade's wider purposes. In addition to being taken as forced laborers and as a resource to barter elsewhere, captives were often integrated into Plains tribes to buttress their populations. The female advantage of childbearing here is obvious. In the old tradition of trade alliances, furthermore, a woman might be given as liaison, an intimate and reproductive link between groups.

Women captives, that is, were living reminders of enduring patterns of Plains life—its most ancient tradition of wide-ranging trade, the movement of peoples through, into, and out of the region, and the fluid relations among the many participants, including those on either edge of the Plains world. The shifting possibilities and meanings of captivity could be seen at the individual as well as the collective level. In 1760, the twenty-one-year-old Maria Rosa Villalpando was one of fifty-seven persons taken by Comanches when they sacked a fortified home near Ranchos de Taos. She left behind an infant son. She was traded to Pawnees along the Platte River, and had another son, Antoine, by 1767, when she took up with a French trader, Jean Sale. Although she produced a son with Sale, she remained a Pawnee captive until he took her to St. Louis in 1770 and married her. There she remained, even after Sale returned to France, the respected elder of what was now a prominent family. She lived until 1830, long enough for her New Mexican son to come calling and put in a claim on her considerable estate.[22]

This type of human movement, with its troubling but mixed meanings, persisted across the Southern Plains even after the United States gained full control of the region and its periphery in the Mexican War, as when traders in the 1850s acquired a boy at Quitaque, now in Floyd County, Texas, for a mare, a rifle, a shirt and drawers, a gun and powder, and a bison robe. The items exchanged for this captive remind us that trade in material goods persisted as well. New goods were introduced by Europeans—firearms, textiles, knives and scrapers and other metal tools, coffee, and sugar formed into cones called *piloncillo*, all of it added to what had circulated for centuries and now was swapped within a radius much extended by the far greater traveling power of the horseback traders. Peoples hundreds of miles away felt the rippling effects of what came out of and across the Southern Plains. Portraits of American Indians on the upper Missouri by Karl Bodmer show his subjects wearing Navajo blankets and Spanish silver crosses traded up from Comanche country through this newly expanded system.[23]

As for what came directly from the Plains, the most important example was itself a merging of the new and old. Horses were fresh arrivals, yet as animals turning grass into something people could use, they were part of a tradition stretching back millennia. In another sense, they were both a recent and ancient part of Plains life. Horses were children coming home. Their distant ancestors evolved here and sent emigrants to Asia before dying off at the end of the Pleistocene. The Spanish returned with a splendid derivation of those early dog-sized horses, one that was still beautifully suited to the vast pasture of short grasses. The result was a faunal flowering eloquently described by historian Dan Flores.[24] Wild mustangs, their tails shaggy and their manes long and tangled, roamed this region by the tens of thousands. Tens of thousands more were kept by the Comanches, Kiowas, and other tribes. Anthropologists estimate that at least six horses per every man, woman, and child were needed simply to sustain nomadic life. As the human population rose arithmetically, the number of horses grew geometrically.

Beyond subsistence, two other factors made these animals even more valuable on the Southern Plains. The flourishing of the horse culture throughout the Great Plains by around 1780 made these animals that region's most valued item of trade. The country above the fortieth parallel, however, was far less hospitable to horses; annual losses among the herds of the Northern Plains tribes were always high and sometimes devastating. The result was a hungry demand to the north. The Comanches responded by supplying horses, directly and indirectly, from their country. The Cheyennes first saw horses when Comanche traders brought them to horticultural villages along the middle Missouri River in present North Dakota, probably in the 1780s. With permission of Maheo, the All Being, the Cheyennes acquired horses and began their own Plains odyssey. Soon they served as middlemen, herding horses from south of the Arkansas to tribes in the Dakotas and elsewhere. To supply this northward flow, the Comanches and others raided New Mexican settlements, culled animals from their own herds, and captured mustangs running wild.

The System Expanded; or, the Great Devouring

Meanwhile, the bison trade continued, with some new wrinkles. Comanche raids from the Plains into New Mexico had naturally retarded somewhat the trade and movement between the two regions, but in 1786 the viceroy of New Spain, Bernardo de Galvez, recommended opening the long-forbidden horse trade to the Comanches. By then they had the animals anyway, he reasoned. Trade would cultivate friendly dependence and would bring into the New Mexican settlements what they needed badly—bison meat and robes. Governor Juan Bautista de Anza's treaty with the Comanche Chief Cuerno Verde in the same year began an era of much more vigorous exchange, and, for the first time since the rise of Comanche power, large numbers of New Mexicans took the initiative by venturing onto the Plains.[25] Usually they are categorized as *comancheros*, who visited the Comanches with goods to trade, and *ciboleros*, who traveled eastward to hunt bison. In reality, there was never such a clear division; the latter might barter with American Indians and the former often returned laden with meat and raw hides they hunted along the way. The distinction does remind us, however, that some concentrated on the bison trade.

Ciboleros hunted usually in the fall. Josiah Gregg described them in their leather jackets and trousers and their flat straw hats, well seated on their mounts, shoulders slung with quivers of arrows, and their long lances strapped to their saddle pommels, tips waving high above them. They would approach a herd from downwind and when it bolted would ride among the fleeing animals, thrusting their lances past a quarry's ribs and into the heart. The best hunters could bring down up to twenty-five in one such chase. The fall hunt lasted several weeks. Ciboleros sliced and sun-dried the meat and packed it tightly into *carretas*, their two-wheeled carts, by stomping it down with their bare feet, a practice they believed help preserve the product. They spent their evenings feasting on it and swilling raw whiskey a visitor called "as barbarous an alcoholic compound as has ever been made." By one estimate, in the early 1830s they were killing at least ten to twelve thousand bison annually.[26]

Behind the accelerated trade was a greater demand from the two sources that had always driven the commerce. A growing New Mexican population needed more food (specifically protein), and their quickening interest in goods channeled through Chihuahua required more Plains' goods for exchange. The market for bison robes in the United States was also taking tens of thousands of bison annually, especially from the Central Plains. Together these pressures, plus the rise in human and horse populations and other changes, were beginning to erode seriously the resource crucial to the Plains economy for centuries. By the 1850s and 1860s, the numbers of bison were shrinking alarmingly on the Southern and Central Plains.[27]

That decline turned into a collapse with the infamous "great hunt" of the 1870s, as hundreds of hide hunters turned to the Southern Plains after virtually exterminating the herds north of the Arkansas and south of the Platte rivers. Within a few years, the southern herd too was on the verge of extinction, and bison were no longer a factor in commerce. In some ways the great hunt was, as it is usually portrayed, a new and unique assault. A technology of railroads and high-caliber rifles allowed Anglo hunters to gobble up and ship off the animals as never before. The slaughter was inspired by an unvarnished capitalism the region had never felt. Bison hides were put to the new use of industrial leather, and the markets now pulling at the herds were immensely greater, fanning out to factories of the Atlantic coast and Europe.

But when put in context of its deep history, this looks like a new twist of an old, embedded economic mechanism. Before, bison had been exported as food, shields, and robes; now they became machine gaskets and belts. The stored solar energy of grasses, made accessible as an animal in the old way, was now transferred to fit the needs of a new industrial power, but the basic process was the same. It is also worth recalling that the older and newer purposes always overlapped. John Cook doubtless was only one of many who entered the business by first working for ciboleros who hunted alongside the rifle-toting Anglo new-comers.[28] Those Anglos, furthermore, by no means always killed bison only for their hides, leaving all meat to rot, as popular impressions would have it. J. Wright Mooar, arguably the most famous hunter of the Southern Plains, was instrumental in opening the industrial market for bison leather. Yet, while sending hides east to that new market, he also set up an elaborate operation (constructing smokehouses 110 feet long and 30 feet wide) to cure bison meat and soak it in brine so he could market it in army posts and Texas frontier settlements.[29] On the Central Plains, dealers shipping green hides also marketed bison hams by the thousands to places as far away as Albany, New York. Newly arrived farming and ranching families conducted periodic hunts among the herds to feed their families.

In a sense, that is, the cause of the bison's near demise was an abrupt, cataclysmic expansion of a system that had operated for centuries. The Plains was providing the world outside with its abundance, as it had for dozens of generations, only now the hunger was suddenly so voracious and the ability to harvest so enhanced that a resource that had once seemed limitless was reduced in a blink of historical time to the vanishing point.

There was, however, one supremely important new element in this old equation. It was not as obvious as Sharps rifles and railcars, but it was far more momentous for people of the Plains, American Indians and Anglos alike. For the first time, external forces were determining what resources and how much of them would be taken. Life always had

been shaped in tension between outside power and Plains people exert-
ing their own. Now the balance tipped quickly toward the former. It
took two forms. An international market economy inspired the great
hunt; bison hides were shipped to satisfy one particular part of it—
factories—but more generally the hunters were responding to its fundamental mechanisms: the rise and fall of demand and prices, technological innovations, flows and fluctuations of currencies and other
resources, and much more.

The other source of outside power was an expanding nation, the
United States. This nation had a far greater population, more accessible
physical power, and much more economic heft than any that had
touched the Plains before it. The hundreds of hunters who slaughtered
the bison, after all, represented only a small fraction of the nation's
thinnest edge of population. They were the exotic fringe of a network of
economic relationships that now bound the Plains to decisions and
influences thousands of miles distant. People and animals dangled like
baubles on a modern mobile. At first glance they seemed to float free,
but when something jiggled in Chicago or New York or London, bison
and American Indians now twitched.

The most obvious manifestation of this outside force was the army,
and, as with the bison hunters, its full meaning is easily missed. Both
folk tradition and a lot of historical writing have stressed the military's
heroism and its frustrations in running to ground the mounted
Comanche and Kiowa warriors, and on the other side the American
Indians' skills, bravery, depredations, and final poignant loss of independence. These elements catch the human drama of the time, but they
tend to overlook what the army represented in a broader sense. Behind
it was a force infinitely greater than what the American Indians could
muster. In some battles of the Civil War, the government had spent
more lives in half an hour than the Comanches could send into the
field in total. True, the army had been cut drastically back, and its western skeleton crew had its moments of bumbling, but, anytime it chose,
the distant government could have easily mustered and sent whatever
was needed to crush any resistance. As it was it played with the
American Indians, keeping the cost as low as possible until a combination of shrewdness and luck gave some officer the chance he needed.
He turned out to be Ranald Mackenzie, who caught the core of
Comanche and Kiowa warriors at Palo Duro Canyon in 1874 and,
after taking the field, seized virtually all the warriors' horses, kept

several hundred of the best for his men, then ordered the slaughter of the remaining 1,450.

It was the culmination of what has been called the Buffalo War, touched off by American Indian attacks on the hide hunters ravaging the southern herd. The trigger of their assault had been Colonel Richard Dodge's go-ahead to push south of the Arkansas: "Boys, if I were a buffalo hunter I would hunt buffalo where the buffalo are."[30] Some have argued that the hide men were in effect an arm of the military sent to destroy what Phil Sheridan called the "Indians' commissary." This has the situation exactly backwards. The hunters were using the army. Certainly they didn't need anyone in a uniform to encourage them. Their inspiration was summed up by Frank Mayer. With a minimal investment and a bit of luck, he figured he could make triple the salary of the president of the United States—as long as the cavalry was there for some protection, he might have added.[31]

Blaming the loss of the bison on the army underestimates by a long shot what the American Indians were up against. For that matter, so does blaming the hide hunters for slaughtering the herds and the army for ending armed resistance. Behind the hunters and the soldiers, two great forces reached into the Southern Plains after the Civil War—a dynamic and voracious international capitalist market economy and a newly consolidated apparatus of state power. The potential clout of each was far greater than any the Plains had ever known. Working in concert, they were unstoppable. A few hundred agents of the first force consumed what had sustained Plains peoples for centuries—the bison, matchless mechanism of converting useless grass into the stuff of a good life. The second force sent a relative handful who caught up with the American Indians and took away the one requisite of independence—the horse, the animal that turned grass into movement and grace. In the full perspective of market and nation, these events must have seemed barely worth a note. And on the long timeline of the South Plains, the end came as a quick perfunctory slap.

Old Patterns, New Shapes

The past century and a quarter have seen a playing out of these themes, some millennia-old, some from a few centuries back, and the last, the intrusion of outside power, quite recent. From the beginning, people have sniffed out rich resources and have sent them out to others. For scores of generations, they have also turned the necessity of movement into the means of wringing more out of the country. Twice these patterns have been expanded. In the seventeenth century, horses tapped more directly into the energy thrumming through the environment, hugely increased people's power to move about, and through those gifts became themselves the Plains' most valuable item of trade. They anticipated other animals that, like the bison, converted into profit the potential of the land, but unlike that indigenous animal these were under human control. Horses, cattle, and sheep all domesticated the Plains' inherent power.

In the second expansion two centuries later, the Plains was pulled into the orbits of national authority and a global market. Those two forces destroyed American Indian independence, but for the waves of settlers who have followed, each also brought considerable, if erratic, opportunity. A recent study calculates that funds channeled through the frontier army were decisive in the establishment of a civilian economy in West Texas in the second half of the nineteenth century. The army also began what has become an incalculably valuable form of government assistance by forging and maintaining paths of human movement. In 1849, Captain Randolph Marcy mapped a route from Santa Fe to Big Spring and northeastward to the Red River due north of Dallas. In the decades ahead westering travelers used it, some to pass through to New Mexico and California and others to take up land on the Plains. Mackenzie's routes during the Buffalo War became major north-south arteries of movement. For long stretches, military roads overlay much older paths, particularly the trails Comanches took to trade and raid. A map showing these various routes is a snarling of intersecting, interweaving lines, and when a modern map is laid on it, we can see how U.S. highways have sometimes followed older paths and sometimes have pushed others across the country, all paid for by federal and state funds and accomplished by a muscular outside technology. After 1955, interstate highways would become the essential avenues of transit and the prime determinants of local economies. Add to roads a century and a quarter of railroad building and, after World War II, the national government's subsidy of air travel to ports that otherwise could never support much service, and we can start to appreciate the massive federal stimulation to the most ancient tradition of the Southern Plains—human movement.

Farmers, global markets, and the national government all helped the rich grasslands of the Southern Plains transform into agricultural fields. This 1908 M. S. Lusby photograph of an alfalfa field near Canyon City, Texas, depicts the result. Courtesy Panhandle-Plains Historical Research Center, Canyon, Texas.

As for the world market, the two exports most connected in the popular mind with the "old" and "new" Plains, cattle and oil, both fed an international demand to become modern variations on the second ancient tradition besides movement—supplying outsiders from the country's abundance. If cattle are domesticated grass-power, petroleum is more sun energy, unimaginably old and trapped underground until recent Plains people pulled it out and exported it, creating booms like that around Snyder, the biggest of its day, that generated huge wealth for some locals and many outside investors, including celebrities such as Bob Hope and Don Ameche. Government and market technologies opened other untapped potential. The most significant was that of agriculture, especially cotton, which with oil and cattle has become a pillar of the regional economy. Arguably, in fact, agriculture might rank with horses, markets, and government as a realignment of the area's potential.

Every new benefit is in tension with an equally obvious vulnerability. A sag in beef demand or a splurge of sales in some other distant Plains or pampas can send cattle prices toward the drain. The oil business is susceptible to factors ranging from political conditions in Venezuela and the Persian Gulf to yuppies' annual opinions of sports utility vehicles. State and national government policies can shake things up terrifically, while influence in the other direction, from the Plains outward, is minimized by a population that is chronically thin and erratic.

American Indians, that is, were only the first to see their independence reduced by these two sources of outside power, and this has made life on the Plains chancier than ever. These new uncertainties are compounded by the oldest one, a climate that shifts dramatically and often withholds something that people need even more than protein and carbohydrates: water. Current economic difficulties and the hemorrhaging of population have followed an especially unfortunate coincidence of new and old vulnerabilities—a slide in the market price of oil and cattle and a devastating drought.

On the other hand, the current hard times throw into stark relief another implication of outside power that is utterly new to the Plains. With the long embrace of government has come unprecedented external support. Besides such direct benefits as income subsidies, aid for children, and health programs, state and national enterprises have provided jobs and, as with the frontier army, the multiplier effect of huge infusions of money. The military tradition continues with army and air force bases. Colleges and universities employ thousands, spend millions, and through research contribute to further innovation. State and federal funding of the ancient tradition of movement is part of the region's lifeblood; in many counties a leading employer is the state highway department.

Ironically, this support also opens opportunities for some, especially the young, to join the exodus from the Plains. Higher education is often a ticket out for those who can come up with the tuition and the grades. The military simultaneously helps prop up local economies and provides young men and women without the funds or inclination for the college classroom a chance to escape. Andres Tijerina is a revealing example of both routes of exit. His father abandoned his family when Andres was five. For a while, his mother supported him and his brother and sister with double jobs until she became ill and the children worked as migrant laborers with a series of relatives. They picked cotton across the Plains of West Texas, living in garages and boxcars, denied access to most public facilities but attending school when they could, always after the fall harvest, until their mother recovered and the family reunited in

San Angelo. Andres and his brother, Albert, were graduated on scholarships from Texas A&M, joined the Air Force, and served in Vietnam. Albert died there. Both Albert and Andres earned the Distinguished Flying Cross. Andres returned as a captain, earned an M.A. in history from Texas Tech and a Ph.D. from University of Texas at Austin, served as executive director of the state Good Neighbor Commission (at thirty-six, the youngest director in state government and the only Hispanic), and has written several books on Mexican American contributions to Texas and the Southwest. He has returned to West Texas occasionally, once to commemorate the naming of a building at Goodfellow Air Force Base in San Angelo after his brother. One of his more vivid memories might serve as a metaphor for thousands of others who have followed similar routes. On a training flight out of Webb Air Force Base, he looked down and realized he was flying over (and eventually away from) fields where he had picked cotton with his brother, sister, aunts, and uncles.[32]

For those who choose to remain on the Plains, federal, state, and local governments provide the backbone of many localities. Government institutions in Snyder pay the wages and salaries of more than half the workforce of the area's major employers. Three facilities alone hire nearly 40 percent of those workers. No wonder, then, that Plains communities have eagerly courted various types of government involvement. Competition for campuses began early. Hermleigh, outside Snyder, made a strong bid for the agricultural and technical college to be established in the area in the 1870s. Its boosters argued that its businesses were the most aggressive, its spirit the feistiest, its climate the healthiest, and its future the most promising. Lubbock, however, got the prize (Texas Tech). Today, Hermleigh's population is under five hundred. Like colleges, military bases are considered economic jewels, and each rumor of one being closed is met with well-justified consternation.

Given the area's celebration of individual independence, the most recent example of eagerly sought government outposts is especially ironic—prisons. In 1986, three years after the oil crash, a local judge in Snyder lobbied successfully for the first state prison unit ever built outside southeastern Texas. An offended citizenry turned him out of office, but since a federal court in 1993 required decentralization of the state system, prisons have become the growth industry of the Southern Plains. They stand outside towns like Snyder, Ware, Wallace, Middleton, Lamesa, and Havens. Without the coils of concertina wire atop their high fences, a passerby might mistake them for especially well-built county fair facilities. As many residents have left these towns, inmates and employees have moved in. Prisoners and workers in the two units of Jones County equal 36.5 percent of the county population.[33] These new arms of government, in turn, prop up others. Local student enrollment in Snyder's Western Texas College (WTC) has declined badly in recent years. In 1980, its basketball team went 37–0 and won its division's national championship, but basketball and football programs have since been eliminated for lack of funds and participants. Total enrollment and credit hours, however, have grown, fed by a new constituency behind bars. Since 1994, enrollments at WTC have grown by thirty percent, the same percentage of inmates among enrollees in the spring 2001 semester. Apparently with plenty of study time on their hands, prisoners are considered by instructors their best and most reliable students.

While outside support has been vital, Plains people as always have cobbled together possibilities to muddle through a difficult passage. Communities today try to capitalize on the one sure thing—people passing through—by offering a chance to stop briefly and enjoy the country. Snyder hosts the West Texas Western Swing Festival ("Come Fiddle around in Snyder"), recognizing the regional origins of the father of western swing, Bob Wills, from Turkey (a bit more than a hundred miles due north in Hall County), which has its own musical celebrations. Snyder also has its White Buffalo Days, in honor of Wright Mooar's killing nearby of one of seven known white bison in the United States. At Knox City ("Seedless Watermelon Capital of the World") visitors can munch on free watermelon during a festival on the last Saturday in July. Hamlin plays on its name to host a Pied Piper parade and dance every fall. Others promise (and deliver) great quail, deer, wild hog, and turkey hunting. Robert Lee (Coke County) calls itself the recreational heart of the Southern Plains, while Coleman claims title to "The Hunting Capital of Texas." Given the prevalent image of the area, however, recreational tourism is not an easy sell. Some towns boast of odd bits of heritage to set them apart. Sweetwater may host the famous annual Rattlesnake Roundup, but Fluvanna, just northwest of Snyder, claims the unofficial world record for the longest rattler, a nine-footer that must have looked like something snipped from a transatlantic cable when shot by a local farmer in his barn. Most towns spice their promotions with assurance of a hearty welcome, although anyone who has experienced the harder side of this country might detect a slightly wry tone. We're invited to Stamford, "where both the mesquite trees and the friendly people are thick," and in Snyder, blistered by nearly a decade virtually without rain, visitors are promised that "the hospitality, like the warm and friendly sun, shines all year long."

Whether tourism will turn out to be part of a solution to today's troubles is much an open question. Some might argue that the combination of ancient uncertainties and modern vulnerability has made the Southern Plains too risky for sensible people. It is equally arguable, on the other hand, that the shifting factors at some point will recombine to bring better times. And surely it is not overly naive to hope that the people of the Southern Plains will adapt once again with some new combination of old trends and future developments to make a reasonable living and even to enjoy occasional surges of prosperity. Just what might come along, obviously no one can say.

It is intriguing to daydream, however, as we look out from the deep past into the decades ahead while listening to stories like those on two recent consecutive broadcasts of National Public Radio's "All Things Considered." One told of Californians' anger during their electrical power crisis when they realized that much of their wattage was being bought at high prices from Texas producers. An arm-waving state legislator suggested California either do something about this banditry or admit defeat and raise the Lone Star flag above the capital at Sacramento. The previous day's program featured a report from the Southern Plains town of McCamey, Texas, an oil boomtown gone bust, which has granted large tax benefits to companies developing hundreds of wind-driven generators. Similar efforts elsewhere have not panned out, but now-familiar forces—new technology, federal tax incentives, state government encouragement, and rising prices elsewhere in the national utilities market—have brought a vigorous revival of interest. While a long shot, McCamey's experiment summons up a delicious fantasy. How lovely it would be if the Southern Plains should regain some economic footing by capturing one more abundant form of energy, converting it as so often before into usable power, and exporting it to those in need, in this case the power-starved residents of the Pacific Coast who look down from airliners into the apparent emptiness of West Texas and who drive across it as fast as possible, goggling at the country's sparseness and complaining about being buffeted by the distilled essence of this country's long story of restless movement—the wind.

Notes

1. Charles Kuralt, *On the Road with Charles Kuralt* (New York: Putnam, 1985), 278.

2. J. D. Figgins, "The Antiquity of Man in America," *Natural History* 27 (May–June 1927): 229–39; Harold J. Cook, "New Geological and Palaeontological Evidence Bearing on the Antiquity of Mankind in America," *Natural History* 27 (May–June 1927): 240–48.

3. Tom Dillehay, "Late Quarternary Bison Population Changes on the Southern Plains," *Plains Anthropologist* 19 (August 1974): 180–96; Darrell Creel, "A Faunal Record From West Central Texas and Its Bearing on Late Holocene Bison Population Changes in the Southern Plains," *Plains Anthropologist* 35 (February 1990): 55–69.

4. Christy G. Turner II and Jacqueline A. Turner, *Man Corn: Cannibalism and Violence in the Prehistoric American Southwest* (Salt Lake City: University of Utah Press, 1999).

5. Katherine A. Spielmann, ed., *Farmers, Hunters, and Colonists: Interaction between the Southwest and Southern Plains* (Tucson: University of Arizona Press, 1991); K. A. Spielmann, "Late Prehistoric Exchange between the Southwest and Southern Plains," *Plains Anthropologist* 28 (1983): 257–72.

6. Herbert Eugene Bolton, *Coronado: Knight of Pueblos and Plains* (Albuquerque: University of New Mexico Press, 1964), 246.

7. On the trade system from Mexico to the Southwest, see Carroll L. Riley, "The Road to Hawikuh: Trade and Trade Routes to Cibola-Zuni during Late Prehistoric and Early Historic Times," *The Kiva* 41 (1975): 137–59.

8. Carroll L. Riley, *The Frontier People: The Greater Southwest in the Protohistoric Period* (Albuquerque: University of New Mexico Press, 1987), 272.

9. Riley, *The Frontier People*, 269; Alfred Vincent Kidder, *The Artifacts of Pecos* (New Haven: Yale University Press, 1932), 249.

10. James A. Brown, "Arkansas Valley Caddoan: The Spiro Phase," in *Prehistory of Oklahoma*, ed. Robert E. Bell (New York: Academic Press, 1984), 241–63; Henry W. Hamilton, "The Spiro Mound," *Missouri Archeologist* 14 (1952): 1–276; Frank F. Schambach, "Spiro and the Tunica: A New Interpretation of the Role of the Tunica in the Culture History of the Southeast and the Southern Plains, A.D. 1100–1750," in *Arkansas Archeology: Essays in Honor of Dan and Phyllis Morse*, ed. R. C. Mainfort, Jr., and M. D. Jeter (Fayetteville: University of Arkansas Press, 1999), 169–224.

11. Riley, "The Road to Hawikuh," 139–40.

12. John Grier Varner and Jeannette Johnson Varner, eds., *The Florida of the Inca* (Austin: University of Texas Press, 1951), 249.

13. Lawrence A. Clayton, Vernon James Knight, Jr., and Edward C. Moore, eds., *The De Soto Chronicles: The Expedition of Hernando De Soto to North*

America in 1539–1543 (Tuscaloosa: University of Alabama Press, 1993), 117, 241, 300.

14. By the eighteenth century, bison were found throughout this area and east of the Mississippi, but during the mid-sixteenth century, their range apparently extended only to the Eastern Plains. The most authoritative study remains Carl O. Sauer, *Seventeenth Century North America* (Berkeley, Calif.: Turtle Island, 1980). See page 226 for Sauer's discussion.

15. Riley, *Frontier People*, 86.

16. Riley, *Frontier People*, 82–83.

17. Mildred M. Wedel, "The Indian They Called Turco," in *Pathways to Plains Prehistory: Anthropological Perspectives of Plains Natives and Their Pasts: Papers in Honor of Robert E. Bell*, ed. D. G. Wyckoff and J. Hoffman (Norman: Oklahoma Anthropological Society, 1982), 153–62.

18. Carroll L. Riley, "Early Spanish-Indian Communication in the Greater Southwest," *New Mexico Historical Review* 46:4 (1971): 304–6.

19. Clayton, Knight, and Moore, eds., *De Soto Chronicles*, 127.

20. For a summary of this development, see Elliott West, *The Contested Plains: Indians, Goldseekers, and the Rush to Colorado* (Lawrence: University Press of Kansas, 1998), 49–54.

21. For an excellent summary of the slave trade, see James F. Brooks, "'This Evil Extends Especially . . . to the Feminine Sex': Negotiating Captivity in the New Mexico Borderlands," *Feminist Studies* 22:2 (1996): 279–309.

22. Brooks, "This Evil," 279–80.

23. Thomas F. Schilz, "Robes, Rum, and Rifles: Indian Middlemen in the Northern Fur Trade," *Montana, The Magazine of Western History* 40 (Winter 1990): 3–4.

24. Dan Flores, "Where All the Pretty Horses Have Gone," in *Horizontal Yellow: Nature and History in the Near Southwest* (Albuquerque: University of New Mexico Press, 1999), 81–124.

25. On this treaty and its background, see Thomas W. Kavanagh, *Comanche Political History: An Ethnohistorical Perspective, 1706–1875* (Lincoln: University of Nebraska Press, 1996), 110–21.

26. The best condensed discussion of *ciboleros* remains Charles L. Kenner, *A History of New Mexican–Plains Indian Relations* (Norman: University of Oklahoma Press, 1969), 98–114. Gregg's description is on 101–2, and the quote on the liquor drunk is on 102.

27. For a discussion of the factors involved in the decline of bison populations on the Central and Southern Plains, see Elliott West, *The Way to the West: Essays on the Central Plains* (Albuquerque: University of New Mexico Press, 1995), 51–83; Dan Flores, "Bison Ecology and Bison Diplomacy: The Southern Plains from 1800 to 1850," *Journal of American History* 78:2 (September 1991): 465–85.

28. John Cook, *The Border and the Buffalo: An Untold Story of the Southwest Plains* (Topeka, Kans.: Crane and Company, 1907), 54, 81–86.

29. J. Wright Mooar interview, Snyder, Texas, March, 1939, Nita Stewart Haley Memorial Library, Midland, Texas.

30. J. Wright Mooar, "The First Buffalo Hunting in the Panhandle," *West Texas Historical Association Year Book* 6 (1930): 110.

31. Meyer quoted in David A. Dary, *The Buffalo Book: The Full Saga of the American Animal* (Chicago: Sage Books, 1974), 103.

32. "Andres Tijerina," in *The Vietnam Experience: A War Remembered*, eds., Stephen Weiss, et al. (Boston: Boston Publishing Company and New York: W. W. Norton, 1988), 182–87; Andres Tijerina, correspondence with the author.

33. Information on prisons in this area provided by Larry Fitzgerald, Texas Department of Criminal Justice.

CHAPTER TWO

When Corporations Rule the Llano Estacado

The Glorious Past and Uncertain Future
of the Southern High Plains Family Farm

JOHN MILLER MORRIS

Where Have All the Farmers Gone?

In January of 2001, a typical cold front rolled down the Great Plains. As the continental polar air mass moved from Kansas and Oklahoma into northwestern Texas and eastern New Mexico, it dipped into the Canadian River Valley, then encountered and poured smoothly across an immense, almost frictionless southwestern tableland—the Southern High Plains, also called the Llano Estacado, or Staked Plains. Cold, dense air sliced underneath the warmer air mass of the Llano region, throwing moist air aloft until a "blue norther" appeared. Unfortunately, there was lightning associated with this winter front. Because civilization on the treeless High Plains is formed by largely vertical structures, lightning is a regular hazard. A massive bolt from this norther hit the old Andy and Melba Brown rural home near Jericho in Donley County, Texas. The family farmhouse burned down. With its destruction another family farm tradition slipped away quietly as well.

In the 1950s, the Brown farmhouse had been lively, full of adults, children, and neighbors, all working the land in an earnest manner—a reflection of another time. The Browns had grown up in a vigorous community with neighbors and acquaintances such as D. E. Leathers at Leila Lake. The Leathers, in fact, were local family farmers so quintessential that they were named—to the cheers of Franklin Roosevelt and a nation—the "Typical American Family" in 1940. After Andy died, Melba married Johnnie Leathers. She moved to Clarendon to live with him, leaving the home place still furnished yet uninhabited. The news that the old Brown house had burned down saddened the remaining farmers of Donley County. Some questioned whether the family farm itself, its way of life, was winking out as well. In this instance, though, it was not an unfeeling agribusiness corporation bulldozing an old home for a scrap of cropland; it was Mother Nature herself that terminated the residence and reclaimed the horizontal nature of the plains.

The disappearance of the Brown house and the heritage of family farming it represented are quietly symptomatic of a long-term shift in agriculture on the Southern High Plains. The trend is the movement from diversified, decentralized, small-scale, family-oriented, and reasonably eco-friendly farm enterprises toward monocultural, centralized, large-scale, corporate-oriented, and presumably more eco-destructive agribusiness. The movement to "bigness" in American agriculture is hardly new; the general process has been under way for most of the twentieth century. But powerful farm programs over the last three decades have made the federal government a major partner in the process. In the 1970s Secretary of Agriculture Earl L. Butz admonished farmers to plow "fencerow to fencerow," a production course that led to a corollary: "Get Big or Get Out." Today, U.S. Department of Agriculture (USDA) government programs profoundly shape and influence modern farming. On the one hand they constitute a political economy seeking to "save the family farmer." On the other hand, almost 70 percent of the payments go to big agribusiness, which further claims the privilege of belonging to "the future."[1]

Yet, the gradual transition from happy, owner-occupied, and traditional family farm to merciless, corporate, and exhaustive farm factory attacks the core of two American ideals: first, it overthrows the historical "yeoman farmer" of Thomas Jefferson and all sentimental populists; and second, it subverts the contemporary environmental or "sustainability" paradigm. The Jeffersonians, of course, lost the demographic argument a century ago; family farmers today are a few percentage points of American society. As for environmentalists and land ethicists, "Big Ag" is largely the problem for them. Wendell Berry argues passionately in *The Unsettling of America: Culture and Agriculture* that the small resourceful family farm not only sustains rural people but also nourishes their communities, particularly communities that value the (sustainable) heritage of "the past."[2] Corporate versus family, big versus small, future versus past—all the dialectics of a complex situation are in place. And these dialectics are thoroughly subject to national demographic trends, changing global economies, and dramatic new technologies.

My extended family has lived and worked on the Southern High Plains for over a century now. We are, improbably enough, still in the business of farming. Many of our former neighbors are not. But there are good reasons why we may also go the way of the old Brown house. The "graying" of farm operators, disappearing rural youth, low commodity prices, high operating costs, exorbitant energy prices, the lack of credit to operators, weird weather, and many other factors make the future look uncertain. And we are a family-corporate farm, a transitional hybrid of the old and the new. A half-century of company experience provides no clear answer to the question of whether cooperative corporate management of land is better or worse than sole proprietorship. We respond to large forces beyond our control. Uncertainty is certain. Our reward is risk. One significant step undertaken in 1998 was to convert hundreds of acres of worn cropland into grassland habitat as part of the government's Conservation Reserve Program (CRP). When it pays to grow eco-friendly grass, the company is happy to be conservationist. Indeed, might not corporate conservation, in partnership with federal programs, contribute to significant new paradigms in the decades ahead?

For better or worse, humankind thoroughly domesticated the Southern High Plains in the past century. Perhaps the chief agency in this dramatic environmental change was the familiar, seemingly simple, family farmer. There were lots of them, and they covered most of the Plains. American farmers came late to the Southern High Plains, an elevated grassland region shared between northern Texas and eastern New Mexico. For most of the nineteenth century, the semiarid Llano Estacado was considered unfit for farming.[3] But farmers did arrive after 1900, and they were amazingly committed to redirecting photosynthetic activity away from short-grass animal grazing and into new domesticated crops. The regional domestication process happened relatively fast, roughly from 1875 to 1910 with new animal genetics, and from 1900 to 1930 with new plant genetics. In the latter period, family labor and small investment melded with bigger networks of corporate endeavor. The dramatic result was the transformation by farmers of the Southern High Plains of a former "uninhabitable desert" into a globally significant food production system.

The arrival and settlement of the family farmer also left a vibrant cultural landscape for the region. A century later, much of that original cultural landscape is gone, dilapidated, or hard-pressed, even as the heritage name Llano Estacado comes back in vogue. Local preservationists have done wonders for sure, but most small-town economies are flat. Local talk in coffee shops can now turn from county poverty rates, business closings, bankruptcies, and demographic declines to even more dire events such as global warming, ice-sheet melting, aquifer depletion, and climatic changes that may increase the aridity for the Southern Plains in general. The Llano Estacado, of course, is simply part of an expanding worldwide debate over conservation-exploitation dialectics. On the surface the Llano of the early twenty-first century is more corporate and less family farm, more intensive use and less extensive use, and more private property and less public access. But what deeper conclusions can we draw from a century of family farm civilization on the Llano? And can history, as an agency of seeing the past, tell us anything about the future?

If corporations rule the Llano Estacado, as they dominate or do rule all significant exchange systems, their reign may be with a heavy hand on the regional environment. In David C. Korten's provocative 1995 book, *When Corporations Rule the World,* he describes the baleful influences that big corporations bring to politics, economics, and especially environmental issues. Korten's globalized food-system corporations are hardly saintly. For the Southern High Plains, however, it need not be sinister transnational companies doing the damage. Already industrial farming in the United States has a poor reputation for protecting land and water, much less practicing humane confinement of animals.[4] Routine feedlot practices in West Texas would be unconscionable in Sweden, India, and perhaps elsewhere. Some modern corporations may well practice "predatory technology" on the Plains, plunder the region's soil or water, and abandon its struggling rural communities whenever convenient to distant owners. Family farmers may do the same at a smaller scale. But theory and moral geography suggest one key advantage to family farms: namely that *successive* land ownership within kinship circles is sensitive to the long-term use—versus short-term exhaustion—of land, water, plant, and animal resources.

Curiously, after exploring the social problems of the modern family farm, I realized that similar questions had been asked once before—almost a hundred years ago. For all the modern moaning about the demise of the idyllic family farm, it was hard-nosed family farmers themselves who displaced the idyllic ranchers of the nineteenth century. In a frenzy of *farm colonization,* thousands and thousands of mechanized agrarians helped themselves to the topsoil with as much zeal as the hard-pressed ranchers had plundered the grass. Moreover, the family farmer crested to glory on the Southern High Plains *at the end* of a long-wave agrarian revolution lasting from 1870 to 1900. One historian sees the transformation of the Texas family farm as a key component in the "The Big Change" that restructured the entire state.[5] Indeed, this period witnessed tremendous change as the state's farms expanded in size and moved inexorably away from old personal subsistence patterns (Daniel Boone) to new regional surplus production (Boone and Sons, Inc.).

Perhaps a new cycle is under way in the twenty-first century, one preoccupied with "Starlink" corn, chemicals, food-processing industries, world trade, information, robotics, bioengineering, and satellite crop visions. Is it fair for mom-and-pop farms to resent a wave of *corporate colonization* from 1980 to 2010? Perhaps it is more pragmatic to implement another technological cycle—of making a new living from the old land—not as ten thousand dispersed farm families but as a few thousand high-tech food system corporations. Of course not all ranchers went out of business in the agrarian boom of the early 1900s, and not all the remaining small family and "hobby" farmers will be absorbed into corporations either.

The number of significant farm operations on the Llano today, some ten thousand (plus another ten thousand small operations) is in rough alignment with the farm boom of 1910.[6] But the larger size and the intensive soil-and-water-mining nature of the current ten thousand primary operations, and the predicted triumph of collective management over individual management, threaten to displace the beloved family farm paradigm as the region's dominant kind of man-land interaction. Already, quaint extensive ranching has become intensive animal feed-lots, and extensive dry land has become intensive irrigated acres. The arrival of large-scale pig farming to the Plains, the extraordinary capital costs for machinery, the invasive and pestiferous species, the reliance on migrant labor pools, and the self-policing regulation policies all amplify modern agriculture's dissonance from nature. The old dream of independence, where farm families lived self-directed lives close to nature, yields to utter dependency relationships, where farmers produce what a corporate system wants for a typically ruthless commodity price. The fear is that "new market realities" are turning traditional family farmers into low-wage, high-risk, rural worker bees. And in fact, the U.S. Census 2000 shows that western and southern Llano counties have 30 percent of their individuals living below the government's poverty level.

On the other hand, recent decades have seen an expansive regional development of the Llano Estacado's health and heritage. Soil and water conservation is widespread, groundwater districts are accepted institutions, no-till farming has taken root, and irrigation technologies are better than ever before. Ground-sensing radar, Geographic Information Systems (GIS), and personal computers are creating new visualizations for the Southern High Plains. Recreational and conservation land use is widespread with Lake Meredith National Recreation Area, Palo Duro Canyon State Park, Alibates Flint Quarries National Monument, Muleshoe National Wildlife Refuge (NWR), Buffalo Lake NWR, and the heritage buffalo herd relocated to Caprock Canyons State Park. Moreover, almost 3.7 million acres of northwest Texas have been placed in the Conservation Reserve Program (CRP) established by the 1985 Food Security Act. As noted earlier, CRP contracts pay farmers to pull land out of crop production and put it back as grassland for many years. County CRP contracts have proved an enormous boost to local wildlife habitat. Urban hunters in turn often buy CRP or other marginal lands, and then they work diligently to increase habitat and wildlife.

For better or worse, when corporations rule the Llano Estacado they will be guiding and implementing many environmental and regional planning responses. If they prove too recalcitrant in being stewards of the land, they may invite heavy regulatory oversight. Agribusiness corporations may also have both power and funds to implement any "sustainability" compromise with capitalism, that is, a theoretical paradigm shift from exhaustive to sustainable farm economies for the mid-twenty-first century. But where are the Southern High Plains headed today—and is it farm families or agribusiness corporations who are showing the true way? To answer this question it is necessary to examine the historic—if not downright symbiotic—relationship of family farmers and corporations on the Southern High Plains. From one turn-of-the-century development paradox (2001) we must go back to another (1901).

Triumph of the Granger: Family-Farm Colonization on the Llano Estacado

In a mere three decades, the dominant human force on the Southern High Plains changed from Comanches to Cowmen to "Cornucopians," that is, from remnant American Indian tribes through a stage of manly ranch empires into baby-boom granger communities. Immediately after the historic U.S. Army campaigns of the mid-1870s (today's disavowed "ethnic cleansing"), Texans and their animals burst onto the Southern High Plains grasslands. There were few farmers among the first pioneers because powerful ranch interests soon bought or fenced the best land and governed the regional economy. Corporate ranching was dramatic and substantial, often pitting puny, individual, pioneer interests against the dreaded power of "the syndicates." From the beginning of Anglo settlement, therefore, corporate culture and imperial outlooks conditioned and characterized the Southern High Plains. The geographer Donald Meinig notes in *Imperial Texas* that much of the rangeland of the Llano Estacado "had come under the control of large companies supplied with Eastern and foreign capital, and railroads had replaced the great cattle trails."[7]

Thus, the principal beneficiaries of pioneer settlement were hardly independent, small, "yeoman farmer" types but rather the land companies, the railroads, the foreign syndicates, and the big-capital ranchers like WMD Lee (LX), partners Charles Goodnight and John Adair (JA), and the politically powerful Farwells of Chicago (XIT). Big ranches and corporate land empires not only held sway over the land, hired hands, and courthouses, but they also operated to contain—nicely or not— unwelcome "nesters" and "hoe-men." Charles Goodnight and other big ranchers opportunely claimed that the regional environment was simply too tough for farmers on the Southern High Plains. But the environment, in combination with ruthless market cycles, soon proved entirely daunting for corporate ranching itself. Episodic drought, poor cattle market conditions, national economic depressions, debts, mismanagement, and environmental difficulties all grievously weakened the old boisterous ranching economy after 1886.

Rancher rule lasted for only a few decades. Today the myths of that period probably bring in more money than the actual ranching or pioneering ever did. Beginning in 1887 and picking up steam in the 1890s and 1900s, new settlement factors and technologies began to crisscross the Llano Estacado. The thin streams of pioneer folk continued and even increased in the 1890s, but they poured less toward the old ranch, trading post, river, creek, or spring sites in the valleys and canyons. The new population trickles centered on or around corporate town-site promotions, especially the railroad towns connected to the larger world of American capitalism. Truly, the arrival of railroads and machine civilization altered almost everything. People left the towns of Tascosa, Mobeetie, and Estacado behind to follow a new spatial logic, one that privileged and responded to real estate, railroads, promotion, and abstract location over older and stricter environmental constraints, such as easy wood and water.

The dominant new settlements of the domesticated plains, cities like Lubbock, Midland, and Amarillo, are deliberate reflections of this corporate spatial discourse. In a usefully flat and monotonous landscape it is not the scenic place that counts, but the intersection of abstract place with corporate needs. Railroad corporations naturally preferred the cost-effective linearity of the endless plains to the colorful wooded canyons and picturesque springs of the pioneers. Corporate town-site agents, such as R. E. Montgomery of the 1887 Fort Worth and Denver Railroad, deliberately strangled the old existing towns. They did so in order to establish corporate rule along their linear worlds. Pioneers, who often bitterly resented this corporate domination, either moved their towns to the railroad (like Old Clarendon did), or withered away in the economic and demographic shakeouts in the decades ahead. Most moved.

By the late 1890s, only a small number of settlers, some thirty-five thousand or so, had taken up residence on the Staked Plains of Texas and New Mexico. Cattle and sheep were plentiful, but finding more than one human being per square mile was unlikely. The U.S. Census 1900 recorded population densities low enough, really, to continue qualifying the vast region, statistically speaking, as a "frontier classification." Since many of the enumerated citizens were urbanites really, congregating in railroad corridor towns such as Amarillo, Canadian, Clarendon, Panhandle, Midland, or county seat towns such as Lubbock, Plainview, Hereford, and Portales, population was indeed sparse out on the ranges. For much of the hinterland there were only scattered, low-wage, livestock workers—and the odd rich boss or better off ranch family. Ranchers accepted the region's lonesome demography as a better alternative, as they saw it, to the environmentally destructive, sod-busting, grass-ruining, calf-stealing, timber-cutting, and game-exterminating encroachments of "hoe-men." They were thankful homestead land in Oklahoma diverted many prospective farmers away from the Staked Plains. The region's lingering nineteenth-century reputation as the "Great American Desert" usefully intimidated others.

All that rancher gloom changed to granger glory after 1900. In fact, the Southern High Plains experienced tremendous growth in the first decade of the twentieth century. This was the era of family-farm colonization. A tidal wave of up-to-date farmers arrived to colonize the Plains, many bringing new paradigms of capital investment and agricultural technology. It helped that a period of decent rainfall ensued, probably a reflection of El Niño Southern Oscillation (ENSO). This better "climate" suggested to newcomers that the land was "not really" a semi-arid range or desert. It also helped that much land was in the hands of bottom-line corporate ranches like the XIT, companies with few desires to keep unprofitable land "in the family" from one generation to another. This second and more profound wave of settlement involved the spatial breakup of old, large, low-profit, worn-pastured ranches and their subsequent retailing as new, small, high-profit, farmland acreage to tens of thousands of "land prospectors." The conversion process itself was corporate in nature, that is, managed by large-scale land colonization firms and methodically abetted by railroads, merchants, and media. Having done their work elsewhere, Midwest land companies (Iowa firms in particular) transferred their attention, visions, capital, mass promotions, slick advertising, and huge operations after 1900 to the Southern High Plains.

Farm colonization recast the region's existing identity. It transformed the economic and demographic base for sure, but also it reshaped local culture from politics to religion. Midwestern values and cultural practices arrived with tremendous force into this prior "southern" and "western" landscape. They were implanted deeply. Even today aspects of the region resemble a Midwest outlier or "little Iowa" so to speak. Out-of-state land promoters such as W. P. Soash, C. O. Keiser, Julien Bassett, and C. W. Post were especially experienced in colonization schemes and mass marketing.[8] Although the early origins of the Llano land boom go back to 1902, the biggest wave of booster-directed settlement poured in after 1905, when entire trainloads of "landseekers" arrived weekly. Tens of thousands of Midwesterners and immigrants eventually came by rail to inspect the cheap lands. Town bands greeted them at the local depot, and slick boosters used fleets of new automobiles to drive the prospects off in style. Out on the flat plains they contemplated gorgeous demonstration farms, good soils, newfangled irrigation wells, easy credit terms, and futuristic farm operations. Many Midwestern landseekers bought the dream, brought their capital, and settled down. For those with less money or credit, homesteading the Southern High Plains was suddenly popular too. Newly reduced filing fees made the experience easy for the young or restless. Homesteaders with little experience or capital needed only to rely on the current beneficial rains lasting indefinitely.

As the old extensive "sustainable" ranch empires were broken up and transformed into intensive family-farm operations, regional population grew rapidly. Total population of the Panhandle (the upper five

Platted by promoter John H. Gee in 1902, Elida, New Mexico, is a significant colonization town of the Southern High Plains that is located twentyfour miles southwest of Portales. Elida's hotel, bank, hardware store, drugstore, lumberyard, and other businesses made money in good years, like 1908, but they struggled when drought times returned. Most towns died out after a few years, but Elida's strategic location on a railroad enabled it to survive. Edward V. Boddy (Boddy & Sons), Elida, New Mexico, Gelatin silver postcard print, 1908, courtesy the John Miller Morris Collection.

rows of northwest Texas counties, anchored by Amarillo) and the South Plains (the next four rows of Texas counties, centered around Lubbock, that lie below the Panhandle), soared by some 100,000 people—to 134,885 by the 1910 census.[9] Indeed, during the early 1900s the Texas Panhandle and South Plains was arguably the fastest growing region of a fast-growing state. New railroad construction advanced hither and yon. The New Mexican side of the Southern High Plains had equally impressive growth. In four east-central counties (Quay, Roosevelt, Curry, and Lea) important railroad and town-site promotions appeared, such as Texico, Clovis, Lovington, Portales, Elida, Ragland, Hobbs, Rogers, Lingo, Eunice, and Tatum.

In addition to the better-financed colonization towns, a bewildering archipelago of ad hoc homesteader hamlets sprang into flickering existence after 1905. A homesteader town of the Plains often started when a country store obtained a designation as a post office. Some rose above humble origins and others quickly died. Consider that in Quay County alone, a fresh-faced 1909 homestead family could choose to live near Ard, Allen, Bard City, Canode, Collinsville, Curry, Dodson, Doris, Lockney, Loyd, Mineosa, Norton, Obar, or Rock Island, among others.[10] Few of these post office hamlets survived more than a decade. Today only a few material hints remain of their former existence, perhaps a forsaken rural cemetery or a circa 1908 postcard with a valuable postmark. In the case of the homesteader towns of Doris, Kappus, and Porter, a Quay County postmark collector can add the notation "Only Recorded Example."

This astounding land rush by largely nonsubsistence farmers depended on *changing* environmental perceptions of the Southern High Plains. After the turn of the century, technology, advertising, and new visual cultures cooperated to dispel the arid and dreadful image associated with the older Llano Estacado. In its place they created the anglicized "Staked Plain"—a young, healthful, inexpensive, and wonderfully fertile region, commonly called the "Promised Land." Prophecies of greatness and Biblical parallels were employed to good effect. Indeed, Christian values and visions were expected to transform a flatland wilderness into a Garden of Eden. By 1908, a Golden Age of farm settlement clearly dawned on the Southern High Plains. This dream of earthly paradise brought not only additional thousands of family farmers, but it also brought mercantile stores, transport facilities, warehouses, machinery, coal consumption, and electricity. And then churches, lodges, schools, the odd college, and sanitariums quickly appeared. Hardworking new-comers from Iowa, Illinois, Kansas, Indiana, and elsewhere, and intrepid immigrants from abroad all bought the regional dream and labored to bring its "Health, Wealth, and Happiness" vision to life. In the process they laid the foundation for the region's strategic transformation into one of most productive agricultural areas in North America.

A large majority of the one hundred thousand new settlers clustered around colonization towns or railroad extension town sites. Colonization towns were obviously speculative enterprises. Corporate interests created most of them, usually in connection with spur or short-line construction schemes. But an individual might get lucky too. In 1902, John Gee platted Elida, New Mexico, as a surer road to wealth than farming itself. He intended his town to serve the central-place theory needs for projected hundreds, maybe thousands, of new farmers in southwest Roosevelt County. While the masses never quite came or lasted, Elida's strategic location on the railroad has kept it alive to the present day. More than fifty such colonization towns sprang up on the Southern High Plains between 1902 and 1914. An amazing twenty-five of these hopeful towns appeared in an arc of eight counties running across the heart of the Llano.[11] Surviving colonization towns for the Llano Estacado included Nazareth (1902), Bovina and Friona (1904), Olton (1908), Crosbyton (1908), Abernathy (1909), Lamesa (1905), Brownfield (1903), and Andrews (1909). Of course many colonization towns, such as Soash, Ellen, Cedric, Virginia City, Montezuma, Spring Lake, and Shafter Lake soon or slowly disappeared. Now only a few old photos suggest their hopes. Those towns that did endure became centers of community life. Streams of colonizers also swelled the existing railroad or county seat communities of Amarillo, Hereford, Canyon, Lubbock, Portales, and elsewhere.

The reality was that corporations, specifically land companies and railroads, made colonization family farming appear both feasible and quite profitable, in good years, on the Southern High Plains. Cattle could walk to market; wheat, milo, and corn could not. Few grangers wanted to haul bulky crops over great distances to reach a distant market. Thus, the interdependence of family farm, land and financing, and railroad transport was absolute: family farm colonizers needed the corporations and vice versa. Their dependency operations were in turn suitably industrialized. Examining hundreds of old photos of the 1900–1914 period, I am struck by the profoundly *industrialized* nature of family farm colonization. The newcomers were hardly no-account, swidden-corn, illiterate subsistence farmers from the Old South, but rather capitalized, innovative, educated, and progressive American families oriented to the future. This sophisticated agrarian pulse, as researcher Frieda Knobloch argues, reflected a stunning and tremendous colonization process applied to the Great Plains environment as a whole.[12]

Then, as now, vociferous complaints about corporate rule—the "big men" against the "little men"—colored social discourse and labor relations. In 1905, the national press took notice of the dwellers of the Staked Plains, "our great inland grazing plain," a place where the old talk was said to be "chiefly of the breeding of Hereford and Durham cattle." In reporter M. G. Cunniff's popular article of that year, "Texas and the Texans," he acknowledged that ordinary Texans once had suffered from overweening corporate rule of the land and economy. The

The Weir family is representative of the typical Midwestern farmers who relocated onto the Llano Estacado. The Weirs are shown here posing proudly with their crops and possessions on display. In contrast to the forlorn "soddies" and crude dugouts of a generation earlier, the Weir farm reflected a more capital-intensive and materialistic approach to farm life on the Plains. George N. Wilkie, Gelatin silver postcard print, 1908, courtesy the John Miller Morris Collection.

problem had seemed intractable, really, until the state's famed railroad commission appeared on the scene in the 1890s. As Cunniff reminded his national audience, local citizens and regional interests used this institution to tame (or so they thought) the dominant corporations of the age. With such a public and regulatory means of balancing individual versus corporate conflict, Cunniff thought a progressive Texas had emerged from stagnancy. Inevitably the state was marching to a "great future."

Cunniff recognized in 1905 that tremendous statewide growth, on the Staked Plains and elsewhere, signified a fundamental transformation under way. The nation's largest commonwealth was moving away from a southern, land-poor, semisubsidence farm system and toward an increasingly sophisticated economy of agribusiness, manufactures, drilling and refining, and industrial production in general. And yet much of this dramatic change, as Cunniff observed for himself, actually belonged to an *increased* expansion of corporate endeavor over the commonwealth. The agents of change that this national reporter saw at work were the cattle kings, big farmers, oil kings, lumber kings, and railroad kings. He saw their dominance, yet he somehow optimistically concluded that "Texas never got out of the grip of the people into the grasp of the corporations." He was a Pollyanna in this regard.

If an eastern reporter believed that corporations dominated the state but did not rule it, perhaps the same could be said for the desert-conquering and town-building family farmers of 1902–1914: they altered and dominated the Southern High Plains, but they did not completely rule it. They brought forth a Garden of Delights, but beyond the dream lay the capricious rule of climate: sudden drought, scores of abandoned towns, and thousands of disappointed and broke small farmers. Homesteading had proved to be a march of folly for many thousands of small dryland farmers, especially in the more arid western Llano. In New Mexico's Quay County alone a dozen or more boomer settlements died in the early 1910s, whisked aside casually by the dry winds of an El Niño Southern Oscillation (ENSO) event. The Texas town of Soash in Howard County went under so fast that it took a large and established land company with it. And this terrific regional bust in agriculture occurred well before the disastrous "dirty thirties" of the Depression era.

Sharp business downturns and drought periodically led to large out-migrations. But the central reality of the colonizer epoch was that corporations and family farmers both hung on and worked together to transform the Southern High Plains. Despite the downturns, within a decade a new agro-industrial empire arose and overshadowed the tired ranches of another age. This new realm featured up-to-date family farms dispersed around linear corridors of steel rails and serviced by centrally placed town hierarchies. Immigration contributed to the ethnic mix as German and Norwegian colonies appeared on the Plains. Farmers adopted increased mechanization, and railroads made money on the coal transported to run the new steam tractors. If resource development was persistent and exhaustive in nature, at least the rates of consumption appeared reasonable.

Many of the newcomers also brought a modernist (if not populist) understanding of "the commons" and the public weal. That is, beyond the usual advent of schools and churches, settlers and farmers also carried important civic and conservation impulses with them. If corporations lured them onto the Southern Plains, it would be up to the colonists, immigrants, and surviving homesteaders to implement any progressive agenda, especially preservation and conservation ideals that they absorbed elsewhere or that enhanced passing the farm to the next generation. Some of their ideas were, of course, simply positive ways of seeing otherwise problematic landscapes. You could not farm a steep canyon, but you might sell a view of it. Indeed, the West has always recognized the value of free-spending curious visitors. Preservation ideals could also help stabilize and diversify an erratic local economy. In this manner, as early as 1907, thoughtful citizens saw connections between sustainable economies and scenic landscapes. When the environment or national economy showed its ugly side, and it soon did both, town dwellers and family farmers alike would need new answers.

The Conservation Response: The Regional Progressives

One summer day in 1879, four years after Charles and Molly Goodnight settled on a remote spur of the eastern Llano Estacado, a pair of touring Englishmen stopped by their JA ranch in Donley County. Nugent Townshend was editor of the English sporting magazine *The Field*; his partner, J. G. Hyde, was a professional photographer. As working tourists, Townshend and Hyde were gathering material about ranching on the Plains. Both men were impressed with the JA's magnificent scale and expansive landscapes. Townshend's narrative appreciation and Hyde's photographs of the pioneer ranch appeared in their subsequent (and influential) 1880 book, *Our Indian Summer in the Far West*.[13] Hyde's first photo, "A Lonely Home in Texas (Grande Vista)," featured a rustic but bold JA dwelling set against a scenic backdrop. It was a pleasant image and one that incidentally summarized the sparse demography. The second Hyde photo, however, was of a sadder nature. Titled "Our Only Buffalo! Grande Vista Ranch, Pan Handle, Texas," it showed a single buffalo calf grazing in the middle ground, all that was left from the vast herds of a few years before. Even this pitiful remnant of the keystone species for the Great Plains would not have survived but for the tender heart of Molly Goodnight. Childless herself, Goodnight had rescued the orphan from its cowboy discoverer, and she had urged her husband to let the animal live on the ranch unmolested.

The forlorn and "last" animal in Hyde's 1879 photo was actually far from doomed. For Charles Goodnight took an interest in the fate of the species after the visit of the Englishmen. And over time Goodnight built up a significant preservation herd from this lowly start, a bison herd that brought him national attention and fame after 1900. In retrospect, Townshend and Hyde had done something more than just publicize get-rich corporate ranch investment on the Southern Plains; they had also served as subtle publicists for a conservation of resources. Hyde's photographs may have helped lure foreign syndicates onto the Great Plains, but they also introduced Molly Goodnight's salvation of a buffalo as a worthy ideal for Victorian parlors. For outsiders, a desirable feature of the western heritage was the nostalgic conservation of an older or preexisting heritage itself.

Research on the early conservation practices of the Southern High Plains is desirable, especially to remind postmodern people that environmentalism is neither new, nor completely antithetical to corporations, nor outside the historic realm of public and private imaginations. Two factors mitigated the worst exploitative practices by family farm colonization: first, a capricious regional environment and climate that soon demanded adaptations; and second, popular notions of safeguarding symbolic or public goods, such as scenic areas, with appropriate attitudes or public stewardship. Taking the first point, corporations cleverly succeeded in attracting family farmers to the Southern High Plains, but keeping them there required something more. The drought of 1907 (and its lingering beyond) obviously altered the simplistic, exaggerated, booster equation by providing a sudden, sharp need for a *conservation horizon*. Researchers of the Great Plains such as Martyn Bowden, John Allen, Malcolm Lewis, and others often note the human perceptual pendulum swinging between viewing the "Plains as a Desert" and the "Plains as a Garden."[14] Railroad and land companies recognized this perceptual seesaw and they feared dry years when the pendulum swung against their preferred visions. They could, of course, continue to ignore or lie their way through bad years, such as with the older talk of "rainbelts" expanding with the arrival of civilization. But it soon dawned on many companies that conservation and adaptation might actually reduce crop failures. And if the failures could be mitigated, then farmers tended to see a "garden" rather than a "desert." The Santa Fe Railroad system particularly embraced this re-evaluative process. In the company's influential regional journal, *The Earth*, it soon promoted a variety of conservation farming techniques and suitable crops.[15]

Dry years, grasshopper plagues, blowouts, and blizzards all encouraged risk reduction and conservation practices for Llano family farmers. Indeed, whether the farmer was originally from humid East Texas or well-watered Iowa, some measure of adaptation simply seemed necessary on the Southern High Plains. An important conservation horizon emerged after 1908, one that served as a perceptual regulator, a choke on poorly suited crops, techniques, and ruinous practices. It was certainly not perfect, but adaptability plus diversification plus technology gave those farmers who wanted to stay a possibility of doing so. The process was greatly helped by a regional genetic revolution, specifically the arrival of new domesticated plants that needed less moisture. German-Russian (Volga German) Mennonite farmers from Kansas, for instance, came to Hartley County to break out and farm an old XIT pasture. They brought with them a secret weapon, a reliable source of success, namely seed stocks of hard red winter wheat, originally from the Anatolian Plateau of Turkey. By 1909, these excellent farmers had some eighty-two thousand acres of red winter wheat in cultivation, now a staple crop for the entire region. Ethnic islands elsewhere on the Plains experimented with other domesticates. A number of important genetic flows came from the semi-arid regions of Africa. Drought-resistant Kaffir and Milo meshed nicely with the climate and suited the needs of ranchers with better bloodlines in livestock. Quantities of these feed grains soon flowed from the Llano. Legend says that the early West Texas cattle feedlot operation began when businessmen saw trains shunting north, carrying off both cattle and feed grains, to be consumed together elsewhere. Why not combine cattle and feed grains on the Plains themselves?

The question of irrigation is more complicated because we now see the Ogallala Aquifer as seriously depleted rather than the God-given superabundance perceived by the family farmers of 1910–1920. Indeed, as John Opie demonstrates in his modern classic, *Ogallala: Water for a Dry Land*, contemporary society is still trying to identify, create, and truly implement a proper conservation response to decades of ground-water mining. Research on the Ogallala Aquifer is vast, of course, a sign of the shallow-water belt's strategic importance.[16] Unquestionably, the 1910–1920 irrigation wells of the Southern High Plains proved a god-send to the early, few, and well capitalized "industrial" farmers. These big farmers financed and furthered the development of hydraulic tech-nology until eventually even small family farmers could come on board.

Unfortunately, the preconceptions of a limitless supply also provoked boundless waste. Early on, boosters held summer "Water Carnivals," advertised occasions when promotional wells poured tens of millions of gallons on the ground solely for the public's amusement and recreation. At Plainview in Hale County, company wells ran at full throttle to cre-ate lavish "false lakes." These artificial lakes demonstrated the "unfailing supply" and also enticed newcomers to think of gentler, wetter climes. Irrigation drilling diffused slowly, because it was expensive, but it spread widely. A regional conservation horizon for the Ogallala Aquifer emerged tentatively in the 1950s and 1960s, a time when thousands of shallow wells sustained family farms on the Llano but then necessarily lowered water tables. For the early 1900s, the value of the aquifer was not its contemplated exhaustion but rather its reliability and "substi-tutability." It was a perfect replacement for less than adequate rainfall.

In contrast to water, a *land* conservation horizon emerged on the Llano Estacado during 1910–1920. It included crop and economic diversification, genetic adaptability, better plow technology, and longer-term thinking. Railroads such as the Rock Island, Santa Fe, and Fort Worth and Denver promoted these new stratagems and increased the connectivity between family farm, ranch, and industry. Indeed, railroads were the "food system" corporations of their day. Charles Goodnight summarily claimed that prosperity on the Southern High Plains owed much to a simple recipe: farming *plus* stock raising equals long-term success. Some ranchers therefore grew hay and other crops. Many family farmers, like William DeLoach, kept some cattle or pigs. A few farmers

Periodically from 1906 to 1909, the colonization photographer George N. Wilkie, of Oakville, Iowa, arrived to work the land booms of the Llano Estacado. Wilke documented the vigorous settlement process in hundreds of outstanding photographs. Many of his promotional images worked to recast environmental perception of the region from notions of a "Great American Desert" to the idea of a "Promised Land" of refreshing waters and amenity landscapes for happy newcomers. Sulphur Park was a favorite recreational stretch along Tierra Blanca Creek near Hereford, Texas. George N. Wilkie, Gelatin silver postcard print, circa 1908, courtesy the John Miller Morris Collection.

even went large-scale with animal husbandry, as at Hereford, an early precursor to the gigantic feedlot operations of today. In the semiarid lands of the Middle East a tripartite network of exchange systems, called the "ecological trilogy," functioned for centuries among pastoral tribes (sheep/camels), farm villages (crops), and a connected urban center (manufactures and services). By 1920, the Southern High Plains of North America supported its own version of an "ecological trilogy," albeit one predicated more on capital and advanced technology. Nevertheless, a tripartite web of relations and interdependencies on the Llano linked pastoral ranches (cattle/horses), family farms (crops), and high connectivity urban centers. Fez, Morocco, and Lubbock, Texas, have their parallels.

An expanding trilogy led to rapid growth, which soon contributed to a more holistic vision for the region. For growth brought with it not only market desires for profit and homestead, but also assorted settler demands for health cures, recreation, hunting, scenic views, sacred sites, swimming holes, medicinal springs, tuberculosis sanitariums, and so on. Over and over again the promotional literature of the era touted the restorative powers of Plains landscape and climate.[17] Health services, recreation, and stewardship of amenity landscapes (like the lovely, if now forgotten, "Sulphur Park" outside of early 1900s Hereford) further invigorated local development—and even attracted some early tourists! Modernists and progressives at the Chamber of Commerce of Canyon City in Randall County saw one local potential. They energetically set out to convert a nearby chasm into a grand public commons, using distant tax monies of course, whence the origin of a movement to "save" Palo Duro Canyon.

The most important local environmental movement in the early 1900s was the conception, formation, and promotion of a Palo Duro National Park Association. Centered in Canyon, Texas, the association began as early as 1906 to agitate for a national park in the upper Palo Duro Canyon. To his everlasting credit, President Theodore Roosevelt had employed his "bully pulpit" to inspire a nation to rethink its man-land relationships. The very idea of conservation was in the air. Local residents were addicted to frequent canyon excursions in any case. The potential for lucrative tourism was obvious to them. By 1908–1909, park advocates had an important friend in the state capitol. Representative John Hall Stephens of Vernon liked the idea, and he introduced several bills in the contemporaneous legislative session. Stephens's bills were duly stymied by the tightfisted fiefdoms of the legislature. But the concept was popular, and advocates tried again for several more years. It certainly helped that national debates on public versus private stewardships now percolated into concerns with preservation of local scenery, biota, soil and water, public recreation, and the "Plains Commons."

Despite the 1908–1911 attention and popular support, it would take two more decades before a compromised Palo Duro Park could emerge, a beautiful (if still ridiculously undersized) commons, and a *state* not national park. In the interim, the obvious obstacle to a people's park was that private landowners, essentially large business interests, owned the scenic canyon. To be sure, Texas had retained its public lands during annexation. But because it rather generously transferred virtually all its interests away (to corporations mostly), the land never had the federal ownership so conducive to park formation in other western states. Any proposed park, large or small, was perforce subject to the hallowed dictates of private property rights. West Texas historian Pete Petersen notes in his history of the state park that "the question of [private] land ownership proved to be a stumbling block."[18] In fact, the question of private property rights versus public stewardship is still a thorny issue for the region, as historian Dan Flores notes elsewhere in this volume.

Two factors combined to resolve the stalled contest between public versus private in favor of the park movement. First, the traumatized and liberalized politics of the 1930s made transfers from private to public domain part of a national recovery. Second, several additional decades of regional aesthetics—art, music, material culture, poetry, and especially photography—had celebrated the canyon, created a romantic vision in the public's eye, and softened the opposition. The major chord, of course, was still the free-enterprise "Promised Land" of the individual farmer, rancher, or town dweller. But now, like J. G. Hyde's photo of an orphan buffalo, a minor chord resonated on the Llano Estacado as aesthetic natures saw a preservationist dream take form as useful public space. As it turned out, the artistic way in seeing (or rather re-seeing) the nature of the Southern High Plains was even good for the economy. But after all, the artists who best saw the Plains thoroughly loved its natural heritage. Their art and artifacts now constitute a significant cultural legacy, a lasting source of human inspiration and regional consciousness. Our new century would do well to study their perspectives.

Perceiving the Plains: The Cultural Creatives

The post-1902 wave of homesteader and colonizer settlement onto the Staked Plains created a remarkable cultural landscape of new towns, farmhouses, and fields. Not all the arrivals were diehard family farmers though. Mixed in with the newcomers were educated, sensitive, bookish, and often talented types—a male and female group conveniently called here the "cultural creatives." Using the abundant natural light of the plains, for example, a largely unsung group of local and regional photographers captured the glory of the colonization process and town settlement. From 1902 to 1915, a score of excellent photographers worked on the Southern High Plains, quietly making magnificent realist pictures of their extraordinary world and time. These photographers not only documented the economic and demographic boom, but also they laid aesthetic foundations for perceiving the Golden Age of the family farm. A recent work by Paul H. Ray and Sherry R. Anderson divides rural mindsets into "traditionalists," "modernists," and "cultural creatives."[19] Borrowing a leaf from this research, many of the early photographers, teachers, poets, writers, painters, and some eccentric farmers of the Llano Estacado were not only "cultural creatives" but also "closet conservationists."

The sudden arrival of tens of thousands of newcomers vastly stimulated regional photography. Promoters, of course, expected photographers to recast the desert into a garden image. But for many photographers the vision of a garden also made room for the primitive, the natural, the sensual, and the geomorphic—a reflection of the persistent vision of nature-as-paradise in American thought.[20] Sam Sherman of Amarillo, Maidens Stennett Lusby of Canyon, George N. Wilkie of Hereford, Norton Baker of Lockney, J. B. Jones of Floydada, E. Brown of Lubbock, J. C. Dallas of Tulia, M. C. Wasson at Post City, George A. Addison of Canadian, R. E. Cochrane of Plainview, Nissley and Byers of Clovis, "Mac" of Shamrock, and Willie Miller of Midland, among dozens of photographers, all labored to capture the aesthetic side of the Staked Plains. They roamed the outdoors with their cameras and tripods. They photographed town and country, plains and canyons, and farm and ranch, all the while taking revelatory pictures of people and place. As their surviving work indicates, photographic perceptions of the scenic, qualitative nature of the Llano Estacado are still useful and valid today. Indeed, their images of nature sites, views, towns, fields, irrigation wells, and country residences are now precious windows into a past way of life, visual documents made during the very recasting of the landscape. And this lively period is where history, technology, and visual culture intersect nicely.

George N. Wilkie, for example, superbly documented family farm colonization on the Southern High Plains. Wilkie was a colonization photographer, a "cultural creative" originally from Oakville, Iowa. When the Iowa land companies came to Texas they brought his outstanding talents with them. From 1906 to 1910, Wilkie not only toured the Southern High Plains, but also shaped new environmental perceptions. Wilkie loved to photograph new towns, young orchards, fall harvests, fine houses, and bustling main streets. He was fond of automobiles, used one extensively for his travels, and often posed prospective colonists and automobiles together. Wilkie's photography dramatically underscores the role these new machines played in conquering "the friction of space," especially in an immense flatland. Wilkie understood that the automobile reduced, or should we say seduced, the normal perception of time and space, perceptually making the "far" seem "near." Land companies soon employed fleets of automobiles to rush prospective purchasers to distant surveys sold on easy credit. Colonists got the impression they were only a score of minutes from the stores and churches of Hereford, when in fact they were often a considerable distance away from town by slow buggy or wagon. Most dispersed farmers on the 1910s Plains got a Model-T as soon as they could afford one. Since the car made the periphery seem more like the core, a new proximate geography unfolded on the Southern High Plains, one that mitigated the old perception of loneliness imbedded in the flatland.

Wilkie further delighted in photographing the environmental amenities he discovered on the Llano. His images of the High Plains geography—the landscapes, hunting grounds, recreations, and landmarks—show a professional appreciation of beauty and scenery. If Wilkie's camera also focused on the 1906–1910 town prosperity and farm fecundity, it was because his images provided important promotional documents to land agents and town boosters. Both groups wanted to change the prospective settler's hitherto unfavorable environmental image of the Plains. Boosters and photographers alike often collaborated in creating a local *geosophy*, a perceived landscape of desire. Accordingly, many Wilkie photographs reflect the fervent environmental, economic, and social optimism that governed the 1906–1910 tide of farm settlement. Boosters strongly believed in their cultural abilities to refashion otherwise desolate ranchland into an agrarian Garden of Eden. And the camera, grounded in realism, did not "lie," or at least not as easily as the 1890s railroad brochures with idealized woodcuts.

Another talented Llano photographer practicing at the turn of the century was Maidens Stennett Lusby. Born in Lincolnshire, England in 1867, Lusby immigrated to Central Texas when he was twelve. Lusby's first interest in photography is unknown, but he was likely exposed to the work and tent studios of the pioneer photographer, Hamilton Biscoe Hillyer of Austin, Texas. Hillyer was deeply interested in outdoor photography, natural history, and gardening, all interests that eventually preoccupied Lusby. This sensitive young man moved to the Panhandle frontier of Canyon City in the spring of 1891. Here he set up in business as a photographer. Lusby was a romantic realist who delighted in documenting the growth and settlement of the Randall County area for two decades. Lusby's photos of agricultural scenes are some of the best in Texas for the time. He constructed a light-filled gallery in Canyon City where he did regular studio work. But he also roamed the landscape to

After moving to Canyon City around 1901, photographer Maidens Stennett Lusby documented the dramatic conversion of ranchland into farms. Creative and deeply interested in natural history, Lusby, an early member and ardent supporter of the Palo Duro National Park Association, photographed local farms, plains, and canyons. A number of his "romantic realist" photos of canyon geomorphology were used to promote preservation ideals and associated goals. Maidens Stennett Lusby, Gelatin silver postcard print, 1907, courtesy the John Miller Morris Collection.

capture the fantastic geomorphology of Palo Duro Canyon, the summer and fall harvests on the High Plains, and the winter trains fighting their way through snowdrifts. With the surge in nearby colonization activity from 1905 to 1910, Lusby soon worked for colonization companies and produced an invaluable photographic survey of the local settlement process.

Naturally he embraced the Palo Duro National Park Association founded in his hometown of Canyon, Texas. In fact, virtually all the association's promotional materials bear reproductions of Lusby photos of Palo Duro Canyon scenes such as "Giants Tower," "Natural Pillars," or "Dreamland Falls." He apparently adored natural history. Known locally as "Mr. Sunshine" for his sunny disposition, Lusby sold out his studio and business around 1913 and retired to a ten-acre farm near Lockney in Floyd County. Here at "Sunshine Gardens" he read books, raised a variety of marketable produce, and allowed local residents to observe the heavens through his telescopes.

In early September of 1916 another cultural creative returned to the Staked Plains. The new instructor at West Texas State Normal School in Canyon, Georgia O'Keeffe, came back to the sky and canyon glories she had known first as an art teacher in Amarillo in 1912. Now, freshly inspired by East Coast aesthetics, she proved extraordinarily sensitive to the primal colors, the elements, the flowers, and especially the sky. O'Keeffe enthused to her friend, Anna Politzer, in a letter dated 11 September 1916:

> Tonight I walked into the sunset—to mail some letters—the whole sky—and there is so much of it out here—was just blazing —and grey blue clouds were rioting all through the hotness of it—and the ugly little buildings and windmills looked great against it.[21]

Within a week of worshipping the sky, the curious new art teacher, often dressed in black, was spending considerable time in Palo Duro Canyon, in daylight and darkness. The decade-old preservation movement for a national park had touted the recreational value of the canyon. But in her roaming and pondering, O'Keeffe soon created an artistic rationale, a new way of seeing the canyon that only involved redefining American art! At Canyon, Texas, O'Keeffe was again living west of the 99th meridian, beyond which, as historian Elliott West noted generally, "the perceptual basics—light, mass, space, color—suddenly shifted in ways both obvious and indescribable."[22] She knew that by conventional

wisdom the flat plains were a "nothing." She even apologized to her cor-
respondents for seeing so much in this nothingness. But her vision was
that the sense of place, the genius loci of the Staked Plains was its inherent "bigness," a perception of nature she reached for in her everyday life
through "livingness."

After reading O'Keeffe's letters from that period, one senses a personal environmentalism bordering on deep ecology. Rather misanthrop-
ically, she contrasted the bigness of the Plains with the smallness of the
people in Canyon, Texas.[23] Nevertheless, borrowing the art critic Robert
Hughes's phrase, the "shock of the new" of the Southern High Plains
opened new pathways for her between art and imagination. For
O'Keeffe, the fences and ugly buildings around Canyon articulated only
a small boundary between culture and nature. Her own work would
deconstruct this boundary. The linear fences and colonization construc-
tions were mere playthings against a larger cosmic vision of "livingness"
with the Plains. The linear and geometric conversions of the landscape
were placeless really—a small barrier to large creativity. O'Keeffe's emo-
tionality was keyed to the sublimity and colors of the plains, the crepus-
cular skies, the earthy canyons, all the astonishing and overwhelming
environmental characteristics that she summarily called its "bigness."

The sublime aesthetics of the High Plains caught fire in Georgia
O'Keeffe's watercolors of the Texas period.[24] Lusby and Wilkie had traveled down similar roads eight years earlier with their photography. There
were other regional artists, in particular the estimable Frank Reaugh,
who sojourned, photographed, and painted these plains and escarpment
canyons. The cultural creatives of the Llano Estacado may have worked
for public schools, town clienteles, and slick land companies, but their
visions and skills often transcended crasser corporate intentions. Wilkie
and Lusby, Reaugh and O'Keeffe all made a little money but empow-
ered a lot of environmental perception. Their visions of the Plains—well
known with O'Keeffe, obscure with Wilkie—reflect a fresh *regional consciousness* and creative identity. Their aesthetics of place remain to guide,
delight, and inform a new century

The 1900–2000 Transition: The C. B. Morris Family Farm—and Corporation

Of the ten thousand Golden Age family farms of 1900–1914, there are
probably only a few thousand or so still in business on the Southern
High Plains of today. Each continuous family farm—strictly speaking,

each lucky survival—of the past tumultuous century has a unique and worthy saga. Even half a century of traditional family farming makes a wonderful narrative, as Janet Neugebauer's edited volume, *Plains Farmer: The Diary of William G. DeLoach, 1914–1964,* makes clear.[25] But the successive land ownership story best known to me is that of my extended family. From great-grandfather to now, I do know how one family managed to keep farming on the Plains—and the price paid. An abbreviated case study can only be a tiny part, of course, of the whole High Plains farm transition from 1900 to 2000. But perhaps the narrative of one family farm can be mildly metonymic, a little story reflecting some truth of the whole.

For over a century, extended families have struggled to make a life and a legacy on the Southern High Plains. A. T. Miller, my great-grandfather, arrived in 1887 to an ocean of grassland. As a Texas Ranger, he did his share in taming the new land. Other family members staked claims, plowed sod, tended stores, and built homes on the treeless highland. They tried to keep their dreams through hard labor, Jesus, and too often a nervous banker. Those who acquired land wove family ties deep into the county landscapes that emerged after the railroads. Families bequeathed a dream along with the land to happy heirs: the line of successive family ownership of land would continue unbroken. One simply did not sell "the land." The land and its idyllic dream flowed through the generations like an enduring Biblical myth. Somewhere in the middle of this land-and-dream is C. B. Morris Company—a family farm for well over half a century converted into a closely held farm corporation for another half century.

For most native Texas families, the old family farm and agrarian dream died decades ago, usually when the rural folks sold out and moved to a nearby city for much better jobs and amenities. Our dream lingers in a northeastern spur of the Staked Plains, on sixteen hundred acres near Clarendon (Donley County), and on one thousand acres of the Rolling Plains north of tiny Thalia (Foard County). After Miller quit the Texas Rangers, he settled near Thalia in the late 1880s, married, bought a section, and transformed himself into a better-off family farmer by the 1910s. He moved to Clarendon to educate his adopted daughter, where she fell in love with another junior college student, Carl Bernard Morris. Carl or "Cap" Morris had grown up as a youth of the 1906–1914 colonization farm boom, principally in the sandy country near Tokio, Texas (1912) in Lynn County. After serving his country in

World War I trenches with the American Expeditionary Force in France, Sergeant Morris returned to Clarendon, married Lena, and went back to farming.

In the 1920s, Cornelia Adair sold to Cap and Lena Morris, my grandparents, some choice land from her JA Ranch in the Clarendon area. Cap Morris was a practitioner of the saying, "If you are tired of working with your back, start using your mind." By the late 1920s, Morris, like his father-in-law Miller, was moving from backbreaking rural labor toward more supervision and finance. Rather than plowing or hoeing, he managed and coordinated a family-oriented system of farm leases and traditional tenant farming in Donley and Foard counties. On the class-conscious plains of Russia or Ukraine, Morris would have been a *kulak*, or entrepreneurial farmer, reputedly exploiting the labor of poor tenants.

There was no disguising, however, the retrograde economic and social horrors of the 1930s Depression and Dust Bowl. The Golden Age of small farm prosperity crashed on the Plains as badly as stock prices tumbled on Wall Street. Like other women, Lena Morris fed canned fruits to the homeless, converted flour sacks into homemade underwear, and made hook rugs. A large number, though, of farm tenants, friends, and even family members left the Southern High Plains, most forever. The people who stayed were scarred by the experience. Notions of *debt* came to mean different things to different generations of farmers. The Morris farms survived largely because they were big enough, solvent enough, conservative enough, and perhaps because they were located in two counties a hundred miles apart. A crop in one county might just off-set a wipeout in the other.

Ironically, about the time Stalin moved to liquidate the kulak class of better-off farmers from the mollisol plains of the USSR, American bankers made a different, more economic decision for their plains. Banks and credit systems slowly squeezed proletarian small farmers and tenants in favor of an emergent, mechanized, and larger landholding class of family farmers such as C. B. Morris. Stalin built his large-scale or *kolkhoz* agriculture system using centralized political pressure. American bankers and creditors built a rationalized larger-scale system with decentralized economic pressure. All things considered, foreclosure notices were an obvious improvement over NKVD machine guns in farm consolidation. And when economic and climate forces reduced family farmers on the Great Plains close to famine (a horrific and man-made disaster in Stalin's Ukraine), the American political system stepped in with federal aid and the Rural Rehabilitation Program. In a recent study of the period, *Down and Out on the Family Farm*, historian Michael Johnston Grant notes that federal aid eased the pain on the way down, but it did not stop the decline of small farmers in competition with larger-scale agriculture.[26]

The family also saved the farm by adopting a "new" 1930s mindset: conservation of resources. C. B. Morris himself embraced conservation to an unusual degree. It was, so to speak, a thinking-man's style of farming anyway. Indeed, conservation practices, crop diversification, and improved mechanization—that is, a thorough rationalization of land, capital, and labor—reduced both economic and environmental risk. Morris not only embraced the New Deal with ardor and service, he also embraced the New Deal rural landscape. He refashioned worn farms with conservation terraces, shelterbelts, rural electricity, more eco-friendly techniques and crops, and he entered local politics as a New Deal Democrat. The movement to sustainability paid off—economically and politically. Thus, the decisions of the 1930s in the USSR and in the USA, that is, whether kulaks or proletarians would rule the fertile steppes and plains of the midlatitudes, were fundamentally different and led to vastly different outcomes.

The 1940s and early 1950s were relatively happy times on the Southern High Plains. The weather improved, the land responded to conservation, and wartime and postwar commodity prices were strong. A new prosperity gradually took hold on family farms in most counties. At Ashtola, not far from Goodnight's former ranch home at Goodnight, Texas, Morris again got interested in diversification. He started up a purebred herd of Galloway cattle that he managed in partnership with a son-in-law, Horace A. Green. Farm life not only looked good, additional family members came on board, including two daughters and two son-in-laws: Mae and Duane Naylor became operators in Foard County, displacing the last of the old tenant farmers; and Naomi and Horace Green did the same in Donley County. In good times family flowed into the business, not out of it.

Half of Cap and Lena's children went to the farms, and half ended up in the cities. Having a healthy percentage of family members trained and prepared to work the land has been, without doubt, instrumental in family-farm longevity. Our eventual death as family farmers was also postponed (rather accidentally it now seems) through a fateful legal decision taken in 1950. Lena and Cap Morris incorporated their mutual and inherited farms into a corporation, the C. B. Morris Company. They distributed stock in such a way as to make minority shareholders of all the eventual heirs. The new legal entity was considered pretty modern at the time; family tradition holds that it was one of the early family-farm corporations in the Panhandle. Despite the underlying corporate legality, things were still run as a large-scale twin family farm. In Donley County, Aunt Oma and Uncle Horace operated a full-blown farm household in the 1950s and 1960s with seven top-notch kids, crops everywhere, cattle, chickens, a huge vegetable garden, wild plum jellies, and the like. In Foard County, Aunt Mae and Uncle Duane raised four smart kids and operated a thousand lovely acres, somehow making a crop year after year in spite of bad weather. Their operations were often critical to the survival of the company.

The mid- and late 1950s, however, were a severe test of the company's need to become "modern" while somehow surviving the "old" droughts, blowouts, bugs, and other environmental challenges. The mid-1950s drought was discouraging to say the least. In Donley County the company turned to the Ogallala Aquifer. In spite of investments in new machinery, both farm operations also used migrant or seasonal labor— the hidden heritage of family farming on the High Plains. Both operations increasingly resorted to anhydrous ammonia, hybrid seeds, cotton strippers, and expensive tractors. Children of the 1950s Llano can thus remember the picking of cotton by migrant hand in one year, and then a banker-financed cotton stripper showing up the next year. Community domino games might remain unchanged from the nineteenth century, but nearby drive-in theaters brought new layers of mass culture to the boondocks. By the 1960s, our irrigation wells pulled harder on the Ogallala Aquifer; it is difficult to imagine the company surviving had they not. As a child, youth, and adult, I found myself chasing cattle, moving irrigation pipe, hoeing, and doing the thousand other verities that went with an urban cousin visiting and sometimes living on a family farm operation.

Lena and Cap Morris both died in the 1960s. Estate taxes and expenses consumed portions of farm income for years. By the early 1970s, though, C. B. Morris Company had evolved into a minor family agribusiness. Despite the adoption of modern machines, technologies, and markets, there was a subversive undercurrent of conservation thinking in the operation. Duane Naylor was a resourceful, even ingenious operator. He liked to recycle in Foard County, and he experimented frequently with seeds and techniques. Horace Green, who operated the Donley County farms, never forgot the Depression. He kept growing cotton for the periodic market bonanza, but he also got involved with the early organic farm companies, specifically Warner Seed Company and Arrowhead Mills of Hereford. Green had a good run at mixed sustainable-exhaustive agriculture in the 1960s and 1970s. A shrewd and intelligent farmer, he reduced risks through integrated management techniques years before the term was invented. At the time he said his type of farming was neither popular nor especially lucrative but that he would still be there when others were busted and gone.

Everyone's attitude shifted profoundly during the mid-1970s and 1980s. First, grandchildren began to return, some (perhaps ominously) with college degrees in agriculture. New stockholders also reached legal age. Shifting government policies and programs, expensive tractors, center-pivot irrigation, dangerous new pesticides, roaring interest rates, wild and fluctuating commodity prices, high fuel and energy costs, and scores of risks and rewards turned the company toward more intense and competitive land uses. Traditionalists were out and modernists were in. Operators planted high-risk, high-reward crops like irrigated corn. The company pushed sentiment aside and tore down a tenant house merely for the scrap of land it occupied. Stockholders borrowed heavily to buy an adjacent farm with its precious groundwater. One very sad day, in the midst of a bad cattle market too, trucks came and carried away the entire Galloway herd. But thus freed of ruminants, former pastures metamorphosed into new cropland—a laborious conversion process, as I know from a long summer's personal experience. The company completed more irrigation wells and explored the underground water options with test wells. In sum, conservation was less important than rising land prices, selling grain to kulak-less Russians, saving face with bankers, and bringing a new generation of go-go farmers on board. We could only get richer! Land prices would soar even higher!

The late 1980s shakeout was severe of course. Farm woes and suffering radiated across the entire Great Plains. Willie Nelson "Farm Aid" concerts and farm protest movements were both popular entertainment, but they did not dissuade a neighbor or two from suicide. Rural land prices fell dramatically as lawyers, dentists, and doctors took their investment money elsewhere. Globalization and unexpected crop diseases proved a relentless challenge. C. B. Morris survived in Donley County largely by betting on and getting government "quotas" in peanuts, an important federal subsidy for growing export peanuts. Peanuts migrated onto the Southern High Plains when more traditional peanut country in the East became so infested with nematodes and diseases as to discourage production altogether. The High Plains was "fresh meat," as it were, for susceptible crops that had degraded other Americans soils. Peanuts truthfully cost a fortune to produce. But growers holding the magic government quotas found they usually paid as a cash crop, provided that the company and operators poured quantities of groundwater, fertilizer, and chemicals onto the land. Supposedly, our export peanuts ended up in the stomachs of millions of snack-hungry soccer fans in Europe. Even conservation itself came back in fashion with the downturn. The company quickly embraced no-till farming as one convenient and efficient 1990s panacea.

Like almost all farm operations on the Southern High Plains, the C. B. Morris Co. increasingly viewed the federal government as a capricious and willy-nilly partner in the production process. The worst kind of crop or commodity price failure is, speaking candidly, one that does not have a large government check following behind it in the mail. But to get that or any check usually involves collaborating, if not sharing some of the decision making, with inquisitive federal agencies and bureaucrats. Of course, few self-respecting, red-blooded American farmers (30 percent of the take) and patriotic agribusinesses (70 percent of the take) willingly own up to any role as voracious welfare recipients. Individual farmers and associations such as the Farm Bureau often impugn "welfare" as an urban concept alien to rural values and beliefs. However that may be, and without ever quite approving its moral necessity, the C. B. Morris Co. joined the prevailing preference for risk reduction by participating in USDA farm programs throughout the 1980s and 1990s. Indeed, "government assistance," "price supports," "quotas," and "disaster checks" became a regular component of the corporate budget, perhaps a fifth of revenue.

By the late 1990s, though, C. B. Morris Company had lost key family operators and family members through relocation, accident, and mortality. Land prices in the hinterland of the Plains were dismally low. Local operators, after the tremendous farm bankruptcies of the past, found it hard to obtain financing. When the peanut diseases refused to stay back East, the company turned one large farm over to alfalfa. Too many adjacent farms lay fallow simply for lack of financing and local operators. In Foard County, as noted, the company placed considerable acreage in the Conservation Reserve Program, spending many thousands of dollars to convert cropland back into grassland habitat in return for annual government checks. Stockholders were also quarreling, sometimes bitterly. Increasingly, it seemed appropriate to dissolve or transform the company in some equitable manner.

C. B. Morris Company has barely, even implausibly, survived half a century of profound change, agrarian dislocations, new stockholders, and gut-wrenching traumas. The company is still in business, neither too big nor too small to go completely broke. At the heart of this survival has been a central (if soulless) reality: corporations can outlive their individual stockholders and/or operators. The willingness of a minority of family members to work the land and a majority of stockholders to help manage the land, both just successfully enough to compete in a brutal, increasingly global market arena, may make some difference. Stockholders, who more often do not live on the land, have to adapt their investment expectations accordingly.

Like thousands of family-farm descendants, the majority of CBM stockholders have made their way to the urban canyons and suburban escarpments of modern Texas. In schools and skyscrapers distant from the Plains, stockholders attempt to keep alive a collective vision—not the old collective called a family farm, but a new collective called the family farm corporation. For better or worse, we have been stuck for half a century with the corporation. Now perhaps it is our myth. Or rather no one has figured out a reasonable way to un-incorporate the family farm, at least without owing enough capital gains on the land as to surrender altogether. And that reality, as sensible as it might be, would bring a larger dream to an end: "Never sell the land." Closely held family farm corporations may put up with more trouble and lower economic returns than nonrelated urban stockholders would ever consider advisable. For this reason *family-owned* corporate agribusiness *may* have a better chance of surviving the odds of the next century.

At a recent meeting, confronted with difficult tax, operational, and capital-investment problems, I wondered how much longer most family members would want to stay in the business. Call farming on the Llano Estacado for what it is now: full-time, high-stakes, heavy-chemical, rural-casino gambling, where "break-the-bank" attitudes usually work in reverse. The fun disappeared years ago, and now the business must work to keep its management, progression, and footing. As a resident family "grass-lovin'" (not many trees available to hug) environmentalist, I recall adding an impractical or idealistic component to some business decisions. Yet, after many centuries of documented farming in the blood, it seems very doubtful that C. B. Morris in its present form will make it beyond another decade or two. High operating costs and low commodity prices equal a persistent financial squeeze. Without farm programs, crop insurance, and disaster payments, company solvency would be questionable. And the corporation has the best kind of land in Texas, "paid for."

The experience of C. B. Morris Co. does indicate the general utility of corporate structures in transferring a family farm operation from one generation to the next. That is, the corporate model has kept the extended family connected to the land, whether its members live on it or not, or whether the connection was wanted or not. And our experience indicates that conservation has not only a place but also a historic heritage. One family farm, in business for over a century, has seen economic expansions followed by environmental and market contractions, counterbalanced by significant conservation shifts, followed by exhaustive expansions, more crashes, and new conservation strategies. A pendulum of sustainable-exhaustive relations, with more machines and decreasing numbers of people, seems to be the pattern.

The traditionalist family farm nevertheless lingers as one of the enduring mythologies of the Southern High Plains. Family farmers talk resolutely about "keeping land in the family," both as a projection of the myth and an acknowledgment of its hold on them personally. Despite most other rational considerations, the notion of selling the family farm, even a stockholder interest in a corporate-style farm, can remain one of the hardest, least impulsive decisions to make. Family operations work fervently to perpetuate their presence on the plains, but too often they do so within a context of troublesome economies, global competition, spouses working off-farm, declines in rural health care, and an aging demographic profile. An overall defiant attitude may prove helpful. Thankfully, any streak of defiance will not extend to the 2002 Farm Program coming out of Washington, D.C. This huge, farm-state inspired program promises more addictive farm welfare than ever. It will certainly prove a cornucopia for large agribusiness, already adept at getting most of the largesse even as their politicians declare honorable intentions to "save the family farm." Directly or indirectly though, a generous farm program benefits almost everyone not actually living in a city.

For the C. B. Morris Co. itself, the extension of the family farm myth from a fourth to a fifth generation is much less certain, much more problematic. Our collective future in farming the plains even looks bleak when almost all the current stockholders live off-farm. Perhaps it is just as well. Old corrals, outbuildings, tumbled-down former tenant houses, and remnant shade groves still signify much CBM property. These relics of yore remind us that many, many families left the farms long before we will have to go. The divide between urban and rural is sharp and cuts cleanly between the generations.

The Llano Farmers of Today

> In terms of agricultural sustainable development, the family
> farm may persist as the best local on-site choice, despite its
> many serious defects and apparent obsolescence.
> —JOHN OPIE, *Ogallala:Water for a Dry Land*

The U.S. Department of Agriculture gathers considerable information on the contemporary land use and farm economy of the Southern High Plains. Indeed, the National Agricultural Statistics System (NASS) now provides a comprehensive set of Internet webtools to explore farm operations by crop, county, and state.[27] For analytical purposes the author used a NASS interactive mapping tool to study a simplified Southern High Plains consisting of four eastern New Mexico counties and twenty-five northwestern Texas counties. After days of playing with the tools and data, I found my vision of modern agriculture in the region resembled the earlier 1910 period of corporate-family endeavor. Both the past and current turns-of-the-century show significant mechanization, ethnic change, intensive production, high capital costs, corporate connectivity (once to nation, now to globe), risk-reduction conservation strategies, and public access and interaction with amenity landscapes.

Based on preliminary study, recent data suggest that the Llano bioregion embraces a mixed sustainability-exhaustive paradigm, primarily by interweaving crop production with cattle production. Charles Goodnight's 1900s stricture that the High Plains was meant for mixed use—for crops *and* cattle—appears to be born out by 1999 NASS data. Family and corporate crop production is, of course, tremendously important to the regional economy. Today the Llano Estacado, hypothetically organized as a new state, would rank about fourteenth among all states in gross agricultural receipts, an income of over $5 billion. However, as the 1998–99 satellite visions of the Llano suggest, the region is still extraordinarily sensitive to drought.

The northern Llano Estacado remains a notable "Cow Commons." An archipelago of feedlot and livestock operations stretches across the northern tier of counties. Family farms are still locally active (and in full production in many of these counties), but the market value of cattle actually exceeds crop revenues. Deaf Smith County, for example, has 669,000 cattle and calves, a reflection of the powerful feedlot industry. Castro County has 289,000 cattle and calves. Contrary to my initial thoughts, the northern Llano is embracing considerable more livestock revenues than irrigated crop income, perhaps a reflection of market demand for beef and declining water tables. It may be instructive, in fact, to plot the expansion of the cattle industry against the slow decline of groundwater-based agriculture.[28] Amarillo provides global connectivity for this Cow Commons with its huge meatpacking plants, food manufacturing, and shipping outlets. At night, of course, the very air of Amarillo smells, sometimes profoundly. There are well over a million cattle pooping off to the city's southwest. A century ago it was slumbering homesteader hamlets off in the distance, not gigantic twenty-four-hour feedlots.

In the late 1980s, professors Frank and Deborah Popper noted the steady demographic declines afflicting most counties of the Great Plains. Large sections of the Plains were wasting away, aging, and declining as communities. The Poppers went beyond identifying the spatial and social concerns by postulating a possible solution: the gradual reconstitution of depopulated grasslands into a comprehensive, dynamic, restocked, and sustainable "Buffalo Commons." At the time, the Poppers' concept was misconstrued widely and treated scornfully at the local level (and still is apparently). The passing of a dozen years or more has done little to redeem the idea for current residents. If anything the Buffalo Commons solution seems even more anachronistic to them, bearing no trace of reality.

Yet, almost unnoticed in a similar interval was the vast, significant, and largely micromanaged patchwork of conservation set-asides appearing in the county-level CRP lands. Some seventeen thousand contracts between northwest Texas farmers and the USDA converted millions of acres of cropland to long periods of permanent, mostly native vegetation. CRP lands are a terribly fractured and privatized version of the pristine Buffalo Commons. But as a compromise they offer something to most of the stakeholders: wildlife gets a break after all, the farmer gets to stay on the land, and taxpayer outlays for set-asides may be less expensive than price supports on typical overproduction. As for the depopulation afflicting many counties, out-migration is not a recent event. As noted earlier, scores of towns and many thousands of migrants were busted as colonization schemes collided with nature's harsher realities after 1907.

On the whole, the size of the modern family farm also increased between 1990 and 2000, indicating that the incremental trend toward "bigness" continues. On the Llano itself, a concentration of full-time farm operations appears in the middle and southern portions of the mesaland. Especially in this middle subregion, sometimes called the Southern Plains, percentages of county agricultural revenue run quite high for crops (not cattle). The high percentages may even reflect an informal family farm "homeland" or center of activity on the Southern High Plains. Such a homeland roughly centers on metropolitan Lubbock, with Crosby, Lynn, Hale, and adjacent counties drawing as much as 70 percent to 96 percent of their agricultural market revenue from farm crops.

Regional data for the 1990s do suggest a mild decline in the number of farm operations per county, perhaps due to bankruptcies, deaths, or sellouts of operations. Many counties declined by several or more percentage points in the number of primary farm operations. Farm numbers tend to show declines in full-time farms in the north and west, but small increases in the east and south. Farm numbers declined least around the Lubbock homeland core, but declines further out from the core were likely, especially in all four New Mexico counties (Quay, Curry, Roosevelt, and Lea). There is the possibility that modern agribusiness is shifting crop production from north to south, perhaps similar to the 1900–1912 colonization shock wave. A few counties, primarily in the South Llano, registered nice gains, suggesting an expanding irrigation economy there. The same data also suggest that farm size has increased in the Llano Estacado's twenty-nine counties.

While the region has about the same overall number of aggressive farm operations as it did in 1910, there have been profound changes in the costs and capitalizations required. An average homesteader in the last century might start a farming life on the Staked Plains with $500 in debt and investment. Currently, the average agricultural capitalization for a High Plains operation is around $700,000 plus $100,000 or more in equipment. The overall disparity in capitalization between large agricultural corporations and smaller operations is significant. Many (if not a large majority) of small family farmers have at least one spouse holding a town, public, or industrial job. A second, even third income is part of modern family farming. Off-farm income arrives throughout the year, is fairly reliable, and clearly works as a diversification strategy to piece together one family income. In contrast, larger farm corporations usually have substantial assets, find better financing, are quick to exploit technology, and are usually better suited to manage the intense capital risks of agriculture. Time and scale generally favor the larger companies in acquiring dominance over significant resource allocations. In a recent instance corporate predator T. Boone Pickens and fellow stockholders acquired vast water rights in the Panhandle. Caught between commodity price squeezes and higher expenses for fuel, supplies, and equipment, the remaining family farmers face a difficult future. Corporate farmers themselves, as smart as they undoubtedly are, are hardly immune to bankruptcy. They too face tremendous challenges in the coming century.

The central problem for the first decades of the twenty-first-century Southern High Plains is to manage a "soft-landing" transition from an *exhaustive* resource paradigm to a mixed *exhaustive-sustainability* resource paradigm. While there are plenty of alternative crops and models, land ethics, and nonprofit suggestions, no one seems to have solved the basic economic and demographic problems, particularly those associated with negative population growth. Answers may include grassroots conservation movements, community support associations (CSAs), heritage tourism, rural development, new technology, global connectivity, and, as I argue, new visual culture. Such a paradigm should include a dialectical resolution of two opposing environmental perceptions: first, a reigning imperial vision of agribusiness, where nature is conquered and commodified; and second, an Arcadian dream of a redeemed, bioregional "commons" landscape (as with the Poppers' Buffalo Commons).

Sustainability on the Southern High Plains will prove difficult. A recent United Nations University series ("Critical Zones in Global Environmental Change") focused on some of the world's most threatened environments—Borneo and the Malay Peninsula, Amazonia, the Basin of Mexico, and the Ordos Plateau of China. For the sixth volume of these "Critical Environmental Regions" books, the series editors released Elizabeth Brooks and Jacque "Jody" Emel's study of the Llano

Estacado. Brooks and Emel's assessment of sustainability for the Llano Estacado begins "by questioning what is to be sustained on the Llano. Was it the resource, the community, or the ecosystem?, we asked. In the end, what would sustainability mean for the Llano Estacado? Sustaining the resource would entail preserving key economic sectors, which would then serve to sustain the region's role in global markets for cotton and cattle. Sustaining the community would imply preserving a way of life and an agricultural production regime. Sustaining the ecosystem is no longer an option."[29] If sustainability itself is multifaceted and slippery, the challenge grows when considering some of the current applications of capitalism: predatory corporate practices (á la pig farms or ground-water exports), the spread of contract farming, generous tax abatement policies to attract corporate investment or wind farms, conservative institutional regimes, and high capitalization costs. It is likely that the Llano bioregion will continue the mixed cattle-grain economy, embrace bio-engineering, show a fresh interest in farm robotics and mechanization, and witness gigantic applications (and perhaps some accidents) of trans-genic crops. Nevertheless, these scientist visions of private corporate land use can and should be modified with large-scale, public-stewardship land allocations. Specifically the region needs new parks, wilderness areas, and heritage centers, including, as I envision it, a projected Southern High Plains Family Farm Heritage Center, a child-friendly, living-farm, inter-active learning center that would leaven the otherwise ranch-crazy way of seeing the past.

Corporations may rule the twenty-first-century Southern High Plains, much as they did in the early twentieth century, but the nature of their current colonization process requires careful thought. New colonization is globalized, genetic, intensive, climate changing, and arguably polluting or exhaustive. As noted, an important part of balancing the 1900s transition was to make room for other modernist needs, such as recreation, sport, community, and art. The 2000s transition also has needs for preserved environmental systems, some of which will likely involve a continually refined conservation movement. This movement, which already exists in parts, needs to emerge from the overlapping, consensual desires of national nonprofit organizations (Nature Conservancy and Sierra Club), Texas state agencies, local movements and heritage centers, and of course from the farm corporations themselves. Indeed, the Arcadian dreams of environmentalists may find sustainable outlets in new parks and variable applications of heritage tourism. In

Donley County, a few savvy local ranchers have learned ways to fatten up, not whiteface cattle, but German, British, and Japanese tourists. Buddy Holly's memory is an ongoing business in Lubbock. Heritage tourism, ranch and farm centers, Internet sites, and eco-friendly state parks may well prove more creative and more widespread in the next century. Cultural trends and environmental perceptions will shape these new spatial outlets, such as "living" farm and ranch interpretive centers, urban-rural monitoring programs, species recovery efforts, and ongoing space-based analysis of land use and climate trends.

If technology looks bright, the dismal science of agrarian economics is hard to see in the looking-glass future. Globalization and class warfare models (big versus small) may accelerate changes already under way. If the trends continually reduce successive family ownership in favor of cut-and-run outside corporations, at least one known and respected pathway to sustainability will prove difficult. Class war arguments are rarely popular with the wealthy rural power elites, who sometimes dominate county fiefdoms. But the polemics of labor versus capital are balancing, insightful, and part of the history of the Llano. Fulminating against dominant corporations is an old western tradition. The useful mediators of future land use dialectics are likely to be urban populations. Midland, Lubbock, Plainview, Portales, and Amarillo maintain a modest measure of urban growth, even if a large proportion is at the expense of diminishing nearby small-farm communities. These oasis cities still nourish romantic horizons for the hinterland. Many of their residents would prefer more sensitive land ethics, even if not exactly volunteering to pay for them. The urban-rural dialogue is nevertheless crucial for the future, because big city voters may make decisions on which elements to sustain in the country: a declining resource, or an older way of life, or a vanishing ecosystem? Even tentative regional planning for the components of a Southern High Plains sustainability paradigm is urgent. Urban funding and political goodwill will be required in the long process.

What is new today is the substantially altered ethnic component in the revived conquest of the Plains. Although the U.S. Census 2000 is still being released, the demographic prominence of Hispanic residents on the Llano is already dramatic. Many counties already or will soon have a majority of residents of Hispanic descent. Clearly ethnic labor is a major factor in the growth of corporate rule on the Southern High Plains. Hispanic in-migration to corporate employers in the meatpacking industry is well known. Some levels of chain-migration between Mexico and the Llano have been spatially significant. Agricultural historian Gary Nall notes that residents from one Zacatecas village have been gradually exchanging old farm labor in Mexico for new farm labor on the Southern High Plains.[30] And in the 1990s, there were other immigrant experiences as well. Catholic Refugee Services in Amarillo assisted Balkan immigrants. Asian migrants were attracted to corporate employment in the food processing industries. Panhandle corporations now attract distant sources of labor, increasing the human and cultural diversity of the region. Farm corporations will likely continue to offer economic opportunities to global or hemispheric migrants.

The future decline of the past family farm may bring a tear to the eye of the sentimentalist, myself included, but the contextual reality of agriculture on the Southern High Plains has been (1902) and will be (2002) corporate. Nor is it the first time corporations have ruled the lands, waters, plants, and animals of the Southern High Plains. The central focus for conservation impulses is likely to be the new relationships between inanimate corporate beings and the very animate if stressed landscapes serving them. Rhetoric about individual "private property" is often zealous, even if the land is increasingly directed by a class of legal *übermenschen* known as closely held corporations. This conversion of family farms into bottom-line, integrated, scaleable, agribusiness enterprises thus poses unique challenges for the conservation/preservation movement. Transgenic crops, bioengineering, satellite surveillance, and robotic pesticide sprayers will constitute a further and massive transformation of the Southern High Plains. It is likely that a projected twenty-first-century bioengineered shock wave will have to mesh with a new conservation impulse in the next few decades, particularly since the climate may be getting worse instead of better, as once desired and claimed.

Arguably the Llano Estacado of 2000–2010 may have important similarities to the Llano of 1900–1910. Both periods reflect immense technological change and transregional connectivity. The role—or rule—of corporations is of paramount influence, and the same approximate number of overall farm operations, some ten thousand to twenty thousand, is at work. Land ownership currently is very "traditionalist" in nature, with private property being taken perhaps more seriously (in an age of liability) than in 1900. The missing ingredient, perhaps, is a politically popular new conservation impulse, one concomitant with the vision of public stewardship, leisure, heritage, and size to match the

Arcadian visions of 1906–1916 or the New Deal of 1930s. Too many residents regard "environmentalism" as a sour, ugly, elitist, distant, collectivist (if not downright Bolshevik) concept for the trammeling of their endowed, individual, anti-statist "rights."

The Future of the Past

The time is ripe then for a resurgent postmodern conservation impulse, one centered as before in "modernist" economies, but grounded in sustainable relations and celebrated in the expressive arts by writers, musicians, indeed all cultural creatives. History, a way of seeing what no longer exists, has a part to play in the imaginative process. Much of the new impulse already exists, either in formal, embryonic, or private fashions. Admittedly, the ugly realities of massive groundwater withdrawals, soil contamination, chemical pollution, pig farming, and so on might constitute a current "corporate desert" perception of the landscape, at least for many environmentalists and land ethicists. Nevertheless, the Llano Estacado has a future, and it might as well be a "Garden" one— once again. Looking to the future, with close attention to the past, I see the outlines of a new twenty-first-century perceptual "Garden" for the Southern High Plains. That the vision and image can swing to the positive is known. Although the cultural parameters of the swing have yet to be fully envisioned, much less politically embraced, still a few reflections may be in order.

New Parks for the Llano Estacado

A key element in a projected twenty-first-century conservation movement includes the expansion and addition of new public parks. The Alibates Flint National Monument, for example, is a regional moneymaker. The tourists come and come. The existing five thousand acres of Palo Duro Canyon State Park near Canyon is also very popular, but it is a spatial will-o'-the-wisp in many respects. The park is simply too tiny, certainly by the bragging rights usually associated with the state, and it is now overcrowded in summers. The addition and preservation of additional components of the sixty-five-mile-long canyon system is entirely desirable. As Dan Flores explains elsewhere in this volume, it once came close to being a big National Park, and could do so again.

The Natural Heritage Program of the Texas State General Land Office has assessed many remaining natural areas of Texas. Historic places and portions of the Llano, such as Las Lenguas or Blanco Canyon or Rocky Dell, and special lands that are already rich in habitat, endangered species, and species diversity, may all lend themselves to new parks, wilderness areas, and wildlife refuges. Indeed, the remnants of the old prairie and grassland biome may harbor significant genetic resources for the future. While species recovery efforts can and do work with private landowners, there is no substitute for much larger habitats with fewer "edge" effects.

Conservation of Farm Community Heritage

As noted above, the Southern High Plains has an implanted preservation and heritage movement. The 1990s witnessed numerous instances of preserving and capitalizing upon the regional and western heritage of the plains. From mom-and-pop downtown stores to generous state funding for local courthouse restoration (a reverse flow of funding from urban to rural cultural investment), the preservation movement is solidly established and justly celebrated. County heritage museums, Main Street revitalization, antique stores, private collectors of farm equipment and tractors, Ebay vendors in small rural towns, and the retailing of western life experiences in general are now part of small-town economies. Substantial numbers of Japanese and German tourists ride horses, eat steaks around campfires, and contemplate the western skies. The Llano, as a land of time, has an enormous capacity to absorb further heritage tourism.

Moreover, the old family farming way of life may itself be of interest to the future. Where can one go to see a functioning colonization or New Deal landscape on the plains? How did our ancestors plant cotton or make wild plum jelly? At Las Cruces, the New Mexico Farm and Ranch Heritage Museum offers an immersion experience to a prior way of regional life. Other architectural and heritage centers on the Llano are certainly a possibility. The traditionalist family-farm "homeland" around Lubbock lends itself to this heritage opportunity, as I suggested earlier.

Post-Postmodern "Cultural Creatives"

If Lusby and Wilkie, Reaugh and O'Keeffe, were the "cultural creatives" of the Southern High Plains landscape in 1910s, who are the ones of today? The happy answer is that there are many artistic types on the plains of today, some with paying jobs. In the regional cities the arts movement is lively and broad-based. The residents of Lubbock often strike this observer as being more personally involved and keenly interested in art than the jaded consumers of Dallas. It happens that some locals turn to art and carry it away with them. Buddy Holly moved to New York, while Joe Ely, Jimmy Dale Gilmore, and Butch Hancock moved to Central Texas after starting the musical trio the "Flatlanders" around a kitchen table in Lubbock. But other Lubbock musicians, Amarillo artists, and Midland writers stayed put. They continue to define cultural horizons appreciative of regional future and past. Imagineers like novelist Elmer Kelton, poet Andy Wilkinson, historian Dan Flores, photographer Wyman Meinzer, writer Patrick Dearen, the inimitable Stanley Marsh III, and many others romance the land in ways the earlier artists would have appreciated and approved.

Spiritual visions of a postmodern congregation of rural people concerned with "livingness" on the High Plains already exist. One highly intelligent agency in the spiritualization process is Father Darryl Birkenfeld's energetic Promised Land Network, a rural outreach ministry of the Catholic diocese of Amarillo. In publications, conferences, symposia, and activities, the Promised Land Network nurtures the earlier Arcadian dreams of farm families. Indeed, it promotes regional creativity to enhance spiritual and sustainable ends. Strengthening and encouraging the creative regionalism of the Llano can only benefit all concerned.

Conservation of Ethnic Landscapes

The dominant commemorative influences of the Southern High Plains arose in the twentieth century. Excepting the Coronado expedition, commemoration centered on the late 1800s Anglo-Saxon arrivals, especially the usual suspects for a state historical marker such as Texas Rangers, pioneer ranchers, military heroes, and epic trailblazers. If the early Anglos got their due along the roads of the twentieth century, then Hispanics likely will see their visions and places honored in the twenty-first century. Beginning in the 1930s, and a major factor in politics today, county percentages of Hispanic population have climbed steadily for seven decades. In looking at the region, geographer Terrence Haverluk finds the Hispanic communities "new" in their orientation and settlement type.[31] But he also notes these Hispanic demographics (approaching 50 percent for some towns) are correlated with higher than expected rates of Spanish language retention. The result in his view is an emergent "High Plains Hispanic Homeland," a hybrid cultural realm, really, that embraces assimilation on the one hand for economic mobility, but on the other hand retains much ethnic identity and often speaks Spanish in the home. Noting strong cultural ties to the Tex-Mex borderland, the historic source of in-migration, Haverluk observes that locals call the South Plains (around Lubbock) "the little [Rio Grande] valley of the north." The importance of agriculture in the regional economy necessarily involves a large number of these Hispanics in farming, farm labor, food service, and food processing.

Shifting regional demographics, whereby a former minority becomes equivalent or even a majority locally, raise important questions. Does the Llano need to re-imagine its past with an eye to the new ethnic future? Already other regions, especially San Antonio, have experimented with framing the issues and debates in "contested history." For the Southern High Plains the possibilities of "hidden heritage" are quite interesting. After all, a modern, initially agrarian, and culturally Tex-Mex migration stream has come from "the Valley" (lower Rio Grande River) to a land that already has a Spanish cultural heritage. But this prior heritage is a different one in many ways, from a different source region (sixteenth-through nineteenth-century New Mexico), and one largely interpreted or ignored by a different ethnic group (twentieth-century Anglos). The older Hispanic heritage of the Llano Estacado lingers in places, including *comanchero* outposts, historic springs, cemeteries, and old *placita* sites. But most historic sites are currently on private property. Some important sites are virtually off-limits, even to researchers. A number of historic places (Rocky Dell) and pre-Anglo personages (Pedro Vial) are neither acknowledged by markers or even a goal of regional planning. Redefining and conserving the lost 1700s or forgotten ethnic heritage sites of the 1800s Llano may provide multiple benefits for a new century, including Hispanic appreciation and tourism from other parts of the state.

With the Alibates flint quarries as paragon, more awareness could also be done for American Indian cultural heritage sites. A few archeologists study the Antelope Creek pueblos in the Canadian Valley, but the public sees little. Yet, one thing the Llano has over many other regions is its sheer duration of cultural time, going back 11,200 B.P. to the Clovis people. The promotion and conservation of the Paleolithic heritage has paid dividends at Clovis, New Mexico, and the Lubbock Lake site, but

other areas and sites await proper discovery, exploration, or due celebration. Finding and conserving the paleo-landscapes will be a suitable
challenge for the future.

The Politics of Conservation

Conserving the land and waters, whether by family or corporate farms,
will involve frequent and intense political elements. Private property is a
strict given for many rural and urban people, even if they do not own
much land themselves. And the vast majority of the Llano Estacado is
private property. Public stewardship of land is certainly not unknown,
but it is less ardently embraced perhaps than in other regions (many
with generous amounts of federal funding or land). The Nature
Conservancy has an enviable record of working with private landowners
for the public good. The expansion of their work and interests to the
Southern High Plains is long overdue.

The late Judge L. Bunton's historic ruling on groundwater flows may
also reflect a new level or expansion of public stewardship, and not just
on the surface. Indeed "public goods" may lie below the surface of the
Llano. After initial resistance, groundwater districts are now part of the
reality for much of the Plains. The pattern of fierce landowner resistance
followed by slow grudging acceptance of new "green" paradigms will
likely continue. This pattern implies that public opinion, media, elections, and, most important, local political leadership will all be instrumental in establishing a regulatory form of conservation, one with
embedded sustainability features. Lastly, the benefits from intelligent
political largesse or "pork" can ultimately catalyze development, much
as Lyndon Johnson transformed the Hill Country with dams, roads, and
electricity.

Green Acres: One Conclusion

While this cold vision of the Llano Estacado suggests that postindustrial
farming will likely displace both traditional family and "nature" farming, it does not mean that the family farmer will disappear either quickly
or completely. Many family farmers are quite resilient and adaptable to
change. They will acquire robotic sprayers and ATVs, use GIS and the
Internet, and plant transgenic crops. Or they may go organic for different economics and market niche share. Other family farmers are well
capitalized (if not already incorporated for liability and estate planning

purposes). Nevertheless many traditional family farmers, like the Bedouin cultures I visited in the 1970s Negev desert, may find their old way of life preserved in future heritage museums far more than on the ground.

"Nature" farming itself has a powerful rationale, one that promises sustainability. It also has a moral geography and humanistic vision that should be encouraged to condition corporate behavior, regulate its pollution, and reduce the excesses and worse practices. Much as British farmers have rethought the wildlife corridor values of traditional hedgerows, High Plains farmers may embrace their "wasteful" playas. And nature farming has two powerful if unseen allies: climate (once drought, now global warming) and declining water tables. The measure of the mitigation will depend heavily on regional planning responses and future public policy formulations. While genetically modified crops largely take hold on the Great Plains, some 4 percent of corn acreage may be planted and marketed as identity-preserved crops, that is, old-fashioned gene pools focused on consumers' "green" expectations.

The transition of the Southern High Plains from a god-fearing, sod-busting, surplus-producing civilization of family farms in 1910 to a more impersonal, globalized, vertically integrated, corporate agribusiness in 2010 still holds a central dilemma: how to balance regional growth and technological development with stochastic and challenging environmental constraints. There were no easy answers in the past. The exhaustion of groundwater and a warming climate may make answers in the future more difficult. The promise of an information revolution and a vastly new bioengineered landscape, however, will predispose cornucopians to look on the sunny side of "food systems."

One answer is obvious: when corporations rule the Llano Estacado they will need a conservation movement—no less in the warming future than in the stubborn past. The general economic, social, and environmental health of the Southern High Plains may depend on a redefined conservation horizon. This sustainable development movement may resemble, in fact, the "natural capitalism" practices in use by progressive large corporations, in which waste is penalized and minimized, and resource productivity is enhanced and maximized. The economics of "natural capitalism" for the family farmer may involve (whether Japan or the High Plains) no-till cultivation, government welfare, and off-farm spousal income.

Almost a century ago the reporter M. G. Cunniff heard Texans declare that their elected, powerful Railroad Commission had done a fine job of reigning in the corporations:

> "It is just as easy to manage the corporations as to have the corporations manage you," say the legislators from the rice fields and the cotton fields, the "piney woods" and the *llano estacado* . . . If other states could have a consciousness as proud and alert as that of Texas—that the commonwealth is bigger than the corporations—half our national problems would disappear.[32]

It is unlikely that the voters will show such spunk again, but depleted groundwater, operating costs, invasive species, and droughts may make "natural capitalists" out of the surviving corporate colonizers of a bio-engineered Southern High Plains. If for no other reason than the tides of public opinion, other corporations will show a friendly face to the environment. The cultural creatives, of course, have known all along that conserving the Llano and preserving its heritage are good for the mind and body.

Notes

1. An important early survey of agribusiness dominance and large-scale institutional biases is Ingolf Vogeler, *The Myth of the Family Farm: Agribusiness Dominance of U.S. Agriculture* (Boulder, Colo.: Westview Press, 1981). Vogeler discusses oligopolies, small-town dependencies, supporting myths, biased federal programs, farm protest movements, contract farming, and tax-loss farming. Vogeler's remarks on the 1970s challenges to family farming are still pertinent.

2. Wendell Berry, *The Unsettling of America: Culture and Agriculture* (San Francisco: Sierra Club Books, 1986).

3. For regional history and origins of the name, see John Miller Morris, *El Llano Estacado: Exploration and Imagination on the High Plains of Texas and New Mexico, 1536–1860* (Austin: Texas State Historical Association, 1997), 162–66.

4. For "shocking truths" about agribusiness and animal abuse, see C. David Coats, *Old MacDonald's Factory Farm* (New York: Continuum, 1989).

5. See the important last chapter, "The Big Change," and farm data appendices in John Stricklin Spratt, *The Road to Spindletop: Economic Change in Texas, 1875–1901* (Dallas: Southern Methodist University Press, 1955), 276–302.

6. Patricia Nelson Limerick and Charles Scoggin note that Colorado's 1990–2000 census growth rate is "almost exactly the same growth rate" as the 1890–1900 census in "Testing the Limits of the Western Dream," *New York Times,* 18 February 2001, A16.

7. Donald W. Meinig, *Imperial Texas: An Interpretive Essay in Cultural Geography* (Austin: University of Texas Press, 1969), 70.

8. A good summary of the regional promotion process is Jan Blodgett, *Land of Bright Promise, Advertising the Texas Panhandle and South Plains, 1870–1917* (Austin: University of Texas Press, 1988). The best case study is Charles Dudley Eaves and C. A. Hutchinson, *Post City, Texas: C. W. Post's Colonizing Activities in West Texas* (Austin: Texas State Historical Association, 1952).

9. See, David B. Gracy, II, "A Preliminary Survey of Land Colonization in the Panhandle–Plains of Texas," *The Museum Journal* 11 (1969): 51–79.

10. See Robert Julyan, *The Place Names of New Mexico* (Albuquerque: University of New Mexico Press, 1996).

11. Castro County (1 colonization town), Parmer Co. (3 towns), Hale Co. (4 towns), Bailey Co. (6 towns), Crosby Co. (4 towns), Lamb Co. (3 towns), Lubbock Co. (3 towns), Hockley Co. (1 town).

12. Frieda Knobloch, *The Culture of Wilderness: Agriculture as Colonization in the American West* (Chapel Hill: University of North Carolina Press, 1999).

13. S. Nugent Townshend and J. G. Hyde, *Our Indian Summer in the Far West: An Autumn Tour of 15,000 Miles in Kansas, Texas, New Mexico, Colorado, and the Indian Territory* (London: Charles Whittingham, 1880). Sixty-two albumen photographs illustrate this rare volume dedicated to the Anglo-Irish capitalist John Adair.

14. Martyn J. Bowden, "The Perception of the Western Interior of the United States, 1800–1870: A Problem in Historical Geography," *Proceedings of the Association of American Geographers* 1 (1969): 16–21; John L. Allen, "Exploration and the Creation of Geographical Images of the Great Plains: Comments on the Role of Subjectivity," in *Images of the Plains: The Role of Human Nature in Settlement,* ed. B. Blouet and M. P. Lawson (Lincoln: University of Nebraska Press, 1975): 3–12; and G. Malcolm Lewis, "Rhetoric of the Western Interior: Modes of Environmental Description in American Promotional Literature of the Nineteenth Century," in *The Iconography of Landscape,* ed. Denis Cosgrove and Stephen Daniels (New York: Cambridge University Press, 1988): 179–93.

15. For an excellent discussion on changing environmental perceptions in railroad advertising, see "The Railroads", chap. 3 in Blodgett, *Land of Bright Promise,* 26–42.

16. See the extensive bibliographic notes in John Opie, *Ogallala: Water for a Dry Land* (Lincoln: University of Nebraska Press, 2000). Two regional classic studies include Donald E. Green, *Land of the Underground Rain, Irrigation on*

the Texas High Plains, 1910–1970 (Austin: University of Texas Press, 1973), and Charles Bowden, *Killing the Hidden Waters* (Austin: University of Texas Press, 1977).

17. A typical 1906 land promotion brochure for Canyon, Texas, assured Iowa and Indiana homeseekers that the climate was "always pure and conducive to good health." Keiser Brothers and Phillips, "The Texas Panhandle" (Washington, Iowa: Needham Printery, 1906), 3.

18. Peter L. Petersen, "A Park for the Panhandle: The Acquisition and Development of Palo Duro State Park," in *The Story of Palo Duro Canyon*, ed. Duane F. Guy (Canyon, Tex.: Panhandle-Plains Historical Society, 1978), 157.

19. Paul H. Ray and Sherry Ruth Anderson, *The Cultural Creatives: How 50 Million People Are Changing the World* (New York: Harmony Books, 2000).

20. Robert Mugerauer, *Interpreting Environments, Tradition, Deconstruction, Hermeneutics* (Austin: University of Texas Press, 1995), 57–115.

21. Jack Cowart and Juan Hamilton, Letters selected by Sarah Greenough, *Georgia O'Keeffe, Art and Letters* (Boston: National Gallery of Art with Bulfinch Press,1987), 156–57.

22. Elliott West, *The Contested Plains: Indians, Goldseekers, and the Rush to Colorado* (Lawrence: University Press of Kansas, 1998), 159.

23. See Roxana Robinson, *Georgia O'Keeffe, A Life* (New York: Harper and Row, 1989), 157–59, 171–72.

24. An excellent catalogue and portrait of O'Keeffe on the High Plains is Sharyn R. Udall, *O'Keeffe and Texas* (San Antonio: Marion Koogler McNay Art Museum, 1998).

25. Janet Neugebauer, ed., *Plains Farmer: The Diary of William G. De Loach, 1914–1964* (College Station: Texas A&M University Press, 1991).

26. Michael Johnston Grant, *Down and out on the Family Farm; Rural Rehabilitation in the Great Plains, 1929–1945* (Lincoln: University of Nebraska Press, 2002).

27. Visit USDA website *www.usda.gov/nass/aggraphs/cropmap.htm* and related NASS websites and interactive mapping tools. Extensive and up-to-date USDA data collections exist on the Web.

28. Emel and Roberts note an extensive arc of groundwater declines exceeding one hundred feet. Jacque Emel and Rebecca Roberts, "Institutional Form and Its Effect on Environmental Change: The Case of Groundwater in the Southern High Plains," *Annals of the Association of American Geographers* 85: 4 (December 1995): 671.

29. Elizabeth Brooks and Jaque Emel, with Brad Jokisch and Paul Robbins, *The Llano Estacado of the U.S. Southern High Plains: Environmental Transformation and the Prospect for Sustainability* (New York: United Nations University Press, 2000), 139.

30. Garry L. Nall, "A Century of Industrial Agriculture in the Panhandle,"

presentation, Texas State Historical Association, 104th Annual Meeting, Austin, Texas, 2 March 2000. The author is greatly indebted to Dr. Nall for his informed discussion of corporate agriculture on the High Plains of Texas.

31. Terrence Haverluk, "Hispanic Community Types and Assimilation," *The Professional Geographer* 50: 4 (November 1998): 465–80.

32. M. G. Conniff, "Texas and the Texans," *Farm and Ranch* (1905): 7267-288. This quote appears on 7267.

CHAPTER THREE

Droughts of the Past, Implications for the Future?

CONNIE WOODHOUSE

Elliott West's essay in this volume paints a picture of the Southern Plains as a region that, although spare and sparsely populated, has historically been rich with reserves of energy in the form of grasslands and bison. John Miller Morris's chapter chronicles the evolution of the region's agricultural development over the last century. Both essays make clear that climate has shaped the character of Southern Plains life and that drought has been one of the most influential characteristics of this climate. The Great Plains as a whole experiences a semiarid climate because it lies in the rain shadow of the Rocky Mountains. Moisture coming from the Pacific Ocean is largely blocked by the mountains, so most precipitation comes from the Gulf of Mexico in the form of spring and summer thunderstorms.[1] Across the Great Plains, annual rainfall tends to grade from wettest in the east to driest in the west, while temperatures range from warm in the south to cool in the north, making the Southern Plains the hottest, driest part of the Great Plains.[2] Consequently, it is not surprising that droughts are a common feature of the region.

Drought and the winds and blowing sands that accompany drought have played a crucial role in shaping the landscapes of the Southern Plains over the course of tens of thousands of years. They have also influenced its inhabitants, their perceptions, cultures, and ways of life. This essay traces the history of drought in the region during the last ten thousand years, the period of time since glaciers covered large areas of North America, known as the Holocene. The last millennium, in particular, will be the period of greatest focus, with an even more detailed look at the last several centuries.

But first, what is drought? In the simplest terms, drought is a significant lack of moisture availability due to lower than normal rainfall. Drought can be defined in a number of ways, such as by rainfall amounts (meteorological drought); vegetation conditions; agricultural productivity; soil moisture (agricultural drought); levels in reservoirs, aquifers, and stream flow (hydrologic drought); or social and economic impacts (socioeconomic drought). The time frames associated with each type of drought vary. Meteorological droughts are first to be detected and first to be over, followed by agricultural and hydrologic droughts. Socioenomic droughts can occur at a variety of time scales. Droughts that last multiple years and impact all facets of the environment and society will be considered here.

Twentieth-Century Droughts

The major droughts of the twentieth century provide a useful starting point, for they offer a familiar context from which to assess droughts of the more distant past. We assess twentieth-century droughts to determine whether this century's droughts are typical of droughts of previous centuries or whether they are unusual events. In the 2000 annual weather summary for the nation, the National Oceanic and Atmospheric Administration (NOAA) reported that the period from July through September 2000 marked the driest three-month period on record for the Southern Plains. This period was even drier than any three-month period during the 1950s drought. Texas alone reported one billion dollars in agricultural losses.[3] However, when climatologists assessed the region for drought three months later, little evidence of drought remained.[4] This proved to be a short-lived, but very costly, drought. Other relatively short but expensive droughts have occurred in the Southern Plains in recent years. A headline in May of 1996 proclaimed, "Drought Impact on Agriculture in the Billions of Dollars," and indeed, drought cost estimates topped $6.5 billion.[5] Although this drought, and a similar one in 1998, lasted less than one year, they had considerable economic impacts. Of course, the losses transcended economics, as they also meant crushing hardships for farm and ranch families.

The north-central Texas record of drought for the full length of the instrumental record, going back to 1895, shows that short, severe droughts like those of 1996, 1998, and 2000 occurred with some regularity, as did droughts of similar severity that lasted several years.[6] However, these droughts paled in comparison to that of the 1950s, which was much more severe and persistent than any other drought in the twentieth century. The Dust Bowl drought of the 1930s was also severe but several short intervals of wetter years somewhat alleviated its impact. If a 1950s-type drought were to occur today, the consequences would be devastating, as demonstrated by these relatively minor recent droughts. Just how rare was the 1950s drought and is such a drought likely to happen again? The instrumental record is simply too short to answer this question, as only one example of such a severe drought (the 1950s event itself) occurred in the one-hundred-and-five-year record.

Fortunately, natural recorders of rainfall and drought exist that reveal information about past climate before the availability of rain gauges and thermometers. These records, called paleoclimatic or proxy records, can be considered surrogates or substitutes for the gauge and thermometer records. Paleoclimatic data may be stored in the rings of

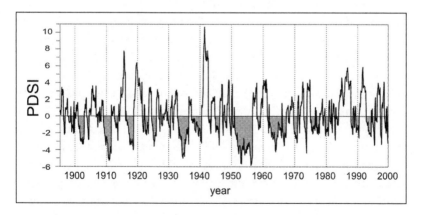

Drought record for north-central Texas by month, 1895–2000. The Palmer Drought Severity index is one of several measures of drought. Values below zero indicate drought. Data from National Climatic Data Center. Graph by Connie Woodhouse.

trees; layers of sand dunes and lake-bottom sediments; in historical documents, such as letters, diaries, and newspapers; and in archaeological artifacts. These records allow us to evaluate twentieth-century droughts in the context of a longer time period and to establish a baseline of natural climate variability. This second matter is especially important. Knowledge of natural baseline climate variability helps us discern when climate changes go beyond what may be expected under natural conditions and what may be due to the influence of human activities on climate. Because of human-induced global warming, records of the past will likely not be analogs to the future, but they can provide a guide to what we may expect and over which the climate effects related to human activities will be superimposed.

The Paleoclimatic Record of Drought

It is perhaps easiest to consider the record of past droughts by working first from the most distant period, for which estimates of climate are the roughest and evaluated in the context of thousands of years, to those of more recent times, for which there are more detailed paleoclimatic data for time scales of decades and years.

THE DUNE RECORD

The Southern High Plains is a nearly flat plateau that extends from the Canadian River in northern Texas to the Edwards Plateau on the south. It is bounded by escarpments on the west (Pecos River valley) and the east (Red, Brazos, and Colorado river tributaries). Sand dunes and sand sheets, most of which are now overlain by vegetation, cover a large portion of the Southern High Plains.[7] However, this has not always been the case. In times of drought, wind-borne deposits of sand created sand dunes and sheets and sand-filled valleys and draws. These dunes, sheets, and sandy valleys all contain a wealth of information about episodes of drought and aridity over the course of the Holocene. Interspersing the layers of sand, representing periods that became too dry to support vegetation, are layers of soil, which reflect periods wet enough to have allowed soil to form and support plant life.[8] The soil layers, which contain organic materials, can be dated with radiocarbon dating techniques. Although the sand itself is not usually dated, the dates from the soil between layers of sand can bracket times of drought. Because there is a lag in time in the geomorphic response to climate conditions (i.e., wet-

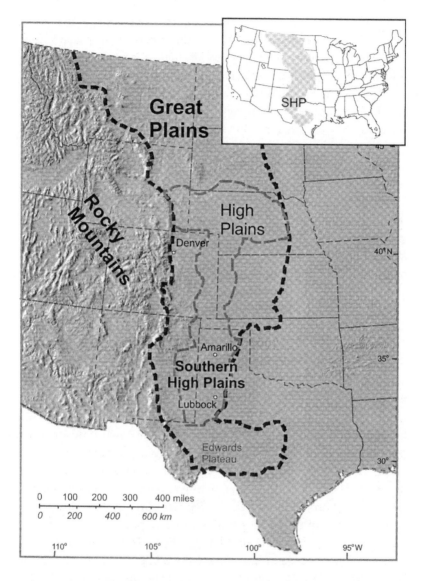

Location of Great Plains (dark dotted line), High Plains (light dotted line), and Southern High Plains. Shaded relief base map and physiographic boundaries adapted from U.S. Geological Survey map I-2206 by Jeffrey Lukas and Connie Woodhouse.

ter climate leading to soil formation and drier climate leading to dune activation), the temporal resolution of this record is fairly coarse. The coarseness is even more pronounced in the earlier part of the record. Radiocarbon dating, since it is not a precise dating method, contributes to low temporal resolution of this record.[9] Still, the sand features provide a more complete chronology of drought and aridity over the past ten thousand years than any other paleoclimatic proxy for this region. Pollen buried in lake and bog sediments and small animal fossils provide additional information, but they do not offer as complete a spatial or temporal coverage.[10]

A time line of drought from sand dune data and lake sediments containing pollen and fossil material shows periods of drought with intervening periods of wetter climate. About twelve thousand years ago, the climate at the very end of the last glacial period was relatively cool and moist, but soon tended toward warmer and drier conditions. The earliest sand sheets dated in the Southern High Plains document the first evidence of regional aridity around eleven thousand to ten thousand years ago. Following this was a period of episodic droughts up until about seventy-five hundred years ago, after which conditions became warmer and drier, culminating in a period known at the Altithermal.[11] This was the warmest, driest period in the last ten thousand years and though most intense in the Southern High Plains, appears to have spread across the Great Plains and into the Rocky Mountains.[12] Incidentally, people occupied the Southern High Plains at this time. At Mustang Springs, Texas, archaeologists have found what they believe to be wells dug down to the water table to reach the Ogallala Aquifer after the springs failed, a good indication of just how severe and prolonged this period of drought was.[13] As West explains in his essay, this period also coincided with a time for which few or no bison bones have been found. Investigators believe the configuration of orbital parameters of the earth at the time contributed to the prevailing conditions of drought and aridity. An increase tilt of the earth likely caused increased solar radiation in summer and, consequently, hotter summers in this part of the world.[14]

The climate became cooler and wetter about five thousand years ago, and although these conditions lasted for about three thousand years, droughts again became more frequent near the end of this period. The dune record shows episodic drought events, severe enough to mobilize sand dunes, throughout the past several thousand years. A more

This time line shows broad temporal patterns of wet and dry conditions from the end of the Pleistocene period, through the Holocene, and to the present. The gridded overlays indicate generally wetter conditions, while the nongridded portions of the time line indicate generally drier conditions. Conditions vary within the wetter and dryer time periods as indicated by the shading. Darker shades indicate greater intensity—drier or wetter— while lighter shades indicate less severe conditions. At the bottom of the figure, the cooler, wetter condi-

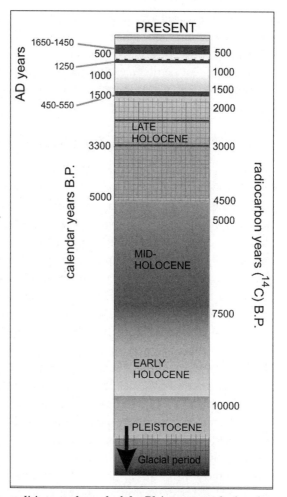

tions tend toward drier conditions at the end of the Pleistocene and after the last glacial period. Episodes of drought in the early Holocene led to increasingly dry conditions that peaked about 7500 B.P. and extended through the mid-Holocene. Wetter conditions, starting about five thousand years ago, prevailed for about three thousand years. About two thousand years ago, conditions started to become drier, with increasing droughts. Horizontal dark lines indicate period of droughts in the last several thousand years. Resolution of data does not allow the identification of individual droughts, but it does show trends to wetter or drier conditions, and periods of overall wetness or dryness. Dates are given in conventional radiocarbon years, calendar years B.P. (B.P. = years before 1950), and A.D. years. Chart by Connie Woodhouse.

detailed dune record available for the last fifteen hundred years suggests droughts occurred periodically, after A.D. 500–600, after about A.D. 1300, and between A.D. 1500 and 1700.[15] There is also evidence for dune activity in the nineteenth century. In the context of the last millennium, however, the twentieth century appears relatively moist, with no widespread dune mobility.

Major Droughts of the Past Millennium

In the last one thousand years, the dune record overlaps with some other paleoclimatic records, such as those from long tree-ring sequences, archaeological data, and lake sediments. These other records provide additional information for two periods of drought documented in the dune record, one in the last quarter of the thirteenth century and one in the second half of the sixteenth century.[16] Although these additional paleoclimatic records are sparsely distributed, and for the most part are not located in the Southern High Plains, the two droughts were widespread enough so that along with the dune record, we can infer their occurrence in the Southern High Plains as well.

Long tree-ring records in the Sierra Nevada, western Great Basin, the southwestern United States, and into the North-Central Great Plains document the thirteenth-century drought.[17] Additional evidence comes from archaeological data for the Dakotas and the southwestern United States, and from lake sediment data in the northern Great Plains and buried stumps in the Sierra Nevada.[18] The availability of tree-ring data, which are precisely dated and highly resolved, makes it possible to pinpoint the years of this drought.[19] In some parts of the Southwest, the drought lasted almost continuously for twenty years (1279–1299), and is sometimes referred to as the "Great Drought."[20] This period of drought coincided with the abandonment of ancient Anasazi settlements and subsequent population redistribution.[21] Although the causes of this reorganization are still hotly debated, and include everything from the overconsumption of natural resources to warfare with other tribes, it is likely that drought was a contributing factor.

A more recent, major drought occurred in the second half of the sixteenth century. This drought has been well documented by tree-ring data for many parts of North America. It appears to have started in northwestern Mexico in the 1560s and spread as far north as Canada. The drought continued across much of western North American until the 1590s, and was most persistent in the southwestern United States and northern Mexico. The impact on humans was likely significant, especially in the Southwest, where the puebloan culture depended on dryland farming. Historical evidence of pueblo abandonment in what is now New Mexico at this time provides evidence for the great impact of this drought.[22]

It is important to note that the droughts of the last several millennia, including the multidecadal droughts of the sixteenth and thirteenth century, occurred under a climate similar to that of today, unlike the mid-Holocene Altithermal dry period. As far as we know, there was nothing very different controlling the climate during these more recent droughts —no great differences in orbital parameters and no evidence for events that might have promoted these drought conditions. The documentation for the droughts of the thirteenth and sixteenth centuries is robust and there is no doubt they occurred. Although these episodes contained some nondrought years, they are clearly unlike any droughts experienced in the twentieth century.

Southern Plains Drought of the Past Four Hundred Years

Trees from northeastern New Mexico and southeastern Colorado provide the foundation for a reconstruction of summer drought for the Oklahoma Panhandle region.[23] The reconstruction extends back to 1595, affording a hint of the sixteenth-century drought, but the record also shows a number of other droughts with which the major twentieth-century droughts can be compared. The 1930s and 1950s droughts, as well as a short, severe drought in the 1960s, appear as major droughts in the last four hundred years. However, there are numerous other droughts in this record that are equally, if not more, severe. In general, about three droughts occur per century that are the magnitude of, or greater than, the major twentieth-century droughts. The nineteenth century in particular (for which there is also dune evidence, as mentioned above), shows two periods of severe drought, 1845 to 1852 and 1859 to 1863, both of which exceed the severity of the twentieth-century droughts. A less severe drought occurred around 1820. The 1845–1852 drought contained eight summers of almost consecutive drought (only 1849 had nondrought conditions). This drought was similar in duration to the 1930s drought, which had nine years of drought with one intervening

nondrought year in this record, but was more severe in terms of intensity. To make matters worse, a severe five-year drought followed this
1840s-era drought only seven years later.

Historical records from early instrumental measurements and travelers' accounts further document the droughts of the nineteenth century. Instrumental records of this time are spotty and discontinuous,
and travelers' accounts suffer from fragmentation, lack of continuity,
and biases. However, both sources provide some assessment of climate
extremes, such as periods of drought. In particular, Stephen H. Long's
1820–1821 expedition reported significant episodes of blowing sand,
indicating drought, in dune fields around the Canadian River. Several
other exploration parties reported blowing sand in the Monahan dunes

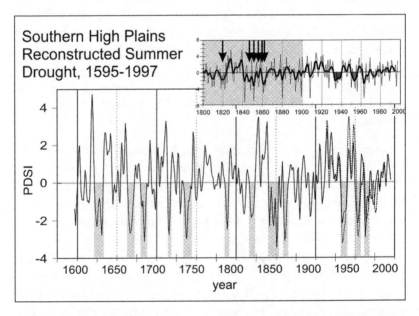

*Reconstructed summer drought, 1595–1997, for the Oklahoma Panhandle
region (black line) and instrumental drought record (dotted line). The lines
have been smoothed to facilitate comparison. The shaded rectangle marks
major droughts. Insert shows the same reconstruction for the nineteenth and
twentieth centuries. Arrows mark years in which historical documents indicate drought. The 1930s and 1950s droughts are shaded. Graph by Connie
Woodhouse.*

in 1850 and 1855 during route reconnaissance across the Southern Plains.[24] Other assessments of conditions from U.S. Army–led expeditions, private emigrants trains to California, railroad surveying parties, and mail coaches, imply droughts in 1845, 1849, and 1850, which also correspond to the tree-ring reconstruction.[25] Military records indicate Southern Plains droughts in 1859 and 1862, while numerous newspaper accounts in Kansas document similar conditions around 1860.[26] Interestingly, these droughts of the 1840s and the 1860s coincide with the decimation of bison in the Great Plains. Although hunting by both Anglo-Americans and American Indians was probably the biggest factor in the bison demise, droughts may have been a contributing factor.[27]

When one examines the droughts of the twentieth century in the context of the past two hundred years, they still appear as major, but those of the mid-nineteenth century may have been equally, if not more, severe. Several, including those of the 1820s, 1850s, and 1860s in particular, may well have exceeded the severity of twentieth-century Southern Plains droughts. At the least, these proxy records indicate that the twentieth-century droughts are not unusual in terms of severity, duration, and frequency.

Summary of the Paleodrought Record

How one assesses the twentieth century in terms of drought severity is relative to the time frame considered for comparison. When viewed in the context of the last four hundred years, the twentieth-century droughts appear to have been relatively mild, especially compared to the nineteenth century. However, the frequency of major droughts (that is, moderate to severe droughts that last four to eight years) has been fairly consistent over time. If the detailed drought record for the past one thousand years (i.e., from high-resolution data such as from tree rings) is considered, a variety of paleoclimatic data support evidence for two widespread, multidecadal droughts in the thirteenth and sixteenth centuries that likely impacted the Southern Plains. Droughts of this nature are more severe than any we have experienced in the twentieth century because of their persistence over several decades. Even the widespread, severe Dust Bowl drought lasted only seven to nine years, while the more severe, but less widespread, 1950s drought lasted five to six years.

The thirteenth- and sixteenth-century droughts, though perhaps broken by some years of moderate climate, maintained drought conditions for twenty years or more. That is something we have not come close to experiencing in the twentieth century.

The dune record, which provides less temporal detail, suggests a slow drying trend over the last fifteen hundred years. Over the entire Holocene period (the last ten thousand years), dune and other proxy data indicate that the driest period took place during several millennia around the middle of the Holocene. This dry period, known as the Altithermal, was generally warmer and drier than any other time during the past ten thousand years. Individual droughts cannot be resolved in this type of record, but it is likely that more frequent severe droughts characterized this period, in addition to warmer and drier conditions overall.

Implications for the Future?

One thing should be abundantly clear by now: drought is a part of natural climate variability in this part of the world. This is due, in large part, to the position of the Southern Plains in the North American continent. The paleoclimatic record demonstrates that this regional disposition to drought has existed for the past ten thousand years.

Although we know a drought when we see it, and can attribute drought to factors such as persistent high pressure over the drought region, our understanding of what causes drought conditions to endure beyond several seasons is far from complete.[28] We do not have a very good idea of what caused the 1950s drought or the more persistent 1930s drought, let alone the multidecadal droughts of the past two thousand years. Obviously, it is difficult, if not impossible, to predict a major drought without this understanding. So what can the paleo record tell us about future droughts?

The record, especially for the past several thousand years, tells us that the twentieth-century record of drought is not particularly representative of prior centuries, even looking back fewer than two hundred years. It also shows that droughts more severe and persistent than the 1950s drought have occurred in the past. Consequently, it is highly likely that drought will continue to be an important factor of Southern Plains climate in the future, and that future droughts may well be more severe than those of the twentieth century.

Global Warming and Droughts

It is now obvious that the earth has warmed over the twentieth century.[29] But what impact has this warming had on droughts? So far, the twentieth-century record shows no trend toward dryness across most of the Great Plains, and some areas of the Southern Plains region, such as northern Texas and the Oklahoma Panhandle, even show an increase in annual precipitation over the twentieth century.[30] However, because there is quite a bit of year-to-year variability in precipitation, it may take some time to discern a significant trend in precipitation that is different from what would be expected under natural variability. Predictions for future climate from General Circulation Models (GCMs) have been somewhat mixed. Recent model results do not show a marked decrease in precipitation over this region in the next century and even suggest a possible increase in rainfall during winter months. However, rainfall is only part of the equation. Predictions for numbers of hot summer days over the next century show an increase of more than 60 percent in the Southern Plains.[31] Even with no decrease in precipitation, higher temperatures may well lead to drier conditions. Another study, which modeled the change in soil moisture in central North America, shows a strong decrease in soil moisture, detectable after about 2030.[32] More locally, modeling work using a dune mobility index shows that predicted greenhouse warming effects on temperature and precipitation have the potential to cause dune and sand sheet reactivation over much of the Great Plains.[33]

In conclusion, paleoclimatic records show that drought has been part of Southern Plains climate for the past ten thousand years. Even without the effects of global warming, it is highly likely that drought will continue to be an important feature of the climate in this region. Future droughts may well be more severe than the major droughts experienced in the twentieth century. These implications should have bearings on the future development and management of Southern Plains water resources and agriculture. They may also affect the region's population growth (or lack of), which will be related to the kinds of opportunities that exist to attract and keep people. However, the natural physical environment of the Southern Plains—what is left of it—will persist, changing over time to reflect changes in climate, whether due to natural variability or human-induced climate change. The region's landscape has been characterized by sand dunes and sand sheets in the past. It is not inconceivable that it may look that way again at some point in the future.

Notes

1. Roger G. Barry and Richard J. Chorley, *Atmosphere, Weather, and Climate,* 5th ed. (London: Methuen, 1987).

2. John R. Borchert, "The Climate of the Central North American Grassland," *Annals of the Association of American Geographers* 40 (1950): 1–39.

3. National Oceanic and Atmospheric Administration, Climate of 2000 Summary; available from *http://lwf.ncdc.noaa.gov/ol/climate/research/2000/ann/us_summary.html.*

4. The drought map for the six months ending in December 2000 can be found at the National Drought Mitigation Center Web site, available from *http://www.drought.unl.edu/monitor/spi/spi00map.htm.*

5. For the full text of this article see *http://agnews.tamu.edu/dailynews/stories/DRGHT/smith.HTM.*

6. The Palmer Drought Severity Index (W.C. Palmer, "Meteorological Drought," U.S. Weather Bureau Research Paper, no. 45 [Washington, D.C.: U.S. Department of Commerce, 1965]) is one of the most commonly used of a number of indices that have been developed to quantify drought. PDSI values are derived from measurements of precipitation, air temperature, and local soil moisture, along with prior values of these measures. Values range from -6.0 (extreme drought) to +6.0 (extreme wet conditions), and have been standardized to facilitate comparisons from region to region. A PDSI value for any given month also will reflect conditions for prior months (generally nine to twelve months), as it is a cumulative measure.

7. The area covered by sand dunes and sheet is more than ten thousand square kilometers, or about 10 percent of the Southern High Plains. Vance T. Holliday, "Stratigraphy and Geochronology of Upper Quaternary Eolian Sand on the Southern High Plains of Texas and New Mexico, United States," *Geological Society of America Bulletin* 113 (2001): 88–108; Daniel R. Muhs and Vance T. Holliday, "Origin of Late Quaternary Dune Fields on the Southern High Plains of Texas and New Mexico," *Geological Society of America Bulletin* 113 (2001): 75–87; Wayne Palmer, "Meteorological Drought," U.S. Weather Bureau Research Paper No. 45 (Washington, D.C.: Department of Commerce, 1965).

8. Mobilization of dunes is dependent on adequate amounts of wind, a sand supply, and the availability of sand to become entrained in wind. In the Southern High Plains, the local Blackwater Formation sediments are a ready source of sand, and the sand-moving potential of winds has been estimated to

be typical of those in many of the major deserts of the world that contain large sand seas. D. H. Muhs and V. T. Holliday, "Origin of Late Quarternary Dune Fields on the Southern High Plains of Texas and New Mexico," GSA *Bulletin* 113, 75–87; Steven G. Fryberger and G. Dean, "Dune Forms and Wind Regime: A Study of Global Sand Seas," in *USGS Professional Paper* 1052, ed. Edwin D. McKee (Washington, D.C.; U.S. Department of the Interior, 1979), 137–69; Carol S. Breed et al., "Regional Studies of Sand Seas Using Landsat (ERTS) Imagery: A Study of Global Sand Seas," in *USGS Professional Paper* 1052, 305–97. The key factor in dune stability or mobilization in this region is the presence of vegetation, which, in turn, is related to climate. It appears that a small change in climate, reducing the ratio of precipitation to potential evaporation, can cause the vegetative cover to die and lead to an onset of eolian activity. Daniel R. Muhs and Vance T. Holliday, "Evidence of Active Dune Sand on the Great Plains in the Nineteenth Century from Accounts of Early Explorers," *Quaternary Research* 43 (1995): 198–208; Holliday, "Stratigraphy and Geochronology."

9. Radiocarbon dates are not exact dates but are interpreted as the probability of a date within a range of years. See Raymond S. Bradley, *Paleoclimatology: Reconstructing Climates of the Quaternary,* 2d ed. (New York: Harcourt/Academic Press, 1999). Ranges are typically plus or minus 5 percent. See Raymond S. Bradley, *Quaternary Paleoclimatology: Methods of Paleoclimatic Reconstruction* (Boston: Allen and Unwin, 1985).

10. Steven A. Hall, "Late Holocene Paleoecology of the Southern Plains," *Quaternary Research* 17 (1982): 391–407; Rickard S. Toomey II, Michael D. Blum, and Salvatore Valastro, Jr., "Later Quaternary Climates and Environments of the Edwards Plateau, Texas," *Global and Planetary Change* 7 (1993): 299–320.

11. Ernst Antevs, "Climatic Changes and Pre-White Man," *University of Utah Bulletin* 10 (1948): 168–91; Ernst Antevs, "Geologic-Climactic Dating in the West," *American Antiquity* 20 (1955): 317–35.

12. Walter E. Dean et al., "Regional Aridity in North America during the Middle Holocene," *The Holocene* 6 (1996): 145–55; David J. Meltzer, "Human Response to Middle Holocene (Altithermal) Climates on the North American Great Plains," *Quaternary Research* 52 (1999): 404–16.

13. David J. Meltzer and Michael B. Collins, "Prehistoric Water Wells on the Southern High Plains: Clues to Altithermal Climates," *Journal of Field Archaeology* 14 (1987): 9–28; David J. Meltzer, "Altithermal Archaeology and Paleoecology at Mustang Springs, on the Southern High Plains of Texas," *American Antiquity* 56 (1991): 236–67.

14. Vance T. Holliday, "Middle Holocene Drought on the Southern High Plains," *Quaternary Research* 31 (1989): 74–82; John E. Kutzbach and Peter J. Guetter, "The Influence of Changing Orbital Parameters and Surface Boundary Conditions on Climatic Simulations for the Past Eighteen

Thousand Years," *Journal of the Atmospheric Sciences* 43 (1986): 1726–59; R. S. Thompson et al., "Climatic Changes in the Western United States Since 18,000 yr. B.P.," in *Global Climates since the Last Glacial Maximum*, Herbert E. Wright, Jr., ed. (Minneapolis: University of Minnesota Press, 1993): 468–513.

15. Holliday, "Stratigraphy and Geochronology."

16. For an overview of the droughts, see Connie A. Woodhouse and Jonathan T. Overpeck, "Two Thousand Years of Drought Variability in the Central United States," *Bulletin of the American Meteorological Society* 9 (1998): 2692–714.

17. A number of proxy records document this drought, including tree-ring chronologies and/or reconstructions. For southwestern Nebraska see Harry E. Weakly, "Recurrence of Drought in the Great Plains during the Last Seven Hundred Years," *Agricultural Engineer* (February 1965): 85; for northern New Mexico see Henri D. Grissino-Mayer, "A 2129-Year Reconstruction of Precipitation for Northwestern New Mexico, USA," in *Tree Rings, Environment, and Humanity: Proceedings of the International Conference, Tucson, AZ, 17– May 1994*, ed. Jeffrey S. Dean, David M. Meko, and Thomas W. Swetnam (Tucson: Radiocarbon, Department. of Geosciences, University of Arizona, 1996), 191–204; for the Four Corners area, see Martin R. Rose, Jeffrey S. Dean, and William B. Robinson, "Dendroclimatic Reconstruction for the Southeastern Colorado Plateau," in *Final Report to Dolores Archaeological Project* (Boulder: University of Colorado, 1982); and for the White Mountains of California, see Malcolm K. Hughes and Lisa J. Graumlich, "Multimillennial Dendroclimatic Studies from the Western United States," in *Climate Variations and Forcing Mechanisms of the Last Two Thousand Years*, ed. Phillip D. Jones, Raymond S. Bradley, and Jean Jouzel (New York: Springer, 1996), 109–24. In the Nebraska tree-ring data, this drought extends from 1276 to 1313, the longest drought in the past 750 years.

18. Archaeological data from the Great Plains and Four Corners areas provide documentation of this drought; see Reid A. Bryson, David A. Baerreis, and Wayne M. Wendland, "The Character of Late-Glacial and Post-Glacial Climatic Change," in *Pleistocene and Recent Environments of the Central Great Plains*, ed. Wakefield Dort, Jr., and J. Knox Jones (Lawrence: University Press of Kansas, 1970), 98–115; Donald J. Lehmer, "Climate and Culture History in the Middle Missouri Valley," in *Pleistocene and Recent Environments of the Central Great Plains*, 117–29; Wayne M. Wendland, "Holocene Man in North America: The Ecological Setting and Climate Background," *Plains Anthropologist* 23 (1978): 273–87; Robert C. Euler et al., "The Colorado Plateaus: Cultural Dynamics and Paleoenvironments," *Science* 205 (1979): 1089–100; Jeffrey S. Dean et al., "Human Behavior, Demography, and Paleoenvironment on the Colorado Plateau," *American Antiquity* 50 (1985):

537–54; Jeffrey S. Dean, "The Medieval Warm Period on the Southern Colorado Plateau," *Climatic Change* 26 (1994): 225–41; Kenneth L. Peterson, "A Warm and Wet Little Climatic Optimum and a Cold and Dry Little Ice Age in the Southern Rocky Mountains, USA," *Climatic Change* 26 (1994): 243–69. This period of drought is also reflected in unprecedentedly low lake levels reconstructed from dated stumps rooted in several areas that are now flooded by streams and lakes in the Sierra Nevada of eastern California. See Scott Stine, "Extreme and Persistent Drought in California and Patagonia during Medieval Time," *Nature* 369 (1994): 546–49.

19. In tree-ring analysis, each and every tree ring is assigned an exact calendar year using a process called crossdating. Marvin A. Stokes and Terah L. Smiley, *An Introduction to Tree-Ring Dating* (Tucson: University of Arizona Press, 1968). Thus, tree rings are precisely dated (i.e., no dating error is assigned). The term "highly resolved" means that tree rings provide information at a very high temporal scale (compared to something like the dune record), typically annual to seasonal.

20. Andrew E. Douglass, "The Secret of the Southwest Solved by Talkative Tree Rings," *National Geographic Magazine* 56 (1929): 736–70; Andrew E. Douglass, "Dating Pueblo Bonito and Other Ruins of the Southwest," *National Geographic Society Contributed Technical Papers, Pueblo Bonito* no. 1 (1935); Emil Walter Haury, "Tree Rings—the Archaeologist's Timepiece," *American Antiquity* 1 (1935): 98–108.

21. Douglass, "Dating Pueblo Bonito"; Dean, "The Medieval Warm Period."

22. The following dendrochronological studies document this drought: Charles W. Stockton and Gordon C. Jacoby, "Long-Term Surface Water Supply and Streamflow level in the Upper Colorado River Basin," *Lake Powell Research Project Bulletin*, No. 18 (1976); Rosanne D. D'Arrigo and Gordon C. Jacoby, "One Thousand Year Record of Winter Precipitation From Northwestern New Mexico, USA: A Reconstruction From Tree-Rings and Its Relationship to El Niño and the Southern Oscillation," *The Holocene* 1 (1991): 95–101; Rosanne D. D'Arrigo and Gordon C. Jacoby, "A Tree-Ring Reconstruction of New Mexico Winter Precipitation and Its Relation to El Niño/Southern Oscillation Events," *El Niño: Historical and Paleoclimatic Aspects of the Southern Oscillation*, ed. Henry F. Diaz and Vera Markgraf (New York: Cambridge University Press, 1992): 243–57; Henri D. Grissino-Mayer, "A 2129-Year Reconstruction," and D. W. Stahle et al., "Tree-Ring Data Document Sixteenth-Century Megadrought over North America," *Eos* 81 (2000): 121–25.

23. Drought, in the form of a drought index called the Palmer Drought Severity Index (PDSI), was reconstructed from tree rings by calibrating the annual tree-ring measurements with the drought index value for a set of years in common to both records, 1910–1949. Stepwise regression was used to

generate a calibration model (regression techniques are commonly used for reconstructions), Harold C. Fritts, *Tree Rings and Climate* (New York: Academic Press, 1976). The model (i.e., the tree rings) explain 72 percent of the variance in the observed PDSI record. An independent set of years in common, 1950–1990, was used to test the model. In the test years, the model explained 39 percent of the variance. Over the full period (1910–1990), the model explains 57 percent of the variance in the observed record. The tree-ring estimates of drought tend to underestimate extreme values, as a function of the regression technique, and thus are conservative estimates of climate.

24. Muhs and Holliday, "Evidence of Dune Sand." Muhs and Holliday compiled travelers' reports of blowing sand in an effort to document eolian events in the nineteenth century; they used some of the same accounts as used by Jim Fenton in "The Desert Myth Dies Slowly on the Staked Plains, 1845–1860," *Panhandle-Plains Historical Review* (1990): 45–74. They assessed the blowing sand reports with regard to current dune conditions and came to the conclusion that dune activity was greater during the intervals around 1820 and the 1850s than it has been in the twentieth century. There are difficulties in gauging the response time of dune vegetation and sand to drought, but the degree of activity appears to have exceeded that occurring during the 1930s drought, suggesting the severity of the nineteenth-century droughts around 1820 and 1850 exceeded that of the 1930s.

25. Fenton recorded perceptions (including those of climate) of nineteenth-century explorers by reviewing accounts of some twenty crossings of the Staked Plains from 1845–1860. Accounts reflect the state of vegetation, water supplies, and occurrences of dust storms and "northers."

26. Cary J. Mock, "Drought and Precipitation Fluctuations in the Great Plains During the Late Nineteenth Century," *Great Plains Research* 1 (1991): 26–56. Mock compiled records kept by surgeons and volunteers at military hospitals (mainly to address questions about weather and health) in the Great Plains for 1851–1890 to examine seasonal precipitation extremes. He grouped the early stations by region, and his Southern Plains region most closely matches the Southern High Plains, although most of the stations he used for this region are in central/eastern Texas and central Oklahoma. L. Dean Bark, "History of American Drought," in *North American Droughts*, ed. Norman J. Rosenberg (Boulder, Colo.: Westview Press, 1978), 9–23.

27. Dan Flores, "Bison Ecology and Bison Diplomacy: The Southern Plains from 1800 to 1850," *The Journal of American History* 78 (1991): 465–85; Elliott West, *The Way to the West: Essays on the Central Plains*. (Albuquerque: University of New Mexico Press, 1995); Andrew C. Isenberg, *The Destruction of the Bison: An Environmental History, 1750–1920* (New York: Cambridge University Press, 2000).

28. For more information on factors contributing to drought and the prospects for predicting drought, see Randall M. Dole, "Prospects for

Predicting Drought in the United States," in *Drought: A Global Assessment*, ed. Donald A. Wilhite (New York: Routledge, 2000).

29. "Intergovernmental Panel on Climate Change (IPCC) Third Assessment Report," in *Climate Change 2001: The Scientific Basis*, ed. J. T. Houghton et al. (New York: Cambridge University Press, 2001).

30. "Climate Change Impacts on the United States: The Potential Consequences of Climate Variability and Change. Overview: Great Plains." The National Assessment Synthesis Team, U.S. Global Change Research Program 2000, available from *http://www.usgcrp.gov/usgcrp/Library/ nationalassessment/overviewgreatplains.htm*.

31. Aiguo Dai et al., "Climates of the Twentieth and Twenty-First Centuries Simulated by the NCAR Climate System Model," *Journal of Climate* 14 (2001): 485–519.

32. Richard T. Wetherald and Syukuro Manabe, "Detectability of Summer Dryness Caused by Greenhouse Warming," *Climatic Change* 43 (1999): 495–511.

33. Daniel R. Muhs and Paula B. Maat, "The Potential Response of Eolian Sands to Greenhouse Warming and Precipitation Reduction on the Great Plains of the USA," *Journal of Arid Environments* 25 (1993): 351–61.

CHAPTER FOUR

A Tale of Two Water Management Districts

Saving a Working Future for the High Plains

JOHN OPIE

Is everything connected to everything else? For the last forty years, environmentalists have answered this question in the affirmative. It is not always borne out on America's High Plains, though, where rainfall measures twelve to twenty inches a year—not enough to support crops of maize, wheat, alfalfa, or soybeans. For centuries, America's largest groundwater system, the Ogallala or High Plains Aquifer, was not a component of the long-standing shortgrass arid plains ecosystem. Rather, it was the hands of man—actually the pumps of man and woman—that eventually drew it from its hiding place.

The Ogallala Acquifer is an amazing and elusive resource. It extends under 170,000 square miles of land stretching from the Dakotas down into western Texas. If we laid the Ogallala under Europe, it might extend north-south from Copenhagen to Rome, or east-west at its widest point between Paris and Munich. The Ogallala contained 3.3 billion acre-feet before forty years of irrigation consumed a third of the water and half of the useable water. An acre-foot is roughly 326,000 gallons. The Ogallala's water would fill Lake Huron, one of the smaller Great Lakes, with enough water remaining to fill one-fifth of Lake Ontario. My estimate is that the Ogallala Aquifer alone contained at least 2 percent of the entire world's supply of fresh water.

If the territory of the United States had been frozen in place about 1800, the Ogallala would have belonged to France in the north and Spain, Mexico, or the independent nation of Texas in the south. Would they have needed Ogallala water? Probably not, if the French had remained in the business of beaver and buffalo skins and the southerners in cattle ranching. Instead, by means of the Louisiana Purchase, the Mexican-American War, and the annexation of Texas, the High Plains became United States territory.

Even so, as early as 1810, early explorers described the Plains as the Great American Desert, unfit for human habitation. Soon, the westering wagon trails and railroads raced across the Plains to the sublime regions of California and Oregon. Not until the 1870s were eastern farmers and German immigrants lured onto the Plains by a season of unusually heavy rains, by the myth "rain follows the plow," which the limited science of the day reinforced, and by the free distribution of public land to farmers if they promised to labor on their 160-acre quartersection for five years or more. All three concepts proved wrong and pushed Plains settlers into hardship, famine, and failure. In fact, Plains farmers enjoyed only two true seasons of prosperity. The first came during the first two decades of the twentieth century with the help of ample rains and high wheat prices. The second began in the 1960s, with intensive irrigation and intensive federal government supports, both of which are in decline today.

The presence of a vast body of groundwater under the Plains only became known early in the twentieth century. The few early irrigators on the Texas High Plains concluded that the Ogallala was an inexhaustible resource. It was once believed to flow in vast cavernous torrents from the Arctic or pool in a large underground lake. Later, it became clear that the water stood mingled with vast beds of sandy gravel, having collected there gradually with the uplift of the Rocky Mountains. It was not being replaced—recharged—in any significant manner because it lay under bedrock where no rainfall or surface streams could reach it. Thus it is fossil water, perhaps ten thousand to twenty-five thousand years old.

Lack of technology kept the water underground despite desperate needs during the 1930s Dust Bowl. Only after World War II did technological innovation introduce a combination of deep drilling, efficient water pumps, and power from converted automobile engines. Intensive

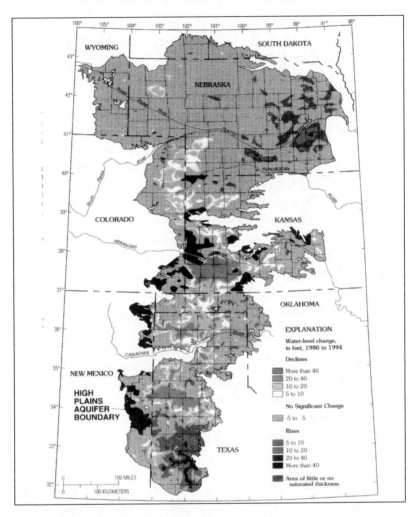

The Ogallala Aquifer (also called the High Plains Aquifer) underlies approximately 170,000 square miles of one of the major agricultural areas of the world. It once contained 3.3 billion acre-feet of fresh water. An acre-foot is one foot of water spread over one acre, or 325,851 gallons. Irrigation from the Ogallala has become intensive, and, since the 1950s, has consumed about a third of the aquifer. Another third remains for potential future use, and a third is unusable because of depth or quality. This map from the U.S. Geological Survey shows the rapid rate of aquifer decline between 1980 and 1994, especially in southwestern Kansas and the Texas–Oklahoma Panhandle. Estimates suggest no more than twenty years of continued irrigation across most of the High Plains. Washington D.C.: Fact Sheet FS-215-95, U.S. Geological Survey, U.S. Department of the Interior, November 1995.

irrigation, from a trickle in the 1950s to a flood by the 1970s, resulted in high yield crops—even more corn per acre than in the Midwest. As a result, over 170,000 wells pump the aquifer today.

For a long time the size of the resource tranquilized irrigators. The three billion acre-feet of water in the gravel beds of the Ogallala made the groundwater seem inexhaustible. Intensive irrigation, however, meant an average drawdown of Ogallala groundwater of two feet a year. In Texas, for example, between the 1940s and the 1980s, the average water level declined nearly 10 feet a year. Some landowners started out with 300 feet of aquifer below them, others only 50 feet. High consumption also brought conflict over property rights and freedom of action. Overlapping drawdown "cones" between wells located too closely to one another made aggressive irrigators rush to flood their fields with groundwater before lowered levels gave them dry wells. In the 1990s, no one wanted to talk about the disappearance of irrigation along some of the edges of the aquifer. Any return to dryland farming was mostly unacceptable and alternative crops went untested. Through the efforts of local water districts, water management did improve in the 1980s, 1990s, and into the early twenty-first century. Drawdown was not eliminated, but it was reduced to an average of one foot a year, a level with which most irrigators could live.

In most of the states overlying the Ogallala, the water is dedicated to "beneficial use," defined as agriculture. In Texas, the Underground Water Districts Act of 1949 provided that districts "make and enforce rules to provide for conserving, preserving, protection, recharging, and preventing waste of the underground water."[1] By 1978, the Texas Supreme Court moved to prevent groundwater waste: withdrawing groundwater could be "negligent" and "willfully wasteful."[2]

For several decades in the second half of the twentieth century, irrigation created widespread prosperity on the Plains. It was wonderful when plains farmers could speak of "rainfall on demand." A good supply of groundwater under a farmer's land not only assured him of on-demand water for crops, it also doubled and tripled his real estate value, his power to borrow money for equipment and seeds, and seemed to assure his economic future. Such security is extraordinary in agriculture, which is so seasonal and vulnerable to the vagaries of climate.

Most High Plains farmers agree that their golden age of intensive irrigation, approximately from 1960 to 1990, came to a painfully premature end because of wasteful irrigation practices. In the 1990s they struggled to use more efficient technologies and extended the life span of irrigation from the aquifer. The water economy of the High Plains (except for the water-rich but less fertile Sand Hills of western Nebraska) evolved from its "exploratory-expansionist" phase to its "mature conservation" phase.[3] Peak heavy use may have occurred between 1978 and 1983 when the acreage irrigated reached an overall high point of 17 million, which declined slightly to 16 million acres in the 1990s.

Plains farmers are as dependent upon irrigation as cigarette smokers are upon nicotine. They cannot break the habit without paying a heavy price. Nor can corn and alfalfa survive without their seasonal fix of thirty inches. Cattle in feedlots each demand a bare minimum eight gallons a day, often soaring to fifteen gallons a day. New megahog facilities containing thousands of animals threaten Ogallala groundwater pollution for the first time. When groundwater becomes impossible to pump, there will be a ripple effect on so-called externalities.[4] Suppliers of irrigation equipment will shut down. Annual loans based on land equity will fall through the floor. Population decline will accelerate and social services such as schools and hospitals will disappear. More than forty years of "water on demand" created a lulling security that masked the enormity of the historically strenuous struggle to grow abundant crops under Dust Bowl conditions.

The future will be challenging, even aside from today's collapse of wheat, corn, and soybean prices. Computer modeling of global warming introduces large-scale desertification to the Plains, far more than any Dust Bowl. This would draw water levels down to a catastrophic 3 feet a year, roughly the water a crop of corn or alfalfa needs. At present the picture is getting worse: five years ago the range of warming in the twenty-first century was a rise of 1.8 to 6.3 degrees Fahrenheit. A January 2001 report doubled this to 2.5 to 10.4 degrees.[5] Such changes would be magnified on the Plains to accelerate and intensify desertification.

Proposals for the abandonment of the Plains to light grazing or empty grassland first came up in the 1920s, but farmers, even if they were failing, resented a federal resettlement program during the 1930s Dust Bowl because it pushed them into "reservations" as if they were American Indians or imitated Soviet collectivization. Decades later in 1987, land use planners Frank and Deborah Popper tried again with a radical proposal.[6] Let us finally admit, they argued, that more than a century of repeated farm abandonments, dust bowls, costly government interventions, and environmental destruction have resulted in the

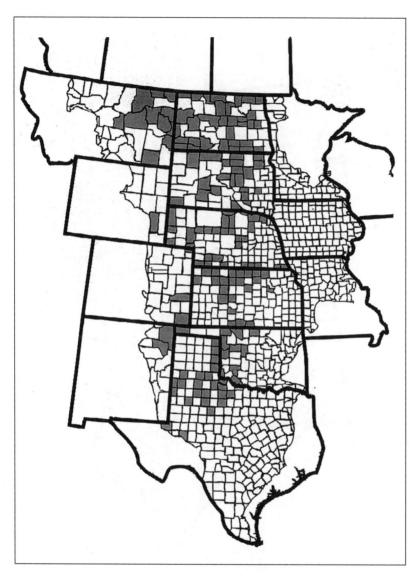

This map, based on census data, shows High Plains counties that had a population loss of 15 percent or more from 1980 to 1998. The Ogallala region has been particularly affected, despite heavy irrigation. Such decline has been continuous since the 1950s and is predicted to continue indefinitely. In comparison, the overall U.S. population grew 21 percent during the same period. Courtesy Great Plains Restoration Council.

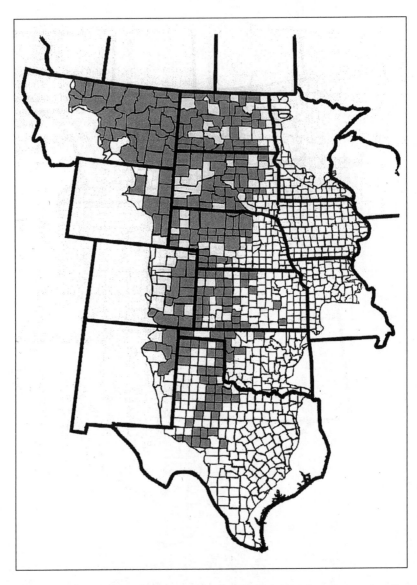

This map depicts High Plains counties with six persons or less per square mile in 1997 (compared to the entire U.S. average of seventy-five persons per square mile). Some areas now have less than two persons per square mile. The counties have been called "frontier counties" because the six-person measure had provided the historic definition of a frontier region. It was first applied in 1893 by Frederick Jackson Turner, who declared the frontier closed based on 1890 census data. Courtesy Great Plains Restoration Council.

failure of the American experiment to extend traditional farming onto the High Plains. In this view, the most realistic responsibility—even a moral duty—toward the Plains and its people was to acknowledge the reality of continuous decline before the troubles become even more grievous. The Poppers identified a county-by-county wide swath of hopeless decline in 139,000 square miles across the Plains from Texas to North Dakota that was already reverting to its pre-agricultural condition. One of the Poppers' main criteria was population decline to less than six persons per square mile: many counties of the High Plains from the Canadian border to the Llano Estacado have fit this category since the 1990 census. The emergent "Buffalo Commons" would become open land and a wildlife refuge, "the world's largest natural and historic preservation project," with more income generated from tourism than agriculture.[7] The Popper description of a "desettlement" crisis became prophetic: the 2000 census described the continuous dwindling of Plains population below frontier status of six persons per square mile. Their Buffalo Commons seemed to take hold, including the increase of buffalo herds to perhaps 300,000, and dramatic increases in American Indian population, which has risen in a few places by more than 200 percent.[8]

A bizarre final stage in Plains agribusiness could be producing a similar outcome. Industrial hog confinement operations involving tens of thousands of animals brought on noisy and impassioned debate. As recently as 1990, a Plains county in Kansas, Oklahoma, or Texas produced only a few thousand hogs in widely dispersed locations—mostly as a sideline by wheat farmers. But in less than a decade, a county such as Texas County in the Oklahoma Panhandle became inhabited by hundreds of thousands of hogs bred and raised in industrial sheds. A hundred thousand hogs produce the waste of 170,000 additional people, an overwhelming number in a region where a town of 25,000 is a metropolis. Major issues became the management and disposal of animal wastes first in lagoons and finally liquid dispersal on a neighboring field. For the first time in its geological and human history, the Ogallala Aquifer faced pollution that could last forever. Not the least was the insult of strong smells that local farmers and townspeople complained destroyed their quality of life. Geographer Owen Furuseth in 1997 concluded that confined animal production had created a new agricultural geography—an imploded or collapsed landscape. The impacts are highly localized but divide the agricultural landscape into habitable or uninhabitable zones.[9]

A multinational corporation, Seaboard Incorporated, is a major hog producer in the central Oklahoma Panhandle, with numerous operations in and near Guymon in Texas County. Buffers between hog confinement sheds, their adjacent lagoons, and waste treatment fields might well depopulate entire neighborhoods or keep human habitation from entering such "dead zones." Local residents are urging a buffer of two or three miles between a habitable structure and a hog confinement operation because of smells and real air pollution; the current regulated distance is between a quarter-mile and three quarters of a mile.

In mid-1998, the Plains states of Texas, Oklahoma, Kansas, and Colorado debated and passed legislation that regulated hog pollution. It could restructure the region. Kansas requires setbacks up to five thousand feet between a residence and a hog confinement operation. Where liquid waste is applied to cropland, which is mostly the case, it could be sprayed no closer than one thousand feet from a habitable structure.[10] The actual geographical impacts are currently unknown. These regulations acknowledge large buffers that effectively create unpopulated zones wherever hog confinement operations abound. In this surprising turn, the Poppers' prediction of the depopulation of large areas of the Plains may come true, but not as they predicted. In the meantime, depletion of groundwater continues.

The Tale of Two Groundwater Conservation Districts

It is ironic that the very success of heavy irrigation from the Ogallala aquifer forced actions to protect the continued flow by reducing the flow. As it turns out, local populist management may be the answer, bringing a three-step transition from destructive development to conservation management to sustainable development. A grassroots democracy tone was long ago set in an 1878 statement by John Wesley Powell: "The people in organized bodies can be trusted. . . . residents should have the right to make their own regulations . . . the entire arid region [should] be organized into natural hydrographic districts, each one to be a commonwealth within itself . . . the plan is to establish local self-government by hydrographic basins."[11] Regional water management districts have used a combination of grassroots democracy, technological alternatives, new agricultural science, and intensive management to reduce groundwater consumption. These agencies can be useful examples on a worldwide basis, as international organizations and commissions look to democratic sustainability of regional irrigation and environments under severe stress.

This is a tale of two such water management agencies. In Texas, the High Plains Underground Water Conservation District No. 1 (henceforth Texas District 1) is headquartered in Lubbock. One person, Wayne Wyatt, was its manager from 1978 until his death in December 2000. The district and its manager became synonymous with the best in traditional groundwater management, using technological fixes and improved groundwater management. On the other hand, there are alternative approaches being tested at the Northwest Kansas Groundwater Management District No. 4 (henceforth Kansas District 4) headquartered in Colby under the long-term leadership of another Wayne—Wayne Bossert. It pioneered cloud seeding. Out of District 4 came the controversial proposal made in 1990 for zero-depletion while significant groundwater remains, instead of the inevitability of zero-depletion when the water runs out. Kansas District 4 is on the northern edge of the Southern Plains, but both districts encompass large parts of the same Dust Bowl region of the 1930s stretching from northwestern Kansas to the southern edge of the Texas Panhandle.

The original objective of Texas District 1 and Kansas District 4 was the profitable consumption of groundwater, as remains true of all Plains water management districts. On the High Plains, "groundwater management" is very often a surrogate phrase for "economic development." Even today, with well-meaning local control, groundwater mining still exceeds recharge by five to ten times.

Wayne Wyatt: Texas High Plains Underground Water Conservation District No. 1

In the late 1940s, Texas High Plains farmers drilled wells to the Ogallala, installed pumps, and began to prosper. They lobbied vigorously against any attempts to regulate their consumption of groundwater.[12] Plains farmers are determinedly independent and Texas irrigators unsurpassed in their sense of personal freedom. The issue headed over the rights of private property. In 1947, the local *Southwestern Crop and Stock* journal editorialized, "it is unsound to advocate to a farmer that he curtail pumping when with top market prices he can pay for his irrigation installation in the first year of its operation."[13] A November 1948 editorial pronounced that "West Texans can consider the water their own—

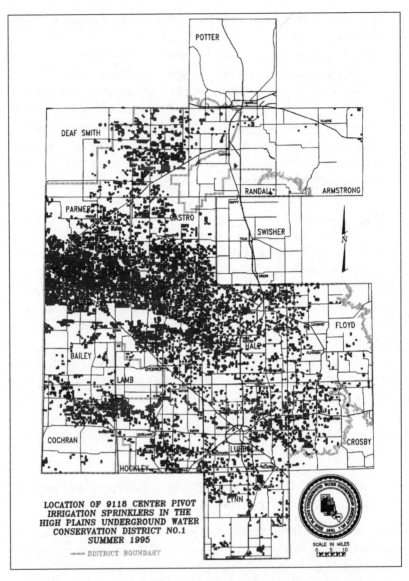

LOCATION OF 9118 CENTER PIVOT
IRRIGATION SPRINKLERS IN THE
HIGH PLAINS UNDERGROUND WATER
CONSERVATION DISTRICT NO.1
SUMMER 1995

━━━ DISTRICT BOUNDARY

SCALE IN MILES
0 5 10

*This map depicts the center-pivot irrigation circles (small dots on the map)
that dominate irrigations from the Ogallala Aquifer in the High Plains of
the Texas Panhandle. The patterns reflect availability of groundwater
depending upon its depth, amount available, and the equipment used. This
map would inform potential irrigation farmers and groundwater district
managers as to likely overcrowding and overconsumption, as well as locations unlikely to produce irrigation. Courtesy the High Plains Underground
Water Conservation District No. 1, Lubbock, Texas.*

to use or waste as they please."[14] But in 1949, Texas set a precedent by legislating the first underground water conservation districts on the High Plains. The motive was not conservation per se, but rather to assure the continued profitable industrialization of a depressed region. District No. 1 would be headquartered at Lubbock where depletion was at its worst. The district was to issue drilling permits, control well spacing, regulate water consumption, develop workable recharge (to refill the aquifer), and prevent water waste. Most important, a board of local irrigators would govern the groundwater district. Individual landowners would continue to have exclusive rights to their water, but it would be managed water.

Virtually no one accepted the notion that the irrigator should give up his personal right to underground water. One Hockley County irrigator represented public opinion when he told the local newspaper, "I favor no control, but if we must have it, let it be local." Management by a state board was out of the question; federal control was unthinkable. Yet virtually everyone agreed with a 1950 editorial of the *Tulia Herald* of Swisher County: "Which is better, a super abundance for a few years and then nothing or reasonable abundance for many years?" As the local debate heated up, the Amarillo *Sunday News-Globe* in a special report on 28 May 1950 quoted one farmer, "What's caused this underground water crisis. . . . Abuse of our natural resources, that's what caused it. . . . It's those who want to squeeze every last drop of wealth from the land every year." But another said he was "somewhat puzzled about all this excitement over the wells going dry. . . . My well has been going good since 1936, and it's still going strong." Another reflected the dominant mood: "All the water under my land belongs to me. No government, no association, nobody can tell me how to use it. I've never wasted any water in my life. I couldn't afford it. . . . I don't intend to live in a country full of Hitlerism laws."[15]

Once formed, the district tried to reassure farmers of their private property rights. One of its brochures cites a March 1956 editorial by Allan White in the district's newsletter, *The Cross Section*, promising suspicious local farmers that "Hitlerism" is not on the way: "The Water District was not created to do away with the rights of the individual but rather . . . to maintain those . . . rights and . . . provide for orderly development and wise use of our own water." The brochure also claimed that "the powers that can be exercised by districts under this law supplant and exceed the ground-water regulatory powers of any other unit of government, either state or federal."[16] The district's structure reinforced the concept of popular representation: a five-member board of directors supported by five-member committees from each of the fifteen counties, totaling a grassroots network of eighty elected officials.

In a regional vote on 29 September 1951, two entire counties, Lubbock and Parmer, and parts of eleven other counties (Lynn, Lamb, Hockley, Deaf Smith, Floyd, Castro, Bailey, Armstrong, Randall, Potter, and Cochran) voted to form Texas's first groundwater management district. Significantly, three of the most intensively irrigated counties, Hale, Swisher, and Crosby, refused to join. (Later, in May 1967, parts of Hale County did join, followed in April 1969, by parts of Crosby County. However, in January 2001, Swisher County once again overwhelmingly rejected membership in the district.) Eventually the new district served an area of 8,149 square miles, or 5,215,600 acres. The High Plains Water Conservation District No. 1 opened its doors in April 1952 and on 1 February 1953 set out its first regulations covering all full-scale irrigation wells (pumping 100,000 gallons per day or more). Compliance was voluntary. In the meantime, land "under pump" expanded from 650,000 irrigated acres in 1946 to 2.7 million irrigated acres in 1954.[17] The district regulations did not provide any immediate relief. Between 1951 and 1958, the average water level fell 28 more feet. In 1954, at least six farmers who started irrigating in 1953 were back into dryland farming.

Even while Ogallala waters showed important declines in District No. 1's territory, local irrigators still had mixed feelings about extensive water management. "When you start talking about a man's water, you get into real trouble." According to a 1975 survey, seven out of ten irrigators supported the way the local district was doing its job, although one farmer reflected the minority view when he said, "All I want is to be left alone. If I can't make it on my own I'll go out of the farming business. This is the way it ought to be with everything. Survival of the fittest." But most agreed with the irrigator who supported local regulation "because I fear large corporate farming operations . . . that can drill too many wells . . . would get all the water."[18]

From 1978 until his death in 2000, Wyatt was manager and groundwater hydrologist of the High Plains Underground Water Conservation District No. 1 in Lubbock, Texas. He saw the best of times and the worst of times as farmer, irrigator, and district manager. Born in Girard, Texas, on 5 August 1935, Wyatt began his farming career when he was in high school. "In the early fifties," he explained, "we were in the most severe drought we had ever seen. Our production was virtually zero. I bought cows for $400 and sold them for $175 after buying alfalfa and feeding them for two years."[19] Family friends staked him to an education at Texas Tech University, where he studied agriculture and ended up in hydrology. He also struggled with barebones farming on rented land with his brother, who was two years older. Only years later did he discover his landlord secretly cosigned loans they received for tractors and combines to help out the two young men. In the 1950s, he remembered, "there was no federal support, no deficiency payments, nothing. I was living off mother and dad, living at home. Dad survived but he was a pretty tough gent. I didn't survive." He concluded that the older generation stood their ground for the sake of the farm lifestyle more than for the promise of any financial success. "Well, let's squeeze this back to my dad. He was good as a farmer. He didn't worry about making money or not. He made a damn good crop he could be proud of."

Out of his own youthful experience Wyatt agreed that a young farmer today is even less likely to succeed in the still-harsh Dust Bowl country without friendly cash aid. The picture is worse now because of heavy debts for land and equipment. "Ten years ago you could have a crop failure and in two years be out." Wyatt said, "You could manage to pay off your debt and be back into an opportunity for profits. [Today] you really got to have four out of five good years. Now if you have crop failure or something, it takes you ten years to recover." Despite the recognized virtues of irrigation, farming remained a high-risk undependable activity. The High Plains is still one of the toughest place to farm in the United States. "Climatic conditions, hail storms, personal management skill, and plain old circumstances—a single isolated bad misjudgment," Wyatt observed, "would get people into a hell of a mess." Despite all the improvements, the 1980s and 1990s were more troublesome to farmers than the 1970s, and no farmer interviewed believed that the twenty-first century promised better days.[20] Wyatt concluded that High Plains irrigation was still flourishing in its own golden age that began after World War II. He said that beginning in the 1990s irrigation faced a gradual, but inevitable, decline. He concluded that "our conservation program is about twenty-five years or more too late."[21] In the foreseeable future, Ogallala water will become scarce enough and costly enough that even the best irrigators—now defined as the most water-efficient irrigators—will have to reduce the acres they water.

Love of farming, even in thin times, and loyalty to harvesting "a damn good crop" despite dry land and scarce water, made Wayne Wyatt's job at Water District No. 1 satisfying. He was comfortable in his pleasant air-conditioned office in an unpretentious one-story building on a shady side street near downtown Lubbock. He started with the district as a field representative in 1957, six years after the district was first established. A year later he found himself in Austin as a staff member of the Texas Water Development Board (TWDB), and soon headed several sections, including water level, groundwater quality monitoring, groundwater data, and water importation. He returned as general manager of Texas District 1 in February 1978, where he soon became known for technological know-how, management skills, and political savvy that made the district a leader in state, national, and international water conservation innovations.

By 1982, the district's newsletter, *The Cross Section*, reported that wasteful open ditches were a thing of the past in the district. It boasted water savings through tailwater recapture, dropped sprinkler heads on center pivot systems to reduce evaporation loss, control of well spacing, and cost-in-water tax depletion allowances.[22] From the first it had been clearly stated that the mission of the district was not groundwater preservation, but its "most efficient use." The district was also the administrative center for well permits, driller's logs, and record keeping on drilling, spacing, and production of wells.[23] To this, Wyatt added that the district disseminated scientific data and reported on new technologies to encourage water efficiency and guarantee continued prosperity for regional irrigators.

Based on the premise, according to Wayne Wyatt, that "we're going to run out of money [to pay for deep pumping] before we run out of water," the district provided detailed hydrological atlases for each of its fifteen counties, "for development, production and use of the water" as well as to "determine limitations which should be made on withdrawing underground water." He continued, "If you have 100 feet of saturated thickness, you ought to get 1,000 gallons per minute. If you go down to 50 feet of saturated thickness, you might be able to get 200 gallons per minute. You would have to drill additional wells to maintain center-pivot irrigation equipment. Say you're drawn bone dry down to 25 feet. You can figure out well yield is only 50 gallons and 50 gallons would probably not be economical. At that point the irrigator would say no, I'm through irrigating." Since at least 50 percent of land value depends upon the capacity to irrigate, the results would be devastating. Wyatt concluded that the high point was reached in 1983, when top quality irrigated land sold for $800 an acre. Ten years later, prices fell

15 to 20 percent. Dryland farming is no alternative when it comes to land values.

The district devotes a great deal of attention to irrigation efficiency (water use and cost related to crop prices) to keep the water running, particularly in light of pumping costs that are likely to go up four to ten times. This includes soil moisture monitoring, irrigation scheduling to water crops only at critical growing periods, water reuse systems, recharge (marginal) through local small "rainwater storage" lakes called playas, furrow dikes (rediscovered from 1930s conservation practices), low- or no-tillage practices (also practiced since the earliest dryland farming days), and the science of crop water consumption. As elsewhere, when irrigation reaches its "mature" phase, the trend is away from historic overpumping and toward minimum-water-use conservation.

The 1997 Texas Water Conservation Report

Wyatt's work prodded the Texas state legislature into a water planning study centered on a surprisingly long-term assessment. In 1997, its mandated regional water plans showed foresight by setting a planning horizon of fifty years from 2000 to 2050. On this long-term scale, the goal was to "project water supplies sufficiently in advance of needs to allow for appropriate management measures."[24] This planning horizon may be too problematic. On the one hand, it raises levels of uncertainty to almost total uncertainty, similar to economics that discount the future by 2 percent a year. On the other hand, we can learn more about the future by including past history that created our current momentum. The time horizon might instead be 1960 to 2050 to include the history of modern irrigation, or even 1870 to 2050 to cover all of Plains settlement—from hardscrabble frontier settlement to late twentieth-century prosperity and possibly back to a hardscrabble frontier. At the very least, we cannot begin in midstream in 2000. We have the opportunity to look back to see the prospects after forty years of regional groundwater management.

The 1997 Texas legislation, as applied to the Llano Estacado, produced crisis documents. The language, which has a bureaucratic coolness, masked the gravity the planners saw in the situation. The Executive Summary of the Llano Estacado Regional Water Plan emphasized "drought conditions" and the need for "sufficient water."[25] It was no longer appropriate to consider expanded consumption of water. The primary objective was to conserve groundwater for the harder times yet to come. Elsewhere, the Executive Summary wrote not of development and growth, but used words like "stabilize" the Plains economy to assure its "viability and longevity." This is not optimistic language if the opposites are "destabilize," "not viable," and "lacking longevity." The water plan can only serve the needs of the region, it said, "specifically to meet the water needs during drought." It added, "Since there is little opportunity to increase the region's water supplies through conventional water development, emphasis has been placed upon water management strategies to increase efficiency of water use in irrigation."[26] The document turned to uncertain tactics: precipitation enhancement (cloud seeding) and brush management, both of which can only offer single-digit percentage improvement. The document's data admitted that demand for groundwater already exceeded supply in some areas and that this condition would spread to most of the region by 2020 with 30 percent undersupply by 2050.[27]

The crisis language of the Texas study may be based on outdated thinking. Moreover, there are some possible changes in the fundamental assumptions about Plains conditions. If we took a careful look at the climate history of the Southern Plains, we might see drought as "normal" instead of the annual 12 to 20 inches of rain that defined the region as semiarid. In the 1990s, for example, there were more drought years than so-called normal years. In February 2001, climate scientists concluded that global warming was already upon us, which indicated more continuous drought on the Plains than ever before.[28] As to current water management practices, if we forecast restricted or zero-depletion water pumping by, say, 2020, why not do it now and protect more groundwater for future generations? This is essentially the difference between the conventional management of Texas District No. 1 and the zero-depletion master plan of Kansas District No. 4.

Wayne Bossert: Northwest Kansas Groundwater Management District No. 4

Two decades after Lubbock irrigators turned on their sprinklers and watched water levels decline, Kansas irrigators began to enjoy their new prosperity but also faced the same water scarcities. Garden City hydrologist Andy Erhart tried to make water conservation acceptable to farmers faced with higher costs. Protection of Ogallala water, he argued,

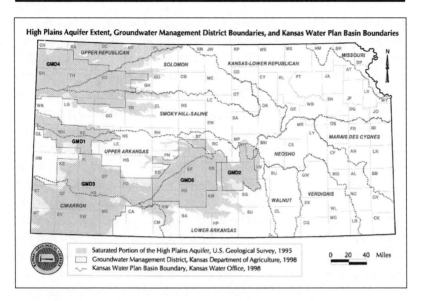

*This map shows the saturated portions of the Ogallala (High Plains)
Aquifer in western Kansas. It also outlines the groundwater management
districts over the Ogallala, of which District 4 is in the northwestern part of
the map. Wayne Bossert, manager of Northwest Kansas Groundwater
Management District No. 4, has taken the lead in zero-depletion management for the long-term sustainability of the aquifer, and hence farming, in
the district's region. Used with permission of Kansas Geological Survey,
2002.*

would protect local agriculture, the farm family, and irreplaceable
resources. As early as 1957, in an article he wrote for a special edition of
the Pratt *Daily Tribune*, Erhart set down some basic priorities. A well-
planned and well-managed irrigation system needed to (1) increase the
efficient use of available water supplies, (2) reduce labor requirements,
(3) prevent excessive erosion, and (4) permit maximum production.[29]
The Northwest Kansas Groundwater Management District No. evolved
out of such thinking.

Zero-Depletion Irrigation: Betting the Farm

Wayne Bossert is a tall, lean man, intelligent and savvy to the point of
being crafty. His western Kansas twang and his love for the people in

and around Colby belie his New Jersey origins. Trained as a hydrologist, he has been the executive director of the Northwest Kansas Groundwater Management District No. 4 since it opened its doors after a public referendum in 1977. In 1990, the district took a drastic step beyond most other Ogallala groundwater management plans: it set a zero-depletion goal to be reached in as little as ten years. This got the attention of local irrigators as if they had been pole-axed. Bossert's logic was simple: despite sophisticated water management strategies, ground-water levels continued to decline.[30] Bossert told a newspaper reporter that "the declining levels meant zero depletion anyway, so why not opt to reach the same goal earlier while retaining an acceptable quantity of water for future management options."[31] Kansas agricultural economist Orlan Buller agreed: "The question is not if, but when and how fast are the adjustments within the region going to happen."[32] Bossert noted that the district's 3600 wells were drawing levels down averaging two feet a year. Worst-case wells had declined as much as 59 feet between 1966 and 1990.[33] Declines averaging more than a foot continued through the 1990s and into the twenty-first century. He courageously (some said it was foolhardy) redirected the concept of efficiency away from cost-benefit of crop yield and toward less water consumption. The results would not be measurable in dollars nor in immediate benefit to irrigation farmers in his district. Instead, he persuaded his district board to give their highest priority to protection of aquifer levels. This was the best local means to perpetuate irrigation-based personal security. Such "rainfall on demand" was a major improvement for regional farmers. It brought them middle class prosperity instead of their earlier frontierlike, high-risk lifestyle.

Bossert admitted that the district's short timeframe deadline could not be met by any traditional methods. The board's aggressive posture came from their belief that early conservation was significantly more valuable than late conservation. It justified its preemptive management policy that set 85 percent efficiency within five years on the basis that farmers were consumers of a state-designated public resource that they used for their profit. Direct action included a yearlong moratorium on water rights development beginning in February 1990. By September 1990, the district board recommended that a cap be put on the amount of water that can be withdrawn, which jump-started the move toward zero depletion. For most areas, withdrawals would be restricted to one-fifth of 1 percent for every foot of water remaining in the ground. For example, a complex mathematical formula determined that if a specially designated management area had an average remaining saturated thickness of 60 feet, it enjoyed three more feet of additional decline before controls kicked in. Such a zone with 125 feet of water would get 11.7 feet of additional decline before regulation took effect. In 1991, Bossert's board set water efficiency standards for typical crops that some farmers might see as marginal: 1.24 acre-feet per acre for corn (instead of almost three acre-feet consumed by some other plains irrigators), .98 acft/ac for milo; .99 acft/ac for soybeans, and .59 acft/ac for wheat. By May 1991, the district board agreed to establish Zero Depletion (ZD) as its goal, defined as a stabilized water table.

Farmers might not accept Bossert's assertion that under the new district philosophy, "any operator who increases efficiency will not have the option of putting the same water on added acres for increased production. He or she will have to sustain the current acreage and production and simply pump less water."[34] An irrigator, saddled with debts for expensive equipment, expects to water heavily until the bills are paid. If water levels reached zero sooner rather than later, Bossert wondered how such major equipment investment could be paid off. "This scenario simply continues the 'overcapitalization' cycle which has caused much of the decline problem in the first place."[35]

The early results were impressive. Bossert reported that in 1994, when total irrigation water use in District No. 4 was 396,396 acre-feet, irrigators consumed only 9,131 acre-feet in excess of actual crop requirements, a mere 1.03 percent of all pumped water for irrigation.[36] Waste and overwatering drastically declined. Bossert insisted that a primary agenda was not to treat the difference (880,833 acre-feet appropriated for agriculture, down from 1,053,297 acre-feet in 1980) as "surplus" water that could be applied to additional acres for more profit, but as groundwater preserved as a future asset. Following Bossert's lead, the statewide Kansas Water Authority considered "water banking," and placed a moratorium on such acreage additions beginning February 1993.[37]

Nevertheless, the district experienced great difficulty in matching its draconian goal with the immediate needs of local farmers to irrigate for their survival. In areas where heavy depletions had been common practice for successful irrigators, they were soon permitted to take more water to protect their economic well being. A tough-minded compromise, reached in 1992, permitted ten more years of decline, sacrificing

22 percent of Ogallala groundwater to protect the remaining 78 percent.[38] Otherwise, Bossert admitted, "some of these [farmers] would hit it [zero depletion] in three years," well before they could make adjustments in equipment and management practices, such as drip irrigation.[39] Flood irrigation wastes 50 percent of its water through evaporation and seepage. Well-managed drip irrigation can reach 90 percent efficiency. Raising irrigation efficiency from 70 percent to 90 percent would extend the life of the aquifer by 20 percent, saving irrigators $7 million. But this high efficiency, using expensive equipment and time-consuming management, would cost about $210 million, a difficult figure that could be justified only over the long term.[40]

Bossert acknowledged that significant issues have arisen out of the new policy: some farmers looked to "irrigation efficiency credits" that could be profitably traded on an open market, like today's industrial pollution rights. Can efficiency upgrading be required if it requires costly equipment? One immediate challenge to the district's plans was a vote against the attachment of water meters to all wells (already mandated for new or refurbished wells) making accurate water level data difficult to obtain. A well-thought-out database was essential, since data from unusually wet years could imply that gains from efficiency may not be significant, and that information from a so-called normal year might not encourage high water use efficiency.

According to the Colby *Free Press*, Bossert's zero-depletion plan "may not mean an end to irrigation, [but] it does herald an end to an age where unrestricted usage endangered the future of water in this portion of the state."[41] In 2000 the water in storage under the district's land was approximately 40.5 million acre-feet. If Bossert met his ambitious goal of 78 percent, he would succeed in saving 31.6 million acre-feet. The newspaper hoped "that the ensuring regulation does not crumble the region's economic structure." Bossert concluded, "An ability to save one's allocation for future use or sale does not promote the 'race to the well' scenario that would be a significant negative factor in all other programs that are driven by a 'systems' or 'trigger' approach."[42] He noted that the district's goal was to "solve the decline problem with as little economic and social disruption as possible," but definitely to solve the problem. Saving the water for future generations took precedence over short-term profits.

District No. 4's plan redistributes costs and benefits among irrigators, businesses, taxpayers, and consumers by placing protection of the aquifer above existing economic, social, and political goals. Nevertheless, the long-term goal is also to protect economic stability for today's irrigators who want to stay irrigators in the future. Nonirrigated agriculture is less desirable because it varies greatly from year to year depending upon rainfall and climate. Not the least, the average value of crop production in northwestern Kansas between 1985 and 1989 was $43 higher for an irrigated acre than for a nonirrigated acre.[43]

As a last resort, Bossert recommended to the Kansas Department of Commerce that the region move "toward a replacement economy of some kind to compensate for the lost agricultural economy."[44] He said that "An ag [sic] approach might be to promote price supports for less water-intensive crops within the federal farm program," meaning less corn and more beans or sunflowers that use less water. A "non-ag" approach might be to make the Ogallala into a perpetual water supply to attract industries that could afford high water prices. Bossert nevertheless sought to preserve an agricultural economy for northwestern Kansas. He advocated a creative multifaceted four-pronged program to keep the farmers on the land: high efficiency irrigation, active weather modification (e.g., cloud-seeding) to increase rainfall 9 percent (thus reducing pumping by 6 percent) and prevent disastrous hailstorms (costing almost $5 million a year in Sherman County alone), incentives (e.g., subsidies) to plant less water-intensive crops, and flexibility in the movement and trading of water rights.

From the beginning, the High Plains water management agencies combined economic development and democratic local participation. However, as Ogallala depletion became more extensive, this combination of economics and politics provided the means to forge long-term water conservation programs. Further, to a remarkable degree, the combination of development, conservation, and localism are consistent with recent global philosophies of sustainable development.

Creating a Geography of Hope on the Plains: The History of a Moral Geography

I treat moral geography here as a political process that is the outcome of public opinion. A moral geography is a public ethical decision—doing the good—made about a particular people and place. In this sense it is Aldo Leopold's land ethic "gone public." Leopold's land ethic evolves from personal stewardship toward the integrity of each local place.[45]

Such an environmental sense of duty encompasses water, land, and people. Localism, when successful, includes an internal logic that must be derived from a particular people and a particular place. Such localism is also reflected, as described above, in the best actions of the two groundwater management districts. It is best applied when it includes an internal logic that uniquely belongs to a particular people and a particular place. Moral geography takes hold when government policy identifies a geographical landscape and its inhabitants in need, and deliberately responds to secure the safety and prosperity of a region.

One question addressed by a moral geography is highly problematic: what is an authentic response to a particular region and what is inauthentic? Americans have historically designated some places as "good," such as Yosemite, and other places as "evil," such as Love Canal. A nuclear power plant is good to some people and evil to others. Although its crops were mostly surpluses, its people low in numbers, and its landscape unspectacular, the Plains were closely identified with America's revered frontier experience and its people with virtuous family farming.

There have been recent attempts to identify moral geography. Philosopher David M. Smith concluded that justice and sustainability must be geographically and historically specific, "grounded in the lived experience of particular people in time and place as well as in the abstractions of philosophical debate."[46] Joan C. Tronto, a philosopher of geography, wrote, "For a society to be judged as a morally admirable society, it must, among other things, adequately provide for care of its members and its territory."[47] Such was the case for the High Plains during the disastrous 1930s, which set the pattern for farm policies ever since.

The plight during the devastating Dust Bowl of the 1930s resulted in a national crusade to save farming on the High Plains. President Franklin D. Roosevelt's New Deal spent more than $2 billion to keep the struggling independent Plains farmers on the land. This willingness by the federal government time and again to shore up the Plains from total human collapse suggests an extraordinary public sense of responsibility (or guilt) toward the vulnerable region. Since the 1930s, Americans have legislated money for agriculture for almost seventy years, one might even say with a degree of compassion. This moral geography offered billions of dollars in a comprehensive program of federal subsidies, price supports, low-cost loans, and crop insurance. This sense of duty helped define aggressive farm bills that Congress passed, the president signed, and government agencies administered.

Success would not come easily. In the early 1940s, rain and war, a strange mixture of good and evil, revived Plains life. But, while grain production in the Texas Panhandle country rose in value to $37,737,000 between 1935 and 1942, it nevertheless cost taxpayers $43,327,000 in federal aid. The nation had to invest $5,590,000 to keep the boom going. Even during the best of times, the agricultural Plains could not break even. Federal intervention of billions of dollars continued to support farmers through the "little dust bowls" of the 1950s, 1970s, and 1990s. These droughts were often worse than the Dust Bowl of the 1930s. By the 1970s, geographer John Borchert could write of "a widespread belief that, though there will be future droughts, there need be no future dust bowl," an affirmation that the moral geography had taken hold.[48] His point was not that the climate had changed, but that government and society had learned to compensate. This support system continued into the 1980s and 1990s but was threatened by doubts raised in the 1996 Farm Bill, which used a draconian plan to eliminate farm supports in seven years. This quickly became a moot point when Congress, under heavy pressure, poured billions of dollars in the late 1990s and the early twenty-first century into Plains agriculture to compensate for severe drought and low commodity prices. People continued to live on the Plains largely because of the federal dole. That is, they are federal clients at taxpayer expense. This costly activity seemed the right thing to do; it sustained virtuous farm families living in a difficult place. Frontier-like conditions persist on the Plains. Its human populations have never gained self-sufficiency. The Plains has contained people put at chronically high risk.

Why this costly attention? In the earliest days of the United States (as well as the earlier colonial era), access to good farmland by ordinary people was a source of equal opportunity and personal freedom. It offered a geography of hope, a pastoral idealism preached by Thomas Jefferson and many others. By the nineteenth century, Americans, and millions of new immigrants, took as an article of faith that life on a family farm—160 acres of diversified production in corn, beans, wheat, hay, hogs, chickens, and cows—was a superior way of life. President Roosevelt specifically referred to this romantic pastoralism when he urged his New Deal to rescue Dust Bowl farmers.

American-style agriculture, which originated in the humid East and Midwest, when transferred to the Plains, was neither inevitable nor permanent. The American family farm has persisted for more than a hundred years on the Plains (and more than two hundred years nationally) as a decentralized "cottage industry" in an increasingly industrialized world. A historic agricultural ethic persisted: the Plains, once family farmers settled them, must not be abandoned. The dry Plains offered a distillation of classic American virtues: farmers were expected to live ascetic, sacrificing lives, with an exhausting work ethic. The Plains would hammer out a purified citizenry. Both human sacrifice (people at risk) and environmental sacrifice (soil erosion) helped the crops grow. Such efforts served God, the nation, and personal integrity; the rewards would be the work itself. Similarly, it seemed to be a national duty to keep these truly representative Americans in the challenging landscape. Agricultural economist John E. Ikerd adds that "many farmers feel special responsibilities to society . . . for providing food, clothing, and shelter for the people. . . . [In return] Society has given special consideration and concessions to farmers reflecting these critical relationships. . . . farmers [have] a set of values that cannot be captured in the dollar-and-cent language of most economic analyses."[49] The response of society to the Plains remains one of the best indicators of whether Americans continue to believe that they have a moral obligation to save the family farm.[50] The Plains remains an extreme region that heightens problems and tests responses.

Today, individual farmers enjoy a privileged position in American society. They are exempt from labor laws about child labor, working conditions, and minimum wages. They receive preferred transportation rates. The farmers' major asset is public goodwill. On the other hand, as agricultural philosopher Gary Comstock reflected in 1987, the playing field was not level for farmers. Owner-operators did not charge full cost for their management services. The constant high risks of hail, drought, and other climate uncertainties did not receive appropriate compensation. The majority of American taxpayers was urban dwellers who did not recognize the challenges of a land-rich, cash-poor workplace. Americans had a public responsibility to compensate America's farmers for their technological efficiency, environmental stewardship, and their intangible quality of life.[51] Policy analyst Kenneth A. Cook concludes that the American public forged a social contract with Plains farmers that recognized the enormous cost they bore to pioneer, endure, and turn the Plains into the American breadbasket. Taxpayers were willing to share the human burden of agricultural production. The contract was to keep the family farm in operation as the place where patriotic virtues of rugged individualism, hardworking industriousness, and personal self-sufficiency were practiced best.[52] In this light, farmers should be judged not by their economic output, but by their responsible use of inputs, such as topsoil and groundwater as well as their own labor, economic risk-taking, and family sacrifice. This is the ethic of personal stewardship that must be acknowledged by acts of public (federal, taxpayer, citizen) stewardship. The vaunted self-sufficiency of good farmers was rarely the case.

Moral geography was applied to groundwater from the earliest days. Agricultural economists Arthur Maass and Raymond L. Anderson observe that "farmers typically refuse to treat water as a regular economic good, like fertilizer, for example. It is, they say, a special product and should be removed from ordinary market transactions so that farmers can control conflict, maintain popular influence and control, and realize equity and social justice."[53] Groundwater has been a public resource owned by each state since the federal government separated water from land in the Desert Land Act of 1877 and turned water over to the western states. Three Dust Bowl states—Texas, Oklahoma, and Kansas—adopted the guideline, "reasonable beneficial use," and by it meant agricultural use. This was not only for economic survival, but because water dedicated to farming was regarded as an essential social good.[54] That is, its free use kept the independent farmer on the land, the productivity of irrigation guaranteed food surpluses, and thus it kept the nation strong and independent. According to a 1936–1937 Oklahoma Supreme Court decision, "beneficial use" and "greatest need" for local "agricultural stability" must control water use in the state.[55]

Beneficial use is difficult to put into effect. Wasteful practices and declining water levels encouraged the creation of local self-governing groundwater conservation districts on the High Plains.[56] A public advocacy group, the Kansas Rural Center, does not believe the issue of waste or beneficial use is simple. Mary Fund of the Center writes, "The term 'beneficial,' though, is still rather ambiguous, since what is beneficial to one person may still be seen as wasteful by someone else. For example, lawn watering to the city dweller is an important use of water—beneficial to lifestyles, self-esteem, and aesthetics, but open to question by some in arid regions, or during drought. In the same vein, irrigating corn with irreplaceable fossil water when we have record harvests and the price is below the cost of production, is also open to question by some people. Therefore, we suggest that in addition to minimizing waste, conservation also implies recognition of 'appropriate use'—the use of water that fits the particular situation, climate, and supply."[57] Regardless, irrigation from groundwater did much to secure farmers on the Plains for another fifty years. Moral geography is still applied to the difficult Southern Plains today where farmers consume Ogallala groundwater to reassure themselves that they have a future.

Conclusion

This essay has focused on practical action and local management as the core of moral geography. Gary Comstock emphasizes the decision-making process as a "sense of direction we call practical wisdom." This involves pragmatic action, a "knowing how to proceed" rather than a "knowing that this is the only right answer."[58] To this expediency we must add the particularity of location. Here we have devoted special attention to particular regional institutions—groundwater management districts—that identified the Plains as a vulnerable landscape with its inhabitants in need and that deliberately responded to save water, land, and people.

The application of a pragmatic moral geography does not expect people to remain dependent. Public support intends to open doors for better local action. A recent shift shows promise toward revived farmer autonomy. The links to a Jeffersonian pastoral idealism remain strong. For example, the visionary agriculturist Wes Jackson founded the innovative Land Institute at Salina, Kansas, in 1972. The institute is committed to keeping independent farmers on the High Plains by returning them to the self-sustaining grassland ecosystem prior to settlement combined with ecologically sound food production. Its primary objective is "to develop an agroecosystem that reflects more the attributes of climax prairie than do conventional agricultural systems based on annual grain crops."[59] The Land Institute, and other alternative operations such as the Kansas Rural Center, advocates agricultural biocentrism. From a biocentric viewpoint, farming cannot be like any other industry. North Dakota farmer Fred Kirschenmann observes that "a farm is not a factory—it is an organism made up of numerous suborganisms, each alive and interdependent, each affected in numerous, complex ways" by outside forces—money, chemicals, technology, market prices—that are invariably disruptive.[60] This move toward self-sustainable farming would redefine the Plains in terms of bioregions, internal carrying capacity, and a sustainable economy.[61]

Moral geographies can be like shifting sands. In colonial and early America, Americans' moral resolve was to domesticate a demonic wilderness. By the time of Plains settlement, farmers who failed to endure on their homesteads believed they had betrayed their duty in the course of Manifest Destiny. Beginning with the New Deal of the 1930s, public policy endorsed the most vigorous attempts to keep stressed farmers on the Plains. From a national perspective, Americans dedicated themselves to protection of beleaguered farmers on the Plains. They concluded that human (and environmental) sacrifice made the crops grow, and demanded restitution. But ecologist Daniel S. Licht points out: "What taxpayers have gotten for their money is continuing habitat fragmentation, ecosystem deterioration, species decline, soil erosion, water sedimentation, depleted aquifers, crop surpluses, rural decay, and demands for more government subsidies."[62] Sixty years of unswerving loyalty to the family farm appeared to unravel with the Farm Bill of 1996.[63] The bill dramatically announced that farmers would no longer be guaranteed their privileged support from the government, although it softened the blow by stretching the reduction over a seven-year period. The Farm Bill also began to chip away at the edges of environmental protection by allowing exceptions to wetland preservation and farmland conservation. Despite pressure for better supports for farming in the 2001 Farm Bill, severe limitations have been written in international trade agreements. This monumental shift raises questions about shifting American values regarding their agricultural geography. By the 1990s, the emergent duty, according to the Poppers and others, was an orderly depopulation of the Plains and a restoration to pre-frontier conditions.

The Heavy Ideological Burden Carried by the Plains

Americans rarely see the High Plains in its own light. They view the Plains through variously colored spectacles that transform the region into a set of predetermined expectations. Historian Donald Worster concludes that distorted views helped induce the Dust Bowl disaster of the 1930s.[64] Geographers have sometimes described such an ideological load as a multilayered or "thick" cultural context.[65] Such a "deep geography" can be richly referential and culturally resonant, regardless of its connection to physical reality. In the case of the Plains, thick contexts changed over time, reflecting different understandings of Plains agriculture as well as shifts in Americans' sense of public responsibility.

One person's signal was another person's noise. What was the Plains? There are at least six possibilities, not mutually exclusive:

1. Was it a geographical zone of tantalizingly good soil but an impossibly dry climate? This suggests that irrigation from the Ogallala was a temporary external input little different from federal subsidies.
2. Was it the historical completion of America's Manifest Destiny, including American exceptionalism, triumphalism, and giantism?
3. Was it a highly productive source of commodities ("the breadbasket and feedbag of the world"), controlled by world markets?
4. Was it a growing pile of debts owed to the bank? Does the credit picture control a farmers' or corporations' actions?
5. Was it a cherished and valuable lifestyle based on the image of the Jeffersonian yeoman farmer?
6. Or is it today the viewpoint of the 1990s megahog industry that sees the Plains as interchangeable with other rural regions, such as the Carolinas, Missouri, and Iowa?

Can one of these mentalities be more authentic than the others? Some geographers like Stephen Birdsall conclude that diverse viewpoints, seemingly equally valid, must be taken to be a "variable regard" of any geographical region.[66] That is, no single approach can unveil all the features of the Plains.

WAS THE SOUTHERN PLAINS TOO FRAGILE A PLACE UPON WHICH TO BUILD A SOCIETY?

The early struggle of men and women on the frontier of the desiccated High Plains has not led to comfortable settlement for later generations, but only to more struggle. The Plains frontier is not yet overcome because the environment has not been mastered; in the long run the Plains environment, because of its climate, may never be conquered. As a result, the old Dust Bowl region has been an inadvertent "experiment station" in crisis management. When the High Plains was settled as an agricultural region it also went on permanent alert, experiencing crisis with no solution and no end. The question for the Plains, according to geographer William Riebsame, and reinforced from the earlier views of geographer A. H. Clark and early environmentalist Paul Sears, is whether the region could ever truly support "the human creation of socially nurturing landscapes" or whether it was a grassland too fragile for European settlers to build a society. Global warming may accelerate the risk.[67] Riebsame concludes that "after a century of settlement and transformation, the Great Plains still spark controversy over the proper human use of semiarid grasslands."[68]

Throughout our history, Americans have routinely engaged in massive environmental transformations. What is less recognized is that Americans have very limited means, even with the best scientific, technological, and political tools, to ameliorate or counteract the transformations. In most cases, Americans have not monitored or understood the changes, and virtually did not even notice them. We have far to go in learning to read our natural and human geographies. For example, when only marketplace rules are applied, the consumption of the environment runs without a governor: the system is constantly slipping into runaway, with potential for great harm before any correction takes place. The engine of change can be slowed down by limiters from other priorities, such as the American reform traditions so aptly described by the environmental philosopher Mark Sagoff.[69] Likewise, a high level of environmental degradation can set limits at the last minute, with great potential for mischief to humanity and the natural world, as became evident on the Plains in the 1930s.[70] Moral geography watches over both people and land at risk.

All Ogallala groundwater management agencies, the Texas High Plains Underground Water Conservation District No. 1, the statewide Oklahoma Water Resources Board, and the regional Kansas Groundwater Management Districts Nos. 1, 3, and 4, have a common mission—not always well-served—to provide a structured means by which to continue indefinitely the development of Ogallala water for agriculture. The Texas and Kansas districts are all heavily committed to controlled water withdrawals by allocation and metering, to careful well spacing, to a continued shift from flood to center pivot irrigation, to strong support of conservation technologies, scientific monitoring of climate and plant evapotranspiration, water replacement through cloud seeding and recharge (admittedly minimal), and to intensive management of water application according to soil and crop needs. New issues are water quality threats from animal confinement operations.

The problem with these reasonable goals is that they do not keep in mind that the Ogallala is in truth an environmental resource that is mostly nonrenewable and is being used up at a very high rate. None of the agencies face up to the fact that pumping water for irrigation is a mining operation as much as coal, gold, or oil. USGS hydrologist John Bredehoeft states it clearly (his italics): *"To the extent that we are mining groundwater, we are running out of water."*[71] Modern Cassandras still speak negatively about the prospects of the Plains. In 1977, the federal General Accounting Office reported dangerously high "ground water overdrafting" on the Texas High Plains and predicted that irrigation would fall from almost 8 million acres in 1975 to 2.2 million in 2020, leading to "significant social and economic dislocations." A return to dryland farming would mean the gradual collapse of the region.[72] In 1984, California law professor Frank J. Trelease complained that most modern irrigators did not recognize that they were mining groundwater that was a nonrenewable resource. "When the water is exhausted (or fallen too deeply) the overlying farmland must revert from irrigated crops back to dryland wheat or cattle grazing."[73]

There are other long-standing views. In 1726, social critic Jonathan Swift wrote, "And he gave it for his opinion, that whoever could make two ears of corn, or two blades of grass, to grow upon a spot of ground where only one grew before, would deserve better of mankind, and do more essential service to his country, than the whole race of politicians put together." According to the modern agricultural policy analyst Earl O. Heady, exclusive attention to protecting the Ogallala from water mining ignores other national and international problems, including population growth, food supplies, and extended drought. He concludes that these problems should overshadow declining Ogallala levels. Unlike more pessimistic analysts, Heady believes that the advent of new efficient technologies, despite lower water levels, will continue to support current food production, and probably surpass it.[74] According to this view, the Ogallala can be sacrificed to serve such "higher" goals. Heady does admit, however, that the surplus conditions of the 1960s, when sixty million acres were held out of production, are not likely to return in the future, putting more pressure to mine water to irrigate farmland. After all, an irrigated cornfield produces 115 bushels an acre, compared to 89 bushels on an eastern humidland farm and 48 bushels on a dryland field.[75] "I am optimistic about our ability," despite declining water levels, he asserts, "to continue growth in agricultural productivity and food production." In a remarkable statement about high farm output, Heady argues for a bullish future at least as productive as the past, based on our ability to extend the irrigator's golden age beyond 2000.[76] To others, this is the perpetuation of a Maginot Line mentality. Societies everywhere have the propensity to prepare for a repeat of their last crisis, as the French did before World War II when they made the Maginot Line a splendid defense for a repeat of World War I. The continued heavy consumption of irreplaceable Ogallala water, no matter how judiciously regulated by state or regional agencies, will make the future of the High Plains different from the past.

Can there be a single authentic (self-validating) view that requires a specific response that is equally authentic? One primary question raised by white European ventures into the High Plains is whether their invasion of the existing "natural" system would endure. That is, would it be a nature-resembling but human-dominated ecosystem (e.g., self-sustaining farmland)? Or could it prosper as a broadly transformed ecosystem (a dependent activity of the larger industrial/metropolitan infrastructure)? Or has the invasion resulted in a degraded system that virtually guarantees failure, if not now then in the foreseeable future of today's generation of farmers?

Americans learned, at the price of great suffering and cost on the High Plains, of the risks resulting from altered ecosystems. When ecosystems are disrupted frequently and stressed in their fundamental features, their natural functions become chaotic and unpredictable. In the view of Wes Jackson and others, an "authentic" (hence moral) geography on the High Plains can be realized not through agricultural giantism, but through sustainability that is resource-conserving, pollution-preventing, environment-restoring, and economically stable. Plains environmentalist Douglas Coffman advises, "Far from signifying failure, easing our death-grip on the dry plains will greatly enhance the natural productivity of the landscape, thus improving long-range prospects for social and economic renewal. . . . Nature must be the chief architect."[77]

This essay remains open-ended because the future of the Southern Plains is uncertain. Texas District No. 1 achieved major improvements in lowering water consumption while sustaining high yields in the fields. So has Kansas District No. 4. Its goal of zero depletion no longer seems radical and impossible. Farmers in their own fields remain the best stewards of the land. We have a far better understanding of environmental management than did people in the 1930s. Yet the momentum of depopulation continues apace. The question of the future of the Southern Plains also depends upon public opinion, described here as a moral geography. What is best for a Plains future is in local hands, but it is also in the hands of Congress and the American people.

Notes

1. Chapter 52, Vernon's Civil Statutes of Texas.
2. *Friendswood Development Company v. Smith-Southwest Industries, Inc.,* 576 S.W.2d 21 (Tex. Sup. Ct. 1978).
3. Robert A. Young, "Local and Regional Economic Impacts," in *Water Scarcity: Impacts on Western Agriculture,* ed. Ernest A. Engelbert and Ann Foley Schevring (Berkeley: University of California Press, 1984), 244–45.
4. P. Barkley, "The Sustainability of Rural Non-Farm Economics in Water Dependent Agricultural Areas," OTA commissioned paper, 1983, excerpted in OTA, *Water-Related Technologies for Sustainable Agriculture in U.S. Arid/Semiarid Lands* (Washington, D.C.: U.S. Congress Office of Technology Assessment, 1983), 137.
5. *http://www.washingtonpost/wp-dyn/articles/A26549-2001Feb19.html.*
6. Frank Popper and Deborah Popper, "The Great Plains: From Dust to Dust," *Planning* 53 (December 1987): 12–18.
7. Frank Popper and Deborah Popper, "The Reinvention of the American Frontier," *Wild Earth* 2 (Spring 1992): 16–18.
8. "'Buffalo Commons' on Great Plains Becomes Commonplace Idea," *The Denver Post,* 21 April 2000, 31; Florence Williams, "Plains Sense: Frank and Deborah Popper's 'Buffalo Commons' Is Creeping Toward Reality," *High Country News,* 33:1 (15 January 2001): 4–5; Patrick O'Driscoll, "'Frontier' Isn't Dying, Just Drifting," *USA Today,* 20 June 2001, 3A; "Unsettled Plains," editorial, *New York Times,* 6 June 2001.
9. Owen J. Furuseth, "Restructuring of Hog Farming in North Carolina: Explosion and Implosion," *The Professional Geographer,* 19 (November 1997): 391–403, and John Fraser Hart, "A Map of the Agricultural Implosion," *Proceedings of the Association of American Geographers,* vol. 2, 68–71.
10. Substitute for House Bill No. 2950, Committee on Environment, Kansas Legislature, Session of 1998, 11 March 1998.
11. John Wesley Powell, *Water for the West,* quoted in *Revised Management Program III: Rules and Regulations, and Policies and Standards* (Garden City: Southwest Kansas Groundwater Management District No. 3, 1986).
12. Donald E. Green, *Land of the Underground Rain: Irrigation on the Texas High Plains, 1910–1970* (Austin: University of Texas Press, 1973), 172–87.
13. All quoted in Green, *Land of the Underground Rain,* 179–83.
14. Quoted in Green, *Land of the Underground Rain,* 177.
15. Quoted in *Amarillo Sunday News-Globe,* 28 May 1950, special section.
16. Abstracted in High Plains Underground Water Conservation District No. 1 brochure, received May 1986.
17. Green, *Land of the Underground Rain,* 188, 189.
18. Frank L. Baird, *District Groundwater Planning and Management Policies on the Texas High Plains: The Views of the People* (Lubbock: High Plains Underground Water Conservation District No. 1, July 1976), 4–5.

19. Interview with Wayne Wyatt in Lubbock, Texas, May 1987.

20. See also Neville P. Clarke, *Texas Agriculture in the 80s: The Critical Decade* (College Station: Texas Agricultural Experiment Station report B-1341, Texas A & M University, 1980).

21. *Rules of High Plains Underground Water Conservation District No. 1, 1954* (Lubbock: High Plains Underground Water Conservation District No. 1, 1954).

22. "The Case for Local Regulation," *The Cross Section* 28 (December 1982): 1–4.

23. Abstracted in HPUDC brochure received May 1986.

24. *Executive Summary, Llano Estacado Regional Water Plan, January 2001,* draft copy received by the author from Wayne Wyatt, Executive Director, LERWP, February 2001, ES-3.

25. *Executive Summary, LERWP,* ES-1.

26. *Executive Summary, LERWP,* ES-3.

27. *Executive Summary, LERWP,* 11–16.

28. *http://www.washingtonpost.com/wp-dyn/articles/A26549-2001Feb19.html.*

29. Typescript dated January 1957, titled, "Conservation Irrigation, by Andrew B. Erhart, Special Edition, *Pratt Daily Tribune."*

30. Correspondence from Wayne Bossert, 19 January 1991; expanded and confirmed in interviews, 4–5 March 1996.

31. Quoted in Kip Lowe, "Groundwater Future a Continuing Concern," in the *Colby (Kansas) Free Press,* 15 June 1990; see also "Groundwater District Halts Water Rights," *Atwood (Kansas) Citizen-Patriot,* 22 February 1990; and reports and publications by Northwest Kansas Groundwater Management District Four, and the author's interviews with Wayne Bossert in April 1991.

32. Orlan Buller, "Potential Economic Effects of a Zero Depletion Policy in Northwest Kansas," paper presented at the Symposium on the Effects of a Zero Depletion Policy on the Ogallala Aquifer of the Great Plains, Ft. Hays State University, Hays, Kansas, 16 April 1991, 13.

33. Data provided by Northwest Kansas Groundwater Management District No. 4, January. See also data on county groundwater decline levels between 1964 and 1994 reported in *The Water Table* (publication of Northwest Kansas Groundwater Management District No. 4) 18, 1 (January/February): 1; 2 (March/April): 3; and 3 (May/June 1995): 3.

34. Correspondence from Wayne Bossert, 19 January 1991.

35. Wayne Bossert letter to Division of Water Resources, 8 October 1990.

36. "Water Use Report Monitoring News," *The Water Table* 18:5 (September/October 1995): 1.

37. "Status of Zero Depletion Discussions," *The Water Table* 16, 1 (January/February 1993): 1; see also "DWR's New Policy Explained," *The Water Table* 16, 1 (January/February 1993): 2; "State Considers Water Banking," *The Water Table* 18, 4 (July/August 1995): 2.

38. Interview with Wayne Bossert, Colby Kansas, 5 March 1996; see also

"Draft Ogallala Decline Committee Recommendations to Northwest Kansas Groundwater management District No. 4," 4 October 1990; Wayne Bossert letter to Division of Water Resources, 8 October 1990; "Declines Committee Makes Recommendation," *The Water Table* 13, 6 (November/December 1990).

39. Mike Corn, "Groundwater District Endorses Zero Depletion Recommendations," *Hays (Kansas) Daily News,* 5 October 1990.

40. "Irrigation Use Efficiency Being Carefully Considered," *The Water Table* 16, 5 (September/October 1993): 1; see also "KSBA Committee Update," *The Water Table* 16, 3 (May/June 1993): 2.

41. Kip Lowe, "Groundwater Future a Continuing Concern," in the *Colby (Kansas) Free Press,* 15 June 1990; see also "Groundwater District Halts Water Rights," *Atwood (Kansas) Citizen- Patriot,* 22 February 1990; and the author's interviews with the District Manager, Wayne Bossert, Northwest Kansas Groundwater Management District Four, April 1991.

42. Bossert, "Approaches to Improved Iirrigation Water Conservation under Conservation by Northwest Kansas Groundwater Management District No. 4," paper presented during "Water Organizations in a Changing West," a conference of the Natural Resources Law Center, University of Colorado School of Law, Boulder, 14–16 June 1993.

43. Buller, "Potential Economic Effects of a Zero Depletion Policy in Northwest Kansas," paper presented at the Symposium on the Effects of a Zero-depletion Policy on the Ogallala Aquifer of the High Plains, Ft. Hays State University, Ft. Hays, Kansas, April 1991.

44. Letter from Wayne Bossert to Kansas Department of Commerce, 4 May 1990.

45. Aldo Leopold, "The Land Ethic," in *A Sand County Almanac, and Sketches Here and There* (New York: Oxford University Press, 1949 [1987 edition]), 201–26.

46. David M. Smith, "Geography and Moral Philosophy: Some Common Ground," paper presented at the annual meeting of the American Association of Geographers, Ft. Worth Texas, April 1997.

47. Joan C. Tronto, *Moral Boundaries: A Political Argument for an Ethic of Care* (New York: Routledge, 1993), 126.

48. J. R. Borchert, "The Dust Bowl of the 1970s," *Annals of the Association of American Geographers* 61 (1971): 1–22.

49. John E. Ikerd, "Agriculture's Search for Sustainability and Profitability," *Journal of Soil and Water Conservation* 45 (January/February 1990): 21.

50. These are the primary arguments in Gary Comstock, *Is There a Moral Obligation to Save the Family Farm?* (Ames: Iowa State University Press, 1987), and David M. Smith, "Geography and Moral Philosophy."

51. Comstock, *Is There a Moral Obligation,* 366, 406, 408.

52. Kenneth A. Cook, "The Environmental Era of U.S. Agricultural Policy," *Journal of Soil and Water Conservation* 44 (September/October 1989): 366.

53. A. Maass and R. L. Anderson, *And the Desert Shall Rejoice: Conflict, Growth and Justice in Arid Environments* (Cambridge, Mass: The MIT Press, 1978), 17.

54. F. Lee Brown, et al, "Water Reallocation, Market Proficiency, and Conflicting Social Values," in *Western Water Institutions in a Changing Environment*, ed. Gary D. Weatherford et al. (Boulder Colo.: Westview Press, 1980).

55. Oklahoma Supreme Court, *Canada v. Shawnee*, 179 OKL. 53, 64 P. 2d 694 (1936, 1937).

56. This is a variant on the social goals of irrigation communities described by F. Lee Brown and Charles T. DuMars, "Water Rights and Market Transfers," in *Water Scarcity*, Engelbert and Foley, 411–13. See also A. Maass and R. L. Anderson, *And the Desert Shall Rejoice: Conflict, Growth and Justice in Arid Environments* (Cambridge, Mass.: The MIT Press, 1978); Kenneth Boulding, *Western Water Resources: Coming Problems and the Policy Alternatives* (Boulder, Colo.: Westview Press, 1980); and F. Lee Brown, et al, "Water Reality, Market Proficiency, and Conflicting Social Values."

57. Mary Fund, *Water in Kansas: A Primer* (Whiting: Kansas Rural Center, 1984), 43–4.

58. Gary Comstock, ed., *Is There a Moral Obligation?*, xxi.

59. Jon K. Piper, "The Prairie as a Model for Sustainable Agriculture: A Preliminary Study," in *The Land Report Research Supplement* 3 (1986): 1; see also Mark Gernes and Jon Piper, "Vegetation Patterns in Tallgrass Prairie and Their Implications for Sustainable Agriculture"; Amy Kullenberg, "Survey of Insects in Native Prairie and Agricultural Plots"; Doug Dittman, "Soil Moisture and Nutrient Patterns in Agricultural Plots and Native Prairie"; and Randolph Kempa, "Seed Systems," all in *The Land Report Research Supplement* 4 (Salina: Kansas Land Institute, 1987).

60. Fred Kirschenmann, "Fundamental Fallacies of Building Agricultural Sustainability," *Journal of Soil and Water Conservation* 46 (May/June, 1991): 168.

61. Doug Aberley, "Mapping the Terrain of Hope," *Wild Earth* 4 (Summer 1994), 62–63.

62. Daniel S. Licht, "The Great Plains: America's Best Chance for Ecosystem Restoration, Part 2," *Wild Earth* 4 (Fall 1994): 36; see also "The Great Plains: America's Best Chance for Ecosystem Restoration, Part 1," *Wild Earth* 4 (Summer 1994): 47–53.

63. Federal Agricultural and Improvement Reform (FAIR) Act of 1996 (4 April 1996), P.L. 104–27.

64. Donald Worster, "Grassland Follies: Agricultural Capitalism on the Plains," in *Under Western Skies: Nature and History in the American West*, ed. Donald Worster (New York: Oxford University Press, 1992), 93–105.

65. Michael Walzer, *Thick and Thin: Moral Argument at Home and Abroad.* (South Bend: University of Notre Dame Press, 1996); and Clifford Geertz, *The Interpretation of Cultures* (New York: Basic Books, 1973).

66. Stephen S. Birdsall, "Regard, Respect, and Responsibility: Sketches for a Moral Geography of the Everyday," *Annals of the Association of American Geographers* 86 (December 1996): 619–29.

67. Dan L. Flores, "A Long Love Affair with an Uncommon Country: Environmental History and the Great Plains," in *Prairie Conservation: Preserving North America's Most Endangered Ecosystem,* ed. Fred B. Samson and Fritz L. Knopf (Washington, D.C.: Island Press, 1996).

68. William E. Riebsame, "The United States Great Plains," in *The Earth as Transformed by Human Action: Global and Regional Changes in the Biosphere over the Past Three Hundred Years,* ed. B. L. Turner II et al. (New York: Cambridge University Press, 1990), 575.

69. Mark Sagoff, *The Economy of the Earth: Philosophy, Law, and the Environment* (New York: Cambridge University Press, 1988).

70. See the extended discussion of environmental impacts in the classic studies by Donella H. Meadows, et al., *The Limits to Growth.* (New York: Universe Books, 1972); and *Beyond the Limits* (Post Hills, Vt.: Chelsea Green Publishing Company, 1992).

71. John Bredehoeft, "Physical Limitations of Water Resources," in Engelbert, *Water Scarcity,* 43.

72. *Ground Water: An Overview* (Washington, D.C.: General Accounting Office, 21 June 1977), 9–14; see also "West Texas and Eastern New Mexico Import Project," *Critical Water Problems Facing the Eleven Western States* (Washington, D.C.: USDI, April 1975); and *Projected Economic Life of Water Resources, Subdivision Number 1, High Plains Underground Water Reservoir* (College Station: Technical Monograph 6, Texas Agricultural Experiment Station, Texas A & M University, December 1969).

73. Commentary by Frank J. Trelease, in Ernest A. Engelbert and Ann Foley Scheuring, eds., *Water Scarcity: Impacts on Western Agriculture* (Berkeley: University of California Press, 1984), 78.

74. Earl O. Heady, "National and International Commodity Price Impacts," in Engelbert, *Water Scarcity,* 227–78.

75. Office of Technology Assessment, *Water-Related Technologies for Sustainable Agriculture in U.S. Arid/Semiarid Lands* (Washington, D.C.: U.S. Congress, Office of Technology Assessment, OTA-F-212, October 1983), 39.

76. Heady, "National and International Commodity Price Impacts," 274, 277–78.

77. Douglas Coffman, "Buffalo Commons: An Encouraging Word," *Wild Earth* 5 (Fall 1995), 31.

CHAPTER FIVE

Exploitationists and Depletionists

Petroleum in the Future of the Southern Plains

DIANA DAVIDS OLIEN

Only two other periods within the history of the American petroleum industry have encompassed as profound change as have the last twenty years, from 1980 to 2000. Between 1859 and 1879, the industry grew from one well at Titusville, Pennsylvania, to a booming new arena with thousands of participants and one industrial giant, Standard Oil. In the two decades following the 1901 Spindletop discovery in Texas, new industry giants appeared and producing regions with vast reserves opened up. Both these periods saw a proliferation of large and small industry participants and a soaring level of exploration and production. By contrast, during the last twenty years there have been two steep downturns resulting in domestic industry contraction, decrease in industry participants large and small, nosediving onshore exploration, and declining domestic production. The industry has restructured and refocused its objectives to shift emphasis to arenas offshore and overseas. For regions like the Southern Plains, in which oil and gas "upstream"— exploration and production—have long been important, these changes of the last twenty years have meant challenging times. If we think about what lies ahead, the place to begin is with these last twenty years and what they can tell us.

There are, of course, some limitations to this approach. We have to reason from existing circumstances: current geological thinking, for example, and technology as it is now or is likely to be in the foreseeable future. When informed observers did this in the 1920s, some of them concluded that America would be out of oil by 1935.[1] In an industry in which innovative thinking and technological breakthroughs can have striking impacts on opportunities, one can never be sure what unforeseen horizons will open up. What follows, then, is based on what is visible now, what we can expect to see if things go in the direction they have been going. It is a "best guess," but a best guess with considerable foundation.

Because the Southern Plains is not a precisely defined region in oil and gas terms, and because it includes a number of producing regions, this essay focuses on the most important of the producing regions of the Southern Plains: the Permian Basin. Covering a large portion of West Texas below the Panhandle and part of southeastern New Mexico, the Permian Basin is a mature producing region whose production has been important since the 1920s. Within it there are numerous giant oil fields, as well as some giant gas fields such as the Gomez field. Not only is it the most important producing basin of the lower forty-eight states, supplying some 12 percent of total daily U.S. oil production, but it has long been the leading arena for applied oil field technology in areas like enhanced oil recovery.[2] It offers us an excellent vantage point from which to study what has been happening in the domestic petroleum industry. If prospects for oil and gas are decreasingly bright in the Permian Basin, they are unlikely to be promising in less prolific regions—though, once again, unexpected developments can set aside such a judgment. Our focus should also be oil upstream, exploration and production, since compared to other regions, refining and petrochemicals are not a major part of industry presence on the Southern Plains.

Price Volatility

The first thing to note about the last twenty years is a circumstance over which industry participants had virtually no control and which was responsible for tremendous losses in the industry: price volatility. Between 1980 and 2000, this volatility was most noticeable in crude oil prices. Notwithstanding the unprecedented surge in natural gas prices of the past year, during most of the last two decades, there was an over-supply of natural gas, a "gas bubble," as industry observers put it, which kept average wellhead prices within a general range of $1.60–$2.60 per thousand cubic feet (Mcf). Between 1986 and 1992, prices averaged below $1.75/Mcf and usually dipped when crude prices fell. But as natural gas prices tended to stay fairly flat, crude oil prices went through wild gyrations. In 1981, the average U.S. price of crude at the wellhead was $30.71 per barrel. In 1982, it slipped down to $28.52 per barrel, continuing to decline until the crash of 1986, when it plummeted to $12.55 per barrel. It rose to over $20 during the Gulf War of 1990, slipped again thereafter, recovered to $18.46 in 1996, and crashed again to $10.80 in 1998. By the end of 1999, the average wellhead price was back to $15.65. Six months later, crude oil trading on NYMEX pushed prices over $30 a barrel.[3]

Obviously the dramatic price crashes of 1986 and 1998 took a heavy toll on the value of industry reserves and on industry profits. During and after 1986, many firms sank in a tidal wave of red ink, never to reemerge. But beyond these relatively predictable effects, the persistence of price volatility worked to discourage investment in exploration and production, particularly on the part of institutional and outside investors, but also on the part of industry players. Since a project that is attractive when oil is $20 a barrel may be a loss when prices are half that amount, price volatility makes it difficult for operators in exploration and production to plan projects and encourages a cautious "wait and see" approach. This is one reason why, even when prices surged upward after 1999, oilmen did not rush to launch another all-out boom in exploration and development. After 1986 and 1998, the prevailing mood seemed to be "better safe than sorry."[4] The industry's reaction to twenty years of price volatility must be kept in mind if we ask whether the oil and gas regions of the Southern Plains will see another great oil boom like that of 1978–1981. The answer is that it's not highly likely. Moreover, should there be another dramatic upturn lively enough to be called a boom, the players taking part will be different and the game will be played differently.

Mergers, Restructuring, and Downsizing

One of the most striking changes of the last twenty years has been what has happened to the major oil companies, the twenty or so largest integrated firms in 1980. First, there are not nearly as many of them now, and, second, they have restructured their exploration and production to shift focus from domestic onshore operations to offshore and/or global objectives. Both developments reflect the increased challenge to maintain profit levels in uncertain times, and both have had and will continue to have a profound effect on the petroleum industry of the Southern Plains.

The thinning of the ranks of the majors and the spate of mergers and acquisitions among them began in the 1980s. Occidental acquired Cities Service in 1982. Chevron took over Gulf, and Texaco took over Getty, in 1984. The same year, two large independents, Superior and Aminoil, were swallowed up by Mobil and Phillips, respectively. In 1987, BP acquired Standard Oil of Ohio. The late nineties brought megamergers: BP, Amoco, and ARCO; and Exxon and Mobil. Now a merger of Chevron and Texaco is in progress. As the ranks of the majors steadily shrank, companies restructured. Sun, for example, spun off its exploration and production into an independent unit, Oryx, which merged with Kerr-McGee in 1998. In 1994, ARCO reorganized to create independent affiliated companies, including ARCO Permian and Vastar. Other companies spun off freestanding units that grew rapidly in importance, like Panhandle Eastern spin-off, Anadarko. These transformations represented a variety of responses to industry recession. The acquisitions of Gulf and Getty, for example, were a far more economical way to acquire reserves than drilling for them. Spin-offs were also a way for companies to identify and let go of branches they no longer saw as part of core strategy or to reorganize for greater cost savings and efficiency. The megamergers can be seen as moves to be ever larger and more competitive in a global industry in which national oil companies with huge reserves, like Petrobras or Lukoil, have become major players.[5]

Becoming more competitive in the more challenging environment of lower prices, however, also required downsizing after mergers and acquisitions that, in practical terms, meant loss of jobs for those merged or acquired whose positions overlapped with those in the acquiring company. Indeed, in response to lower prices and diminished profits, companies of all sizes fell back on what independents had long called a "lean and mean" strategy: doing the maximal amount of work with the minimal number of persons on the payroll. For example, even before acquisition by BP, Amoco had progressively cut back on regional offices and positions. In the Permian Basin it closed district offices in Hobbs, Andrews, and Levelland in 1987, consolidating them in Odessa and Brownfield. By 1992, it cut 8,500 jobs companywide; 5,700 employees had taken early retirement or severance packages, and 2,800 had left in asset disposition. In 1994, Amoco trimmed off another 3,800 jobs. Other major companies followed a similar course; in 1990, for example, Chevron eliminated 1000 jobs, and in 1994 Texaco trimmed off 2,500. Overall, in the decade 1982–1992, the U.S. petroleum industry lost over 400,000 jobs, including 51 percent of domestic exploration and production jobs. Over half the jobs lost were in Texas.[6]

As they downsized, majors also began to sell off domestic production, refocusing on offshore and/or foreign arenas. ARCO, for example, began a program of divesting U.S. production in 1986, selling, as one company executive put it, properties that were "nonstrategic," at the same time it cut back its work force. By 1992, it had sold $700 million worth of leases and was looking to sell a large number of its relatively small Permian Basin properties. Many of these properties were acquired by emerging "mega" independents. At the end of 1992, for example, Anadarko picked up $208.9 million of Permian Basin reserves from ARCO. Denver-based Apache Corporation acquired properties from Amoco in the Permian and Anadarko basins, including secondary and tertiary recovery projects, as well as gas processing plants in Winkler County, Texas. As Devon Energy Corporation vice president H. Alan Turner commented, "A few small companies can move in and fill the void left today by majors going overseas. Those few could grow very quickly." Certainly Devon would grow quickly; by 2001, having acquired PennzEnergy, North Star Energy, and Santa Fe-Snyder, it had emerged as a mega independent with a substantial Permian Basin presence.[7]

What all this has meant is that on the Southern Plains, in the Permian Basin and elsewhere, the majors have retreated, and they are not going to return. Giant discoveries initially brought them to areas like the Permian Basin. Now that the producing regions of the Southern Plains are, in industry terms, "mature," no one expects to find fields the size of Yates or Wasson.[8] The largest companies, including many of the new mega independents like Anadarko and Apache, are going after globally important targets—in the North Sea, in China, off West Africa and Brazil—the kind of field plays that are no longer generally foreseeable onshore in the lower forty-eight. What are some of the implications of this change? Will the larger independents fill the void left by the majors' pullout?

Certainly part of the aftermath of major company departure will be shrinking per capita income in oil-based communities. As one independent oilman pointed out, the jobs lost in Midland with major company departures were $75,000–$100,000-a-year jobs; Midland growth in sectors like retailing and services has tended to create $25,000–$30,000-a-year jobs. A recent report by Angelou Economic Advisers, Inc., showed 60 percent of household incomes in Midland County to be under $50,000 a year; only 7 percent were over $100,000. Close to three-quarters of household incomes in Ector County were less than $50,000 a year. The loss of well-paid major company jobs is not going to be a void independents of any size will fill, because independent companies do not staff on the scale major companies do. To use a Midland example, the termination of ARCO Permian meant the loss of 160 jobs, and the pullout of Mobil after merger with Exxon brought the loss of 170 jobs. Chevron, still maintaining a Midland office, cut back from 236 office workers and 200 field hands to 123 office workers and 135 field hands. By contrast, Anadarko and Apache, with increasingly important regional presence, employ 30 office workers and 100 field hands, and 7 office workers and 99 field hands, respectively. Moreover, some mega independents such as Pioneer and Devon have relocated employees to Dallas and Houston, resulting in a loss of 285 jobs in Midland. No wonder that, as of June 2000, an estimated one-third of Midland office space was vacant.[9]

The Independents' Role

The departure of the majors has profoundly affected industry opportunities for independents, though oilmen differ on how they have changed. For independents that are large and growing larger, the departure of the majors has opened up chances to acquire leases and production once locked in majors' inventories. Midlander James Henry, whose Henry Petroleum is one of the top thirty-two oil producers in Texas, wrote in 1996, "This is the golden age for independents. For the first time we don't have to compete with the major companies. In fact, the majors are helping us by selling some of their smaller, less profitable, fields." He added, "Their garbage is our gold." Independents such as Henry Petroleum have not only picked up properties but also industry talent; geoprofessionals facing layoffs or transfers have, in some instances, chosen to stay in West Texas and have found jobs with independent firms.

On the other hand, twenty years ago majors and independents in many regions shared a sort of symbiotic relationship, wherein independents might sell parts of deals to majors interested in the geological potential of projects, and majors might farm out acreage they wanted tested to independents. As one veteran Midland independent put it, "The removal of the majors and their offices and their support, that's a big factor, because we used to be able to get partnership arrangements with them." Historically, majors and independents often cooperated rather than competed. Moreover, many an independent in the Permian Basin as well as other regions got started by selling parts of deals to and

James C. Henry, CEO, Henry Petroleum LP. The departure of major corporations from West Texas has meant greater opportunity for some independent oil companies. Henry's company, in business since 1969, represents one of those that has taken advantage of the situation. Courtesy James C. Henry.

working with major companies; the absence of the majors may make it harder for newcomers to enter independent ranks.[10] It is not evident that the large independents are filling the role that the majors once had in this region.

As mature regions where exploration is of decreasing importance, the oil fields of the Southern Plains are still important for their production. If underground supplies of water are rapidly waning, a huge amount of hydrocarbons remain underground. What will slow production decline is the technologically enhanced ability to get more and more hydrocarbons out of reservoirs. Historically, on the Southern Plains the major companies have done the research and development for secondary and tertiary recovery—what you can get by stimulating a reservoir when natural pressure and production have declined. Major companies did the necessary scientific work for large-scale application of waterfloods in the fifties and, in the following decades, enhanced oil recovery by carbon dioxide injection. Such experimentation was, and is, beyond what independents can afford, though once recovery methods are proven to work, they certainly apply them. On the bright side, now that much CO_2-related infrastructure is in place, CO_2 flooding has become cheaper and more accessible. On the dark side, most major companies have cut back on research and development in order to cut costs, and it is thus uncertain who will do the next steps in research and development of enhanced recovery processes that will improve this technology further.[11]

Yet enhancing recovery is precisely what is vital to sustaining production on the Southern Plains. In the Permian Basin alone, an estimated equivalent of 8.6 billion barrels of oil remains to be recovered. But, in the absence of new technology directed at extracting more of that oil and gas, diminishing returns will be unavoidable. And, at the moment, no new breakthroughs in recovery processes, comparable to waterflooding or CO_2 injection, seem on the horizon. Some independents hope that federally funded research programs will take up where the majors left off; some hope university research programs will fill the gap. The fact remains that right now no one is doing what the majors once did.[12]

New Strategies in Science and Technology

Independents' strategies on the Southern Plains are not only different from those of the majors in the past, but, for the most part, they bear no relation to those of the old-time wildcatters whose focus on exploration opened up field after field in the first half of the twentieth century. Instead of looking for great bonanzas, the present-day independents are looking for what earlier prospectors overlooked—small structures easily missed, oil and gas in areas where earlier drilling and production technology would not yield attractive returns, strata passed up for those with larger production. Depending on which independent one talks to, what's happening may be called "harvesting" or "gleaning," but it translates generally into going after by-passed or smaller objectives. Independent oilman James Henry identifies himself as an "exploitationist," an operator who goes into existing fields with a full staff of geoprofessionals and uses the most up-to-date science and technology to produce as much additional oil and gas as possible from old reservoirs. The exploitationist does this with as low overhead as possible, making profitable what the majors, with higher overhead, could not.[13]

Applying the latest geoscience and technology is key in exploitationist strategy. In terms of identifying targets, the most valuable geoscientific development of the last twenty years has been the development and application of 3-D seismic technology. 3-D seismic makes it possible to study an underground structure in three dimensions and is far better than earlier seismic imaging at locating small structures, making it possible to evaluate and tap them much more precisely. This technology, however, is based upon interpretation of massive amounts of seismic data. Here the tremendous improvements in computer technology of the last twenty years, in particular the tremendous acceleration in computerized information processing, has been critical to the effective deployment of 3-D seismic data. Computer advances have not only made working with 3-D seismic much more efficient, they have also made it much more affordable, in that one can analyze far more data with far fewer geoscientists. These developments have brought the latest techniques of geophysical science within the reach of even modest-sized independents. The enhanced accuracy of 3-D seismic projections has also substantially reduced risk in exploration, and it is thus one of the most important elements currently driving both exploration and exploitation in the oilfields of the Southern Plains and elsewhere.[14]

Once a small target has been identified, the task of hitting it accurately is critical, and here relatively recent advances in drilling technology have made a significant difference. Drilling can now be done with downhole motors and measurement while drilling; the latter lets the driller know exactly what is happening downhole. These improvements

Computer technology has increased the efficiency of companies pursuing the exploitationist strategy of oil development on the Southern Plains. Photo courtesy Hunt Oil Company.

have not only made drilling more accurate but also faster—and, hence, more affordable in the search for the sort of small targets the exploitationist is after.[15]

With respect to drilling, one of the most remarkable advances of the last twenty years has been the development of much more affordable horizontal drilling. First widely used in the Austin Chalk, this technique is now often applied in heavily fractured or tight sand formations where wells drilled vertically may yield scant production. Horizontal drilling may offer an amount of production that might once have taken dozens of wells to yield, with a well bore that may extend two or more miles laterally. The technique thus opens up new opportunities for production in formations once uneconomical to drill. It may also be used to tap formations passed up earlier by going into an existing well and drilling laterally, and there have been experiments in using it for secondary recovery projects. In short, it has exciting potential in a mature area like the Permian Basin, and exploitationist independents are using it.[16]

Horizontal drilling is crucial in what is currently the brightest spot on the Permian Basin exploration horizon, the search for more Delaware

Basin gas. This play opened in 1999, when Exxon Mobil began drilling horizontally in the Montoya-Devonian formation in Block 16 of Ward County. Ten wells drilled by Exxon Mobil are now producing roughly 85 Mmcf a day of gas. Larger independents like Burlington Resources, Abraxas, and EOG joined in, and action has extended into Reeves County. Typically, wells are drilled vertically to the Montoya and then extended with four-thousand-foot laterals. Not only has this brought in new gas, but the technique can probably be applied in older fields to bring in additional gas.[17] Higher gas prices and escalating demand for gas, of course, make such ventures attractive, just as they have revived drilling for deep gas reserves further north in the Anadarko and Dalhart basins of Texas and Oklahoma. Overall, in terms of drilling, there is likely to be more future action directed toward gas than oil in Southern Plains producing regions.

In practical terms, how do technological breakthroughs translate into an independent exploitationist's operations? First, when an exploitationist considers acquiring a producing property, computers allow an evaluation of its wells and economic potential to be completed in a matter of hours rather than days, meaning thousands of dollars saved. The exploitationist can then use his geoscientific personnel to make a thorough study of the property, using seismic data. He can make a well by well study of production. From all this, he can develop what amounts to a property, or perhaps field, strategy. He may decide to drill some wells deeper or drill additional wells. He may take a well used to inject water in a waterflood and produce oil from it instead. He may take an existing well and drill horizontally out from it. In all of this, however, applied science is his guide.[18]

Over the past twenty years, then, applied science has opened up opportunities, lowered risks, and made operations much more affordable, thus enhancing independent activity. The question is, of course, for how long will it continue to do so? Here again, what one can predict is tied to existing science and technology, and among operators opinions differ widely. James Henry suggests that we may be looking at an exploitationist future of ten to twenty years in the Permian Basin; most other observers tend to see a far longer future for such activity, perhaps as long as hydrocarbons are a dominant energy source, given the size of the region and the reserves it still contains. What industry participants do agree on is that, overall, production will decline. Parenthetically, this decline will impact not only the incomes of oilmen but also of farmers and ranchers receiving royalty checks. Like water, royalty income will be running shorter on the Southern Plains.[19]

Once exploitationists have used all the science at their command, what next? Here industry observers expect "depletionists" to take over. Unlike exploitationists, depletionists will work without geoprofessional staff, keeping employees and overhead to the minimum. By keeping costs cut back to the bone, by doing much of the work of nursing wells along by themselves, they will be able to make a profit on wells producing only a few barrels of oil a day. They are, as one independent put it, at the end of the industry "food chain"; they will operate properties larger operators have abandoned as no longer profitable. As oil fields dwindle into the hands of depletionists, the number of oil field and geoprofessional jobs will decrease still further.[20]

Service Providers and Labor

Oil industry participants include drilling contractors and other service providers, and, like the major companies, their ranks have greatly thinned in the last twenty years. Contractors and service providers were hit hard when plunging oil prices resulted in drastic reductions in what firms could spend on exploration and development. For smaller service providers whose operations were exclusively domestic, the situation was especially dire because companies that could afford substantial levels of investment in exploration and development increasingly spent dollars overseas. For example, in 1991, a year of industry recession, 64 percent of exploration and development spending, including 70 percent of major company spending in that area, went outside the United States. The combination of decreased activity at home and increased activity abroad hit smaller service providers especially hard. Between 1981 and 1989, bankruptcies, acquisitions, and mergers reduced the size of this sector by 40 percent. International Association of Drilling Contractors' membership was 1050 in 1981, but by 1995 it was down to 350. Similarly, in well service there were close to 1000 contractors in 1981; by 1995 this number had shrunk to less than 600. At the same time, hard times encouraged the formation of mega service providers, just as they produced mega independents. In 1987, Baker International Corp. merged with Hughes Tool Co., reducing its work force by 6,500 jobs as it did so. In 1993, Weatherford International, Inc. merged with Tuboscope Vetco International Inc. In 1998, Baker Hughes acquired Western Atlas,

Halliburton acquired Dresser Industries, and Schlumberger merged with Camco International. There are thus fewer service providers, employing far fewer persons.[21]

One element behind the reconfiguring of the service sector has been access to capital. When boom turned to bust after 1981, investor dollars withdrew from the hard-pressed service providers. Growth by mergers and acquisitions let some firms reach a size at which they could begin to look like more stable investment propositions and, hence, attract dollars from larger institutional investors. As Ray Peterson, senior vice president of UTI Drilling put it, "The bigger companies . . . needed to reach a certain critical mass to attract the attention of institutional investors." Despite renewed action in the oil patch since 1999, it is not very likely that there will be a new proliferation of small drilling contractors; not only is it difficult for a small driller to find both investor dollars and equipment—renewed activity having put the latter in short supply—but the particular problem service providers of all sizes face is shortage of labor—and that problem is acute.[22]

Hard times, mergers, and acquisitions have not only meant company layoffs of geoprofessionals and production workers, but massive layoffs in the service sector. As Peterson put it, there really is nothing one can do with a drilling rig crew if they don't have an oil or gas well to drill, and, in all the difficult times from 1982 through 1999, "the industry laid off so many people and just starved them away from our business, that they left our business, got other jobs, and we just really lost our core of people." Now workers are wary of returning to an industry where activity and employment are so unstable. As Peterson observed, "We need . . . to be able to show . . . that there is some security to those people who say, 'OK, you laid me off seven times, now you want me to come back again?'" He added, "The cyclical nature of our industry means that just about the time everyone starts to believe that there is some security, wages are good, this is a good place to work, there it goes down again— lay 'em off." Similarly, Jay Reynolds, president of Rod Ric Drilling noted, "Employees don't feel they have any stability." As a result, as one operator said, it can be hard to find a competent tool pusher, let alone a competent crew. Experienced workers, having left the industry, have found more stable and often better paying employment.[23]

When it comes to recruiting new workers, lack of job security is not the only problem the industry has. During down times, even workers who kept their jobs suffered pay cuts. Wages for field hands have not kept up with wages in less demanding types of work. As Morris Burns of the Permian Basin Petroleum Association put it, "You can't go out and hire rig hands for $7, $8, $10 an hour any more. Twenty years ago that was four times what somebody could make working at WalMart. Now it's $.50 more than they can make working at WalMart." Moreover, young workers are not enthusiastic about work that can be seven days a week, Sundays and holidays, with a hundred-mile or more commute. Also, as more and more young persons have the chance for a college education, blue-collar work like roughnecking has less appeal.[24]

The shortage of blue-collar workers, then, is acute, industry-wide, and extends even to offshore operations. It is also a drag on infrastructure; in 2001 operators who wish to drill or need well workovers have long waits for service, yet another brake on the advent of a boom. The industry is experimenting with training programs, and it has talked of trying to recruit newly released convicts. It has also recognized that in the last twenty years the oil field work force has seen ethnic change, from overwhelmingly Anglo to 90 percent Hispanic, and has begun to advertise for workers on Hispanic radio stations. One well service operator now advertises for workers on Mexican radio stations, and green-carded workers increasingly make up his crews. One can expect the percentage of Hispanic workers in the oil field work force to continue to increase, but that also reflects changing demographics on the Southern Plains, and, more especially, West Texas, as Yolanda Romero points out elsewhere in this volume.[25]

As there are fewer oil industry jobs and fewer workers who wish to fill them, where will workers on the Southern Plains go? People have always moved about on the Southern Plains, but, unfortunately for the region, the likeliest answer is elsewhere. Between 1998 and 1999, a period of severe industry downturn, net out-migration from Midland County was 1809 persons; the net loss of students to Midland Independent School District was 600 students. This dramatic dip in little more than a year is simply a stark example of what has been happening to population in many Southern Plains counties over the last decade. During the 1990s, for example, population in Hutchinson County shrunk by 7.7 percent, Crane County by 7.8 percent, Winkler County by 10 percent, Yoakum County by 11.1 percent, Ward County by 12.3 percent, Cottle County by 15.9 percent, and Upton County by 20.1 percent. By contrast, during the same period, Harris County grew by 15.3 percent and Dallas County by 11.3 percent. As the regional

Federal Reserve Bank reported in 1996, 85 percent of all income earned by oil industry workers in Texas went to persons in the state's metropolitan areas, most especially Houston and Dallas. Workers who have not relocated have found jobs outside oil. In Midland-Odessa the main employment sectors are trade, services, and local government; all three sectors, separately, employ more persons than the petroleum industry. In fact, in November 2000, 16,100 persons in Midland-Odessa worked in local government; only 11,400 worked in the petroleum industry.[26]

Looking to the Future

If we look at the future of oil and gas on the Southern Plains, we can identify some pronounced trends. These trends are not unique to the Southern Plains. In fact, they are visible in onshore exploration and production in the lower forty-eight states. First, the majors will continue to take a diminished role in onshore exploration and production, shifting focus to offshore and overseas operations, although if the federal government opens up the Arctic National Wildlife Reserve, they will be active there. The larger independents will also have an increasingly global orientation, rather than concentrate on domestic operations. Second, independent firms will dominate domestic exploration and production, but, like the majors, they will do more with fewer people, and they will not fund research and development as the majors once did. Thus jobs lost in the industry are probably permanently lost, and the question of who will do necessary research and development remains open. Third, independents will be more focused on production than exploration, and in exploration they will aim for smaller and smaller targets. If exploration and production technology continues to advance, this will permit them to keep lowering risks in achieving these goals and keep making operations more efficient. But if reduced industry spending on technological research and development results in slower technological progress, such strategy will be less workable. Fourth, the industry will continue to strive to retrieve an increasing percentage of hydrocarbons that still remain underground. Here, technological advances to enhance recovery will be important in sustaining activity levels; without them, production and activity levels will decline more rapidly. Fifth, both the ranks of service providers and the size of the oilfield work force are likely to keep shrinking. For communities whose economies are undiversified and squarely tied to petroleum, these trends do not add up to a rosy future.

On the other hand, as veteran independent Arden Grover points out, "Things keep turning up."[27] Historically, there have been many forecasts of doom in the petroleum industry, and many of them have been dead wrong. For an industry so closely attuned to technological change and scientific rethinking, it is prudent to admit that we cannot foresee what might "turn up." Our forecasts are squarely tied to what we can see in front of us; there may be other options less visible at present. The other element impossible to forecast is timing. Will the exploitationist future of the Southern Plains be ten to twenty years, or twenty to forty years? Will it be longer? A tremendous volume of hydrocarbons does remain underground, and if petroleum prices stay high, there will be ample incentive to go after them. What is certain is that we are not going to go back to the oil industry as it was in 1981. This is not your father's oil industry, and we cannot expect the future to repeat the past.

Notes

1. Roger M. Olien and Diana Davids Olien, *Oil and Ideology: The Cultural Creation of the American Petroleum Industry* (Chapel Hill: University of North Carolina Press, 2000), 159–60.

2. Morris Burns, interviewed by Diana Davids Olien, 9 February 2001, Midland, Texas; James Henry, interviewed by Diana Davids Olien, 27 December 2000, Midland, Texas.

3. *Oil and Gas Journal* (hereafter *OGJ*), 26 January 1987, 45; *OGJ* 30 January 1995, 55; *OGJ* 31 January 2000, 51.

4. Robert C. Leibrock, interviewed by Diana Davids Olien and Roger M. Olien, 28 July 2000, Midland, Texas; Arden Grover, interviewed by Diana Davids Olien, 2 February 2001, Midland, Texas; Henry interview; Buddy Sipes, interviewed by Diana Davids Olien, 16 February 2001, Midland, Texas.

5. Sam Fletcher, "Oil Mergers Eliminating Jobs," *Houston Post*, 30 September 1984; James R. Pierobon, "Mobil's 'Hard Line' Style May Change Superior," *Houston Chronicle*, 13 March 1984; "BP Amoco Merger Creates a Third 'Supermajor,'" *OGJ* 17 August 1998, 34; "Kerr-McGee, Oryx Join U.S. Merger Frenzy," *OGJ* 26 October 1998, 38; "Panhandle Eastern to Spin Off Anadarko," *OGJ* 25 August 1986, 34; R. Dobie Langenkamp, "Getting Smaller in a Real World," *Houston Chronicle*, 31 December 2000.

6. "BP's Robert Horton Oversees Broad Change in Firm's Corporate Culture," *OGJ* 10 December 1990, 15; "ARCO to Cut Staff, Regroup in Lower Forty-Eight," *OGJ* 12 August 1991, 37; "Chevron, Unocal Detail Plans for Restructuring," *OGJ* 11 May 1992, 26; *Midland Reporter-Telegram*,

1 July 1987; "Restructuring Rampant in U.S.," *OGJ* 13 July 1992, 18; "Amoco Spells Out Restructuring, Work Force Cuts," *OGJ* 1 August 1994, 27; "Chevron Restructuring U.S. Upstream Unit," *OGJ* 26 February 1990, 46; "Texaco Schedules Broad Restructuring Program," *OGJ* 11 July 1994, 25; A. D. Koen, "U.S. Petroleum Industry Adjusts to Tough Economy," *OGJ* 13 July 1992, 15; "Industry Recession to Persist," *OGJ* 30 March 1992, 24.

7. "Majors' U. S. Retrenchment Causes Sale Property Glut," *OGJ* 24 August 1992, 18; "Devon-Santa Fe-Snyder Deal Tops M & A Action," *OGJ* 5 June 2000, 26–28.

8. Henry interview; Burns interview; Arlen Edgar, interviewed by Diana Davids Olien, 2 February 2001, Midland, Texas; Sipes interview; Grover interview.

9. Sipes interview; "Consultant: It's Midland's Last Wake-Up Call," *Midland Reporter-Telegram*, 21 February 2001; "Major Withdrawal," *Houston Chronicle*, 4 June 2000; Midland Chamber of Commerce, "Midland County Employment Layoff Report, 1998–2000;" Kevin Skipper, "Midland's Employment Earnings Growth Lackluster Compared to State," *Business Journal, Midland Reporter-Telegram*, December 2000.

10. James C. Henry, "Opportunities Await U.S. Independents Willing to Change," *OGJ* 4 November 1996, 53–54, 56; Burns interview; Grover interview; Roger M. Olien and Diana Davids Olien, *Wildcatters: Texas Independent Oilmen* (Austin: Texas Monthly Press, 1984), 173.

11. Edgar interview; Burns interview; "U.S. Upstream Reliance Growing on Cooperative Programs in R & D," *OGJ* 17 April 1995, 17–21; "Downturn Hobbling Upstream Technology R & D," *OGJ* 29 March 1999, 23–24.

12. Henry interview; Sipes interview; Leslie Haines, "Aiming for Permian Power," *Oil and Gas Investor*, June 2001, 67.

13. Henry, "Opportunities Await," 51; Henry interview.

14. Edgar interview; Burns interview.

15. Ray Peterson, interviewed by Diana Davids Olien, 9 February 2001, Midland, Texas.

16. Peterson interview; Burns interview.

17. "Tom Brown, Chevron Join in Hot Play," *Midland Reporter-Telegram*, 4 March 2001.

18. James Henry, interviewed by Diana Davids Olien, 4 January 2001, Midland, Texas (hereafter this interview will be cited as Henry interview 2); Sipes interview.

19. Henry interview; Edgar interview; Grover interview; Burns interview.

20. Henry, "Opportunities Await," 51; Henry interview; Edgar interview.

21. Koen, "Tough Economy," 15; Raji Samghabadi, "Bit by Bit: Bloody but Unbowed, Oil-Service Companies are Reviving," *Barron's* 24 April 1989, 11, 30; Sam Fletcher, "A Slick Move," *Houston Post*, 13 February 1995; Michael Davis, "2 Top Oilfield Service Firms to Merge," *Houston Post*, 16 July 1993;

Scott Nyquist, "Petroleum Companies Should Include M & A Options in Strategy Portfolio," *OGJ* 18 May 1998, 36; "Baker Hughes, Western Atlas Agree to Merge," *OGJ* 18 May 1998, 30; John Kennedy, "How Oil and Gas Companies Fought 1998 and Won," *OGJ* 4 January 1999, 22; "Schlumberger, Camco Sign Merger Agreement," *OGJ* 29 June 1998, 30.

22. Peterson interview; Richard Wheatley, "Crunch Looms for U.S. Service/Supply Sector," *OGJ* 7 April 1997, 28, 30.

23. Peterson interview; Leibrock interview; Gelu Suluguic, "Drilling Rates Soar, But Record Cash Flows Allow Producers to Cover Costs," *Houston Chronicle,* 31 December 2000; John Paul Pitts, "Could Exploration, Seismic Booms Be On the Way?" *Midland Reporter-Telegram,* 4 February 2001; Mella McEwen, "Labor Shortage, not Equipment, Main Problem Facing Drillers," *Midland Reporter-Telegram,* 15 October 2000.

24. Peterson interview; Burns interview; McEwen, "Labor Shortage."

25. Sipes interview; Peterson interview; Burns interview; Henry interview; "Oil Producers Increasingly Desperate for Workers to Fill Jobs," *Midland Reporter-Telegram,* 28 May 2000.

26. Midland Chamber of Commerce, "Net Population Migration— Midland County, TX," "Permian Basin Job Losses," "Industry Sector Employment;" "Texas Growth in the 1990s," *Dallas Morning News,* 9 March 2000; Caleb Solomon, "Where Are the Oil Jobs? They've Gone to the City," *Wall Street Journal,* 20 March 1996.

27. Grover interview.

CHAPTER SIX

Identity and Conservative Politics on the Southern Plains

JEFF ROCHE

Since the 1970s, a conservative brand of politics, characterized by a zealous fidelity to the Republican Party, has dominated the Southern Plains.[1] Voters in this region, which stretches from the heart of West Texas north onto the Great Plains, shaped their politics in stages and created a political identity most comfortable within the most conservative wing of the Republican Party. These conservatives have merged a libertarian belief in limited government and unfettered capitalism with a conviction in the power and righteousness of small-town, Protestant values.[2] As they defined their particular beliefs about politics, citizenship, government, entrepreneurial capitalism, masculinity, family, class, race, individual freedom, and community, a core ideology has emerged. The ideology is characterized by an aversion toward centralization, especially in government; the celebration of local public space; insistence upon the virtue of shared standards and values; individual loyalty to community and responsibility for contributing to the public good—reflected in the region's unusually high voter registration, participation in the electoral process, church attendance, community organizing, and other volunteer activities; and maintaining traditional social and cultural standards.[3] Adapting and refining these beliefs to fit the times and most often trapped within the restraints of contemporary language and, more important, political reality (in Texas, the one-party system, for example), Southern Plains voters have resembled New Dealers, isolationists, anti-communists, Nixon's Silent Majority, Reagan's Democrats, and Gingrich's Republican Revolutionaries. These national labels, however, mask as much as they reveal.

The way that Plains voters have merged their historical/regional identity with their racial/producer identity to become "cowboy conservatives" is far more important. They see themselves as the grandchildren of the last generation to carve out a society from the wilderness. Considering themselves the paragons of small-town virtue and the embodiment of America's producer class, they believe that they are the most able defenders of patriotism, Protestantism, the sanctity of the family, capitalism, and democracy. Over the course of the twentieth century, as they focused their political ideology, they found like-minded brethren across the country, especially in the South and West. Together, these voters, who by 1970 willingly called themselves "conservative," took over the Republican Party and by 1980 transformed American politics to reflect their vision of America—the Southern Plains writ large, if you will.[4]

The future of politics on the Southern Plains, therefore, will tie into changes in local identity—political and otherwise. Every indication points to fundamental shifts in the demography, economy, and ecology of the region. Not only is its population aging, but it is also rapidly diminishing. This is most evident in the rapid demise of thousands of small towns: the fount of Southern Plains political ideology. The cities of the region are growing, but the racial and ethnic makeup of cities like Lubbock and Amarillo is undergoing elemental change. Hispanic residents will make up a near majority of every Plains city in the coming decades. Family farms are dying, usually at the expense of agribusiness conglomerates that operate on an economy of scale. And the region's water supply, fed by the massive Ogallala aquifer, is drying up.

These key transformations will produce not only the means, but also the necessity for future generations to challenge the hegemony of Plains conservatism. Concerns over scarce resources and a changing economy will pit corporate farmers against city dwellers over what historian John

Opie describes as the "moral geography" of the Southern Plains. Regional politicians will find themselves caught in the middle. And a changing national party will only exacerbate the situation. Southern Plains conservatives, most of whom chose the Republican Party because it best expressed their particular political ideology, will strain against the collar of a national party seemingly ready to abandon philosophy in exchange for political power.

The Politics of Creating Historical Identity

To understand future changes, it is imperative to explore how Southern Plains political culture developed and how this culture ties directly to political identity. This essay will focus on the Texas Panhandle, the geographic heart of the Southern Plains and the epicenter of its conservatism. This "last frontier" was largely settled by southerners moving westward in the 1890s and midwesterners moving south in the 1910s.[5] During the 1920s, the Panhandle underwent a major transformation; the population exploded, especially in Lubbock, Amarillo, Plainview, and other cities. Agriculture emerged as the bedrock of a rapidly expanding and diversifying regional economy—which included oil, natural gas, banking, ranching, and transportation. Confronting rapid change, local elites—bankers, lawyers, ranchers, merchants, newspaper editors, educators, and others—attempted to commodify a regional identity that reflected their vision of the future and their interpretation of the frontier past.

Led by West Texas State Normal College historian Hattie Anderson, members of the elite organized to capture and control a particular version of Panhandle history. Anderson, most certainly operating from purely intellectual motives, saw a unique possibility to create a historical society among many of the pioneers who had settled the region a generation earlier. Thoroughly versed in the interpretation of American history most often associated with Frederick Jackson Turner, Anderson saw the Panhandle as a region emerging from a frontier stage of development.[6] Anderson's colleagues at West Texas State, also Turnerians, showed unqualified interest in the creation of a historical society.[7] Their vision, the Panhandle-Plains Historical Society (PPHS), founded in 1921, was an unqualified success. Supported by local merchants, bankers, lawyers, ranchers, and farmers, the PPHS was soon publishing an academic journal and making plans to build a museum. In gathering artifacts, organizing meetings, and distributing literature, the PPHS almost singularly focused on the ranching frontier. By 1930, on the eve of the Depression, the PPHS had ninety-two lifetime members and hundreds more who paid annual dues. They even built, with matching funds from the state of Texas, a museum dedicated to the Panhandle frontier. As historians John Bodnar and Michael Kammen remind us, however, the celebration of the past is a highly politicized process. Those who can control the production of memory can use their version of history to advocate a particular message. Those who controlled the PPHS chose very deliberately to celebrate a history that reflects an underlying set of political beliefs.[8]

The celebration of the ranching frontier demonstrates a Turnerian impulse. Like Turner, the founders of the PPHS stared out into a frontierless America. These (often metaphorical) sons and daughters of pioneers felt that the regenerative fountain of democracy might soon give way to a corrupt, class-based, urban America. Glancing askance at the sudden emergence of cities on the Plains, they pledged to "uphold, forever, the honor of the country [their] forefathers wrought out of the wilderness."[9] Hattie Anderson believed that the PPHS had a "sacred duty" to preserve frontier history and pass it on to "the children of the future [so] that we may maintain our distinctive American characteristics and ideals."[10] The celebration of frontier community provided Panhandle Texans with an identity. They saw themselves as the repository of the American frontier experience. They believed themselves to be more democratic, more moral, and most important, more self-sufficient because of their closer ties to their pioneer past.

The immediate future held an ecological and economic nightmare. The Great Depression, the Dust Bowl, and the New Deal would forever alter the Texas Panhandle, and by fundamentally challenging their self-sufficient, rugged identity, force Panhandle Texans to articulate more carefully their political philosophy. Before the 1930s, Panhandle political culture—characterized by an intense localism, antagonism toward the state government in Austin, squabbles over moral issues like temperance and gambling, and small-town rivalries for local capital and resources—depended on a frontier image to set themselves apart. During the Depression, they relied on their shared pioneer identity to justify their acceptance of a sudden and large federal presence. Moreover, community elites demanded that individuals conform to a stifling community ideal—that of a frontier society under siege.

When the stock market reeled then crashed in fall 1929, local citizens seemed nonchalant, maybe even a little smug. Eastern bankers, middlemen, and commodity speculators—the traditional enemies of farmers and ranchers—had finally received their comeuppance. Clyde Warwick, owner and editor of the *Canyon News*, gleefully reported the crash. "Gamblers," who had no interest in community, men who sought solely to line their own pockets, should receive no sympathy from hard-working Plains people, he assured. *Amarillo Globe* editor Gene Howe agreed; he blamed the crash on those who had "engaged in an orgy of gambling . . . [those who had] lost sight of fundamentals."[11] Besides, many thought, why should they worry about the economic problems of the eastern elite? The local economy was on the rebound; prices were up, and farmers enjoyed record harvests. Panhandle investors, who had put most of their money in ventures close to home, insulated the region from the Depression's impact well into the next summer. The inequitable economy of the 1920s, which rewarded urban stock gamblers while southern and western farmers faced a downward spiral in commodity prices, seemed to be righting itself. Just before the fall harvest, the Texas Panhandle had the strongest regional economy in the nation. The good times ended by the first frost. Wheat, cotton, and cattle prices plummeted, and the Great Depression came to the Southern Plains.[12]

Panhandle Texans looked inward to brave the economic crisis. Amarillo newspaper owner/editor Gene Howe took on the Depression like a knight on a quest. He turned his column into a personal help-wanted section. He opened a soup kitchen that served meals "to go" in an effort to prevent the appearance of "bread lines." The meals, he assured, were not charity; Howe asked that his guests pay him back "at the rate of 10 cents a gallon" once they got "back on [their] feet."[13] The West Texas Chamber of Commerce distributed make-work jobs using local, state, and some federal monies. Amarillo newspaper man Henry Ansley took the Depression in stride and published a book, *I Like the Depression*. He explained that economic devastation had brought families and communities closer together. More important, Ansley explained, the Depression forced men and women to return to an older set of values. Across the Plains, with a brand of frontier noblesse oblige, newspaper editors, bank presidents, large farmers and ranchers, ministers, merchants, and other community elites searched for a way to take care of their communities.[14]

In 1932, when Southern Plains voters turned to Franklin Roosevelt and his promise of a "new deal," many assumed that the new president's plan would resemble their ideas about local relief.[15] When New Deal relief programs brought much-needed money and work to the region, most residents were thankful. They saw the money and programs as a temporary measure meant to resuscitate the local economy.

Slowly and steadily, however, Panhandle Texans grew leery of the ubiquitous presence of Washington. Thousands of men and women worked for the Works Progress Administration (WPA) on a seemingly endless variety of projects—many of them easily recognizable as make-work. The Civilian Conservation Corps (CCC) built roads, buildings, and bridges that made Palo Duro Canyon State Park a reality. (But, as historian Dan Flores demonstrates elsewhere in this volume, the dream of a national park faded.) Initially, local merchants cooperated with the regulations set forth by the National Recovery Administration (NRA) and proudly displayed the Blue Eagle in their storefronts. Public Works Administration (PWA) workers built high schools, roads, stadiums, and bridges across the region. Although many feared these programs were creating a generation dependent on federal largesse, most accepted the unyielding reality of economic disaster. Far more frightening were the dozens of farm programs designed not simply to save the region from the ravages of drought, but to transform fundamentally the local agricultural economy and, inadvertently, the local culture.[16]

Like some sort of Biblical punishment straight out of the Old Testament (which many on the Plains believed it was), the Great Depression was accompanied by a relentless drought, plagues of grasshoppers, cruelly hot summers, and staggering dust storms that often left small deserts in their wake.[17] The Dust Bowl devastated the agricultural economy. By the mid-1930s, farmers faced almost certain ruin. Their plowed fields lay exposed to the heat of the summer sun and the force of the spring winds. The resultant wind erosion created mile-long hummocks of sand, and many places on the High Plains resembled the Sahara. The Southern Plains economy, which had begun its downward spiral in the fall of 1930, grew exponentially worse.[18]

The rapid desertification of the Plains frightened New Deal agriculturalists.[19] This region—the breadbasket of the United States—seemed on the edge of ruin. For many eastern-educated experts, the Dust Bowl represented the logical, perhaps inevitable, consequence of a free-market economy that allowed individual landowners to treat land itself as a commodity. They argued publicly and vehemently that America's frontier experience, with its emphasis on individualism, had created this ecological disaster. Many urged that the entire region be returned to federally controlled grasslands. Others, including the influential Great Plains Committee, recommended government-sponsored cooperative programs that would relocate farmers onto government-owned land. Reform-minded New Dealers saw the Dust Bowl as a chance to fundamentally transform the destructive nature of Plains agriculture.[20]

Local farmers and area boosters looked at the New Deal eggheads in their midst with disbelief. They assured themselves that periodic drought was simple environmental reality and promised the government that a few changes in agricultural techniques would offset temporary ecological conditions. The New Dealers' philosophy and plans for the agricultural and economic rehabilitation of the Southern Plains, they cried, did not reflect the values of the region.[21] Perhaps as a coping mechanism, perhaps as a method to place a contemporary crisis into some context, or most probably both, the people on the Southern Plains turned to the myths of their own frontier as a model for overcoming adversity. Their version of the frontier, however, was more complex than the individualistic account that New Dealers used to critique the Plains economy. Panhandle Texans portrayed frontier values as a combination of individualism and community. While individual initiative and freedom from constraints certainly played a large role in describing their own past, the responsibility those individuals had to the community, especially in times of crisis, was equally important.

The frontier, according to this particular version of the story, was less about individuals carving out a place for themselves on the prairie than about building lasting communities in the wilderness. Individuals willing to shoulder the responsibility of community willingly gave up some modicum of freedom to create a permanent settlement. Perhaps most important and interesting in terms of Panhandle political culture is the fact that in this version of the frontier the heroes are not necessarily the stoic ranchers or wandering cowboys, but rather farmers, shopkeepers, teachers, preachers, newspaper editors, and bankers, women and men willing to sacrifice to build a community for their daughters and sons—the very people facing the Dust Bowl and Depression emerge as the champions of the frontier. These city and county elites fought to preserve the political, economic, and social fabric of their communities. The tension between reform-minded New Dealers and locals bent on preserving their identity went beyond disagreements over the future, because it rested upon diametrically opposing interpretations of the past.[22]

Fully versed in the Plains version of the past, Panhandle Congressman Marvin Jones, chairman of the House Agricultural Committee, spent the 1930s simultaneously working to gain relief for farmers and to fend off New Deal reformers.[23] A neo-Populist, Jones, echoing many of his constituents, blamed the Depression on the maldistribution of wealth and the destruction of agricultural purchasing power.[24] Distrusting most forms of collectivism, Jones's New Dealism centered on the idea that those closest to the soil should make decisions on programs, resource allocations, and agricultural priorities. He lamented "the tendency to center all power and authority in Washington."[25] Jones justified relief without reform on the floor of the House:

> Farmers are the last great American individualists . . . they have been hedged about by organized groups on every side. Had there been no legislation in behalf of these groups, had there been no regulations of commerce, had there been no trade barriers and no monopolies, the farmer would have needed no legislation. Standing on dead level with every other citizen, the farmer could have fought his own battles, protected his own interests, and carved his own niche in the affairs of our common country.[26]

Back home, many worried about the long-term impacts of the government relief that Jones fought so hard to obtain. What would become of the independent farmer ideal, they wondered. Respondents to a 1938 Wheeler County survey agreed that they would accept a lower-paying job before working for a federal relief project. As one man declared, everyone with a "backbone" should "buckle down to labor of some kind and make a go of it without the aid of the government." The wife of the local school principal summed up what many privately held: that the New Deal would eventually produce a "generation of shiftless perverse people."[27]

Republican Cowboys

There were many Panhandle Texans who distrusted government policy from the very beginning. Foremost among these was Panhandle rancher, historian, and political activist J. Evetts Haley. The obdurate Haley, who would remain a fixture in conservative politics for the next fifty years, was among the most literate and passionate of Roosevelt's critics in Texas.[28] Haley couched his criticism by pointing out how and why the New Deal countered Texas tradition. In a 1934 *Saturday Evening Post* article, he claimed that the New Deal cattle program was not a legitimate response to an economic crisis, but rather it was a horrifying threat to individualism, liberty, responsibility, the credit system of the range, the superiority of Plains cattle, and western virtue. Cattlemen, he argued, had not only ranched on the Plains for more than a century, but they had also remained the region's reservoir of individualism and independence. "Before the days of the Brain Trust," Haley complained, "no one would have the temerity to suggest how a cowman should manage his affairs." In another broadside published by the West Texas Chamber of Commerce, Haley railed that the New Deal was incompatible with "true Texas traditions" and "the pioneer's love of independence." Haley's essay reached every small-town banker, editor, merchant, feedstore operator, tractor dealer, and large-scale farmer or rancher in the Panhandle.[29]

As the Depression dragged on, other Panhandle Texans agreed with Haley. *The Dalhart Texan* reported in 1934: "Farmers and ranchers of the North Panhandle, sick and disgusted with government bureaucracy, double-crossing and unfilled pledges on a promised work relief program, muttered to themselves that with another rain . . . Mr. Harry Hopkins, Federal Relief Administrator, and all his drouth and relief cohorts could take a running start and go jump in a lake."[30] Ralph G. Bray, the regional public relations director for the Resettlement Administration (RA) didn't wait for rain; he quit his position in protest over the RA-produced film "The Plow That Broke the Plains." Refusing to work for an administration made up of "bubble blowers, dilettantes, and doctrinaires," Bray accused RA head Rexford Tugwell of using the Dust Bowl to create "cheap sentimentalism" in an effort to gain support "for formulating a lot of Utopian policies and radical philosophies." He warned: "At the rate we are going, under temporizing and theorizing leadership, the country will blow away before we can do anything."[31] *Canyon News* owner/editor Clyde Warwick, who had encouraged Panhandle Texans to look to Franklin Roosevelt for national leadership in 1931, evolved into one of the president's harshest critics by the 1940s. He accused Roosevelt of coming under the undue influence of labor leaders, corporate bigwigs, and even the Communist Party. He explained to his readers before the 1944 presidential contest that "a few hand-picked New

Dealers . . . have been able to manipulate the affairs of the nation for the benefit of the labor racketeers and those who are determined to turn this great nation into a Socialistic camp." The New Deal, he argued, had mutated into an ugly form of socialism.[32]

In the throes of ecological disaster and withstanding a bureaucratic assault on their heritage, Panhandle Texans searched for a language to express their ambivalent feelings toward the New Deal. On the one hand, they desperately needed government programs to survive. On the other, the reformers who created or administered many of those programs not only questioned Panhandle Texans' identity as self-sufficient pioneers, they also threatened to take over the local economy. Panhandle Texans took New Dealers' remonstrations about the failure of the frontier ethic as a personal affront. They searched for models to justify temporary government assistance. Some, like neo-Populist Marvin Jones, saw the federal money as reparation for discriminatory government policy toward farmers and ranchers, and they fought for local control of federal resources. After all, they believed, since farmers were the backbone of American democracy, they deserved at least the same level of protection enjoyed by eastern manufacturers and industrialists. Others compared their present situation to a community under siege.

In this scenario, the beleaguered frontier community proved a valuable metaphor. Just as the federal government cleared the Plains of American Indians to protect nascent frontier society, the New Deal sheltered a moral agricultural community from the vagaries of an unstable economic system brought to the edge of collapse by greedy bankers and stock speculators from the East. The inchoate political ideology that emerged from these debates formed the beginnings of a new style of conservatism. Their conservatism, based on a frontier model of community and predicated on a concept of "deserving" Americans, continued to inform Panhandle politics for the next forty years. Panhandle Texans, conservative and liberal, saw themselves as the heart of American democracy; their fused identity as producers and pioneers would have increased resonance as they climbed from Dust Bowl destitution into an emerging middle class.

The rains returned in 1941, and World War II jumpstarted the moribund economy. After the war—fueled by federal money, marked technological improvements, and massive irrigation—the Panhandle's sleepy farm economy became a giant corporate-based agribusiness machine. As geographer John Miller Morris demonstrates in this volume, even family farms have become small corporations. Land, tractors, combines, seed planters, plows, mechanical cotton pickers, and other farm implements, irrigation systems, barns, silos, taxes, homes, and the other accruements of modern agriculture represent millions of dollars in fixed assets, capital, and expenses. Farmers have to hire workers (often on a temporary basis), arrange transportation for their products, and negotiate loans. And after the day's work is finished, farmers stay up late night after night filling out countless government forms to ensure that they receive inexpensive loans, that they are paid for leaving fields fallow, and that they remain eligible for those government programs that will insure profitability for another year. In short, farmers have become modern entrepreneurial capitalists without abandoning their claims to a producer ethic. Instead, as they began to define their political philosophy during the postwar years, they linked anticommunism (and antistatism) with producerism. Between the 1950s and 1970s, conservatives created a local Republican Party that reflected their ideals of producer-conservatism and devoted itself to rewarding "deserving" Americans.[33]

The emergence of the local Republican Party is crucial to understanding the contemporary political culture of the Southern Plains. In the early years of the 1960s, after years of being trapped within the conservative wing of the Democratic Party, a Plains version of the Republican Party emerged as a powerful political force. The new party gave political voice and electoral power to conservatives outside the pre-existing Democratic system. It is important to note that the men and women who created the Panhandle Republican Party were conservatives first; they chose the Republican Party as a vehicle to put their political philosophy into practice. Further, they built their party from scratch so it was not as diluted by compromise as many other conservative cells of the GOP. Their identity as conservatives and Republicans was directly tied to their identity as Panhandle Texans.

Those who built the local GOP worked from the grassroots. They were as devoted to electing county chairmen as they were to supporting a particular gubernatorial, senatorial, or presidential candidate. Grassroots mobilizing first meant finding like-minded (conservative) people. Then, these conservatives had to articulate exactly why they needed to put in the time and effort—not just to vote, but to serve as precinct captains, to man phone drives, to organize fund raisers, and to work on local campaigns. As Republican organizer Richard Brooks put it: "We wanted very much to establish a two-party system in the state . . . quite apart from who the candidate might be at any given moment in any given place. We worked hard to get that done at the local level."[34]

The women and men who built the GOP drew from overlapping sources of support. First and foremost was an organized and angry group of anticommunists who looked with horror at the fluid nature of world politics, an unsteady social structure at home, and a government seemingly unwilling to stem the tide of rapid change. They often vented their outrage through local chapters of the John Birch Society (JBS), which was extremely popular. Amarilloans elected two different Bircher mayors during the 1960s. JBS billboards ("Impeach Earl Warren!" and "Get U.S. out of the United Nations!") graced the Panhandle skyline for decades.[35] From this base, conservatives brought together several different groups. They encouraged a small, unorganized cadre of "presidential" Republicans who had been in the area (mostly in the northern Panhandle) since the 1910s—usually the sons and daughters of Midwestern settlers—to support a local ticket. As the Democratic Party moved slightly to the left in the postwar years, many conservative Democrats grew angry enough to seek out local alternatives and looked toward this new party. And a new generation of voters, who were children during the Depression and had no particular allegiance to the Democratic Party, had grown into the middle or upper-middle class. These voters based their politics on their pocketbooks and were receptive toward the conservative Republican message. *Tulia Herald* editor H. M. Baggarly scolded these new Republicans:

> [His] grandfather lost his shirt during the depression of the thirties. His father took advantage of the New Deal reforms and under the liberal government we have had for the last 30 years has wound up on easy street. Both were Democrats. Now this young man is attending college with a fat check from home coming every week, drives a convertible, and lives like a millionaire's son . . . and is the president of the Young Republicans at his college! Had the Republicans been in the saddle the past 30 years and given us the kind of government this man now preaches, he probably would be hoeing cotton on a sharecropper farm somewhere, praying for a Democratic victory.[36]

Building their party around a set of conservative principles associated in the 1950s with Ohio Senator Robert Taft and in the 1960s with Arizona Senator Barry Goldwater (and eventually with California governor Ronald Reagan), Panhandle Republicans were primarily concerned with issues of fighting Communism and federal deficit spending, reducing the national debt, protecting American interests abroad, and reducing the centralization of government.

Wisely, the leaders of the nascent Republican Party focused their early efforts on local, nonpartisan elections. Three early victories demonstrated their organizational aptitude and the receptiveness of their neighbors to a conservative message. In 1961, a young successful real-estate builder named Jack Seale, an admitted member of the John Birch Society, won the mayor's race in Amarillo.[37] Perhaps most impressive was the election of Ken Kohler, a Republican, to the Texas Legislature. When J. Edgar Wilson, a Democrat who had been elected in 1960, died after the 1961 session (the Texas Legislature meets only every other year) and could not return for a special session, the Amarillo/Canyon district had no representative. Young Republicans put together a campaign. They quickly named precinct chairs, ward captains, and county commissioners, organized a canvassing team, and held fund-raisers to buy ad time on local television and radio stations. In short, they put together a political party. Their efforts proved successful; Kohler won the election with a small plurality over Wilson's widow.[38] Panhandle Republicans also proved valuable in electing the first Republican senator from Texas in the twentieth century. Running in a special election to fill Lyndon Johnson's vacated seat in the United State Senate (in 1960, Johnson ran for both vice president and for re-election to the Senate and won both races), conservative John Tower put together one of the best campaigns in modern Texas politics. Tower eked out a close statewide victory but overwhelmed his opponents in the Panhandle. Demonstrating clearly the shift in the political climate and the hard work of local Republicans, just seven months after the national election Tower won 54 percent of the Panhandle votes and took nineteen counties, including Randall, Potter, and Lubbock—the largest counties in the region.[39]

Panhandle Republicans' early efforts primed them for what they hoped would be their big moment—the 1964 presidential campaign. The nomination of conservative hero Barry Goldwater infused their party with new recruits and enthusiasm. As Goldwater himself once noted, Texas provided the best place "in the nation to study . . . the GOP grass roots."[40] Goldwater's message resonated on the Plains. His ideas offered a clear alternative to the liberal policies that many believed were ruining the nation. When he stressed the importance of moral values and community, Panhandle Texans cheered. Goldwater's philosophy, summed up in *The Conscience of a Conservative* (1960), described a new brand of political conservatism. It was more than a simple anticommunist tirade or a censure of liberalism; it was an upbeat delineation of the value of individualism and the importance of tradition. His message managed to stress a brand of laissez-faire capitalism that the small-town merchant, teacher, the middle-class farming family, the newspaper editor, and bank president could support. This was exactly the same argument that conservatives on the Southern Plains had made for thirty years. Richard Brooks explained: "[*Conscience of a Conservative*] was a rallying point." Southern Plains conservatives, like Goldwater, he said, "should be concerned about the welfare of other people; to help make life better for them in any way possible, but a strong central government with a Socialist approach was not the right answer."[41]

Goldwater's maverick persona also proved popular in the Panhandle; his image as a rugged modern westerner tied in perfectly with their brand of cowboy conservatism. The grandson of Arizona pioneers, Goldwater flew jets, rode rapids, and collected western Americana. At certain public appearances, he wore cowboy boots, a cowboy hat, and a bolo tie. His photographs of the American West appeared regularly in the pages of *Arizona Highways*. He was the near-perfect package to deliver the message of conservatism to those Panhandle Texans who were uninterested in the paranoid fantasies, gloom and doom prophecies, and the authoritarianism of the John Birch Society.

Goldwater's most important contribution, however, was unhinging the word *conservative* from its association with wealthy easterners and attaching it to the West. Goldwater's conservatism, with all its frontier trappings, gave the people of the Southern Plains something positive to support. *Conservatism*, as a word, was still flexible enough to incorporate a variety of meanings. It was more than a simple economic philosophy or anticommunist fervor. It came to mean an adherence to small-town values (especially local attitudes toward morality), middle-class or petite bourgeois sensibility, the producer ethic, whiteness, and Protestantism. Goldwater's campaign tapped into this wellspring of political attitudes.[42] Between 1960 and 1972, more and more people began calling themselves conservative. In October 1964, 38 percent of Panhandle Texans used the label to describe their politics. A similar poll taken in 1968 showed an increase to 53 percent. By 1970, 82 percent considered themselves conservative.[43]

Since 1964, voters on the Southern Plains have rapidly converted their party allegiances to the Republican Party. Importantly, however, conservatism is an ideology and the Republican Party is an organization. The fundamental challenge for Southern Plains conservatives will be to overcome what will become an increasing distance from the national Republican Party. As the last few national elections have shown, the American electorate has divided fairly evenly along partisan lines. Consequently, national candidates and platforms have become less blatantly ideological. Each must fight for the votes of the mysterious middle—those voters whose primary concerns seem to change with the season: education, social security, the national debt, drugs, violence, health insurance, the environment, energy. In an era of made-for-television candidates, bumper-sticker political philosophy, and carefully edited ten-second platforms, political ideologies are cumbersome and not always beneficial to national parties. But on the Southern Plains, conservatives discovered their ideology first and created their Republican Party second. This situation can only lead to conflict between a national party seeking that magic 3 or 4 percent advantage and ideological purists seeking a vehicle to spread their convictions.

The Politics of Whiteness

Even as the local and national Republican parties grow distant from one another, changing demographics and rapid urbanization will revitalize the Democratic Party. In part, this will be based on a changing racial or ethnic composition of Panhandle voters. In the 1950s and 1960s, as the GOP grew in influence on the Southern Plains, the region was characterized by a small-town or suburban, white, middle-class homogeneity. The local GOP—and in many ways the national party—have crafted their messages to appeal to just such a constituency. Since the 1960s, however, the Panhandle has changed and will continue to change in crucial ways. First, although still overwhelmingly white at the beginning of the twenty-first century, the ethnic and racial demography has begun a fundamental shift. The white population is aging (already the oldest in Texas), and the hundreds of small towns in the Panhandle are losing population, fast. The region's two major cities, Amarillo and Lubbock, will undergo massive transformations over the next few decades. Amarillo, for example, is expected to almost double in population. Lubbock, using the same scenario (the growth patterns that emerged between 1980–1990), will grow very little, only about 3 percent. More important, the racial and ethnic composition of these cities will change drastically. In 1990, Amarillo's population was 80 percent white (down from 90 percent just twenty years earlier). The city had a 5 percent African American population and a Hispanic population of 13 percent. In 2030, the white population will represent only 44 percent, the African American population will remain at 5 percent, the Hispanic population will explode to 45 percent. Lubbock will experience a similar transformation. The white population—68 percent in 1990—will drop to 42 percent, the African American population will remain at 7 percent, and the Hispanic population will double from 23 percent to 46 percent.[44]

These are not sudden trends; the racial demography of these cities has been slowly changing since the 1950s. And it has been impacting the politics of the region for at least that long. The resultant racial and ethnic changes will have a huge impact on local political culture and create an opening for a resurgent, urban-focused, and racially diverse Democratic Party. I am not arguing that voters will join the Democratic Party simply because of their racial or ethnic identity. I am arguing, however, that politicians can no longer ignore or exploit race as a political issue. As historian Yolanda Romero reminds us in the essay that follows, for most of the twentieth century, Southern Plains politics has been dominated, often blatantly, by a struggle to preserve the racial status quo. From the beginning, land agents who recruited midwesterners and southerners to settle the region sought white bourgeois farmers who had the experience and responsibility to establish the agricultural potential of the Southern Plains and the capital for local investment. Hoping to re-create the brand of homogenous communities that characterized much of the Northern Plains, land agents shared with their clients a particular vision of what their new neighbors should look like, how they should act, what type of church they should attend, and what they should do for a living. Land agents welcomed certain ethnic communities and forbade others. Whole communities of Poles, Swedes, and Norwegians formed instant settlements, while African Americans, Italians, Italian Americans, and Hispanics were rarely allowed to purchase land.[45]

Land agents particularly discriminated against African Americans. An early Lubbock land company brochure invited people to come and settle where there were "no negroes and where you do not have to keep the door of your corn-crib and smokehouse locked, where you can leave

your home and remain away for weeks at a time without fear of returning to find that a horrifying tragedy has befallen your loved ones in your
absence." The ad welcomed, however, successful "liberal" white farmers. It was clear exactly who the agents sought for neighbors, as well as
what sort of behavior would not be tolerated in the young communities.
Southern racism merged with Midwest bourgeois culture.[46]

Most people of color on the Southern Plains lived in the urban centers of Amarillo and Lubbock, both tightly segregated cities. In Amarillo,
African Americans lived in the "flats" and Hispanics lived on the city's
"east side." Residents faced a ninety-dollar fine if found in the "wrong"
part of town. City leaders in early Lubbock tried to keep out African
Americans altogether. A 1909 newspaper editorial warned that "Negroes"
spread like "Johnson grass" and argued for rigid exclusion laws. By
1923, city ordinances segregated African Americans within specific
neighborhoods. Fifty years later, Amarillo and Lubbock remained two
of the most residentially segregated cities in America.[47]

On most of the Southern Plains, however, the lack of significant
numbers of people of color often masked racial animosity. As Romero
argues, racial politics can thrive in a predominantly "white" region.
Even as the civil rights movement challenged the institutions of white
supremacy across the South and Texas, the people of the Southern
Plains rarely resorted to violence or the brand of fire-eating malice that
characterized their southern neighbors. They faced no sudden influx of
minorities into schools, restaurants, movie houses, or public parks. In
fact, laws requiring separate schools for black and white students presented a financial burden for local taxpayers.[48] Obviously, a large percentage of those on the Southern Plains were not more enlightened or
tolerant than Texans generally. Their support for civil rights stemmed
from their insulation. De facto segregation and the overwhelming majority of whites in the region—most counties had black populations of less
than 5 percent—enforced a degree of white hegemony that no segregation statutes could match. Even as NAACP chapters in Lubbock and
Amarillo pushed for local changes, their activities in those cities simply
did not affect whites scattered over the rest of the region.

An emerging culture of African American protest in the region
would not only soon challenge the racial structure of the Panhandle, but
it would also merge race with political identity for many voters. In
Canyon, Texas, black students protesting at West Texas State University
(WT) shocked local whites. The "local" college where parents sent their

children had seemed safe from the unsavory influences that seemed to characterize campuses across the country. In 1967 and 1968, black students participated in a march down Canyon's main street in honor of the recently slain Martin Luther King; protested against a fraternity's use of Confederate symbols in university-sanctioned events; elected a black homecoming queen; and demanded the desegregation of the faculty, a Black Student Union, and black studies courses. Before the college protests, whites had rarely considered the politics of their whiteness or pondered their racial identity. They maintained the delusion that *their* "negroes," unlike those sitting in at diners or marching across the South or rioting in cities, were content.[49] After the WT campus protests, whites on the Southern Plains, like many urban ethnics in the Midwest or Northeast, suddenly had to reconfigure their definition of race relations. And, as historian Dan T. Carter persuasively argues in his award-winning biography of George Wallace, racial conservatism escaped the confines of Dixie.

For many, the national Democratic Party was on the wrong side of the civil rights issue. In 1968, former Alabama Governor George Wallace, running a rattletrap segregationist, third-party presidential campaign, won almost 22 percent of Panhandle votes. As late as October, Wallace was clearly a threat to Nixon in the region, regularly polling 45 percent of the vote. In important ways, Wallace's political message blended perfectly with the emerging political ideology of the Southern Plains—a militant defense of community and community values against outside forces. Supporting, even if not voting for, ex-Democrat Wallace marked an important step for a significant segment of Panhandle voters. In his campaign rhetoric, Wallace demonstrated a clear relationship between conservatism and race.[50]

School busing provided an ideal outlet for the articulation of this new form of racial politics. Whites on the Southern Plains consistently disapproved of any form of busing. In 1972, 91 percent of those polled in the Panhandle were anti-busing. Three years later, when Congressman George Mahon sent out a sample ballot asking his constituents if they would support a constitutional amendment that would prevent forced busing, 100 percent of respondents reacted affirmatively. Their comments reveal an understanding of post–Civil Rights movement racial politics. Most respondents avoided racist diatribes and focused on the logistical "foolishness" of busing. The responses for favoring the proposed amendment were varied. People stated that busing was "stupid to begin with"; it cost too much in gas and oil, it added another layer of bureaucracy to the local school system, and it detracted from the sanctity of the "neighborhood school."[51] In Plainview, local citizens rallied to form an organization, Concerned Citizens against Forced Busing. Plainview native and former gubernatorial candidate Marshall Formby argued that busing "could have unmanageable social consequences." Although these types of reassurances proved common in areas where busing programs disrupted the existing school and social systems, Hale County had a black population of less than 5 percent.[52]

In Amarillo, local African Americans endured the difficulties of busing. City officials gerrymandered school districts to protect all-white Amarillo High School and closed all-black Carver High School. This process isolated the growing Hispanic population within the newly built Caprock High School. Most African American students were then bused to Tascosa High School, in a working-class neighborhood. Black students and their parents were completely dissatisfied with the arrangement. One unidentified man claimed that the students were "expected to be white." One woman later recalled the level of ignorance she witnessed among her white classmates. "A lot of kids would walk up to you and want to feel your hair . . .and they would touch it and say I wish my hair could do that. They would rub you to see if the color would come off."[53]

Tascosa High School was rough. Its mascot was the "Rebel," "Dixie" was the unofficial school song, and each year students elected a "Southern Belle" and flew the Confederate battle flag at sporting events. As black students walked down the halls, they heard muttered epithets and threats and felt cold stares on their backs. In the bathroom they saw "Get a Nigger" and "Bus them back to Africa" scrawled on the stalls. The principal expected trouble at every turn and kept an unusually close eye on black students. He even labeled "rakes," combs used by black students on their Afros, as weapons and forbade their use. Violence broke out on several occasions between white and black students. Eventually, Amarillo police officers were assigned to patrol the school.[54]

A local black minister, V. P. Perry, explained the change in white attitudes between the 1950s and 1970s:

> Whites turned from the Red Herring to the Black scare. Black movements and organizations were suspect. Even the music peculiar to black people was viewed as a Communist plot to

degenerate white youths. Integration was a dirty word. Whites saw it as a Red conspiracy to change the balance of White power to Black domination. Fear replaced reason. Hate supplanted love. Benign neglect led to polarization.[55]

The politics of race had come to the Southern Plains. For the next thirty years, Southern Plains politicians used a new language to express the not-always latent racism of constituents. Issues of affirmative action; redistricting congressional districts, school boundaries, and voting precincts; immigration restriction; welfare; crime and the criminal justice system; and education could all be used in a not-so-subtle gambit at white votes. In the years to come, the racial politics on the Southern Plains will, by necessity, change. As the region becomes less homogenous and more urban, the good-old-boy politics of protecting the all-white small-town community will, to be blunt, not work. City and county officials in Lubbock and Potter counties, realizing this, have recently practiced a new more racially sensitive brand of politics. City commissions of both places are much more racially diverse than they were even a decade ago. And these changes will only intensify in the future as the changing racial demography and growing urbanization of the Southern Plains fundamentally alter the political culture of the region. For most of the twentieth century, the Amarillo and Lubbock economies were largely an extension of surrounding agricultural and oil industries. Consequently, these cities reflected the cultural and political attitudes of their rural neighbors. City, state, and national politicians usually resolved urban-rural conflicts in favor of agricultural interests. For example, in the 1950s the Mexican government forbade Lubbock-area farmers from using Mexican nationals as farm workers in the bracero program because local restaurateurs, landlords, and beauty shop owners had treated the braceros so poorly. The agricultural community, desperate for the labor, pressured city government officials, their representatives in the state legislature, and even Congressman George Mahon to intervene on their behalf and not only to lift the ban, but also to force local business owners to treat the workers with more respect.

In the future, savvy Panhandle politicians will recognize that only as a Democrat will an office seeker have the maneuverability to gain the campaign money from agribusiness and the votes from urban dwellers. Democrats do not have to appeal to social conservatives determined to maintain the illusion of lily-white, small-town communities, nor to economic ideologues resolved to limit federal involvement on the Plains. As representatives of a practically "new" or at least a resurrected party, these Democrats will have the freedom to make appeals to the federal government for the massive expenditures needed to preserve the Panhandle's agricultural economy and the autonomy to actively seek out urban voters with a different agenda. Moreover, a growing distance between local conservatives—who claim ideological purity, and yet can justify federal intervention in the name of community—and a national party less committed to ideology will weaken the Republican hold on the Southern Plains. The way is then cleared for a politician not tied to the dominant party to appeal to voters who understand that the political structures created during the twentieth century will not hold up in a drastically different Southern Plains.

So much of the political ideology of the Southern Plains relies on a particular identity; Panhandle Texans have seen themselves as the last of a breed. As pioneers (or at least the descendants of the last pioneers), they consider themselves responsible for upholding a mythic code of self-reliance, individuality, preservers of a rough-hewn sense of community. Whenever this identity has come under fire, especially from "outside" forces, residents have responded by further crafting, defining, and articulating their particular political code. They continue to defend the myth that they live in communities of white, small-town, Protestant, yeoman farmers even as the economy is ruled by huge agribusiness conglomerates, the region becomes more urban with every passing year, and the racial and ethnic dynamics are in the midst of monumental change. There should be no question that the myth of cowboy communities will continue on the Southern Plains. In the coming decades, however, a new political identity is sure to emerge, one more urban, Catholic, working-class with enough votes to disrupt the conservative hegemonic control of the region.[56]

Notes

1. I would like to thank Dan Flores, Jack Morris, Diana Olien, John Opie, Fred Rathjen, Yolanda Romero, Elliott West, and Connie Woodhouse for their perceptive comments and suggestions on an earlier draft of this essay. I would also like to thank Andrea Boardman and David Weber for their efforts in putting together the Future of the Southern Plains Symposium that brought together this group of scholars to discuss the future of the region that

we all have grown to love. I reserve special thanks for Sherry Smith for her tireless efforts in organizing the conference, for shepherding a very diverse group of scholars, for her tremendous efforts in editing this essay, and for helping to create a book that should prove valuable to scholars of Texas, the Plains, and the West for years to come.

2. Postwar conservative politics is the subject of several recent monographs and is undergoing a significant interpretive shift. For more on the historiography of conservatism, see Alan Brinkley, "The Problem of American Conservatism," *American Historical Review* 99 (April 1994): 409–29; Michael Kazin, "The Grass-Roots Right: New Histories of U.S. Conservatism in the Twentieth Century," *American Historical Review* 97 (February 1992): 136–55; Leonard J. Moore, "Good Old-Fashioned New Social History and the Twentieth-Century American Right," *Reviews in American History* 24 (December 1996): 555–73. See also John A. Andrew, *The Other Side of the Sixties: Young Americans for Freedom and the Rise of Conservative Politics* (New Brunswick, N.J.: Rutgers University Press, 1997); Sidney Blumenthal, *The Rise of the Counter-Establishment: From Conservative Ideology to Political Power* (New York: N.Y. Times Books, 1986); Mary C. Brennan, *Turning Right in the Sixties: The Conservative Capture of the GOP* (Chapel Hill: University of North Carolina Press, 1995); Matthew Dallek, *The Right Moment: Ronald Reagan's First Victory and the Decisive Turning Point in American Politics* (New York: Free Press, 2001); Sara Rose Diamond, *Roads to Dominion: Right-wing Movements and Political Power in the United States* (New York: Guilford Press, 1995); David Farber and Jeff Roche, eds., *The Conservative Sixties* (New York: Peter Lang, 2003); Robert Alan Goldberg, *Barry Goldwater* (New Haven: Yale University Press, 1995); Jerome Himmelstein, *To the Right: The Transformation of American Conservatism* (Berkeley: University of California Press, 1990); Godfrey Hodgson, *The World Turned Right Side Up: A History of the Conservative Ascendancy in America* (Boston: Houghtin Mifflin, 1996); Rebecca E. Klatch, *Women of the New Right* (Philadelphia: Temple University Press, 1987) and *A Generation Divided: The New Left, the New Right, and the 1960s* (Berkeley: University of California Press, 1999); Lisa McGirr, *Suburban Warriors: The Origins of the New American Right* (Princeton: Princeton University Press, 2001); Rick Perlstein, *Before the Storm: Barry Goldwater and the Unmaking of the American Consensus* (New York: Hill and Wang, 2001); Jeff Roche, "Cowboy Conservatism: Texas Panhandle Politics, 1933–1972" (Ph.D. dissertation, University of New Mexico, 2001); Greg Schneider, *Cadres for Conservatism: Young Americans for Freedom and the Rise of the Contemporary Right* (New York: New York University Press, 1999); Jonathan M. Schoenwald, *A Time for Choosing: The Rise of Modern American Conservatism* (New York: Oxford University Press, 2001); and Kurt Schuparra, *Triumph of the Right: The Rise of the California Conservative Movement, 1945–1966* (Armonk, N.Y.: M .E. Sharpe, 1998).

3. In this essay, I use the term "political culture" to describe the process

people use to "articulate, negotiate, implement, and enforce the competing claims they make upon one another and upon the whole." The discourses and symbolism through which citizens make claims upon one another offer legitimacy and/or authority to individuals, groups, interests, or institutions. See Keith Baker, *Inventing the French Revolution: Essays on French Political Culture in the Eighteenth Century* (New York: Cambridge University Press, 1990), 4. See also Roger Chartier, "Text, Symbols, and Frenchness," *Journal of Modern History* 57 (1985): 682–95. For a concise discussion on the evolution of cultural history, see Lynn Hunt, "Introduction," in *The New Cultural History* (Berkeley: University of California Press, 1989).

4. In important ways, the people of the Southern Plains exhibit the cultural characteristics described as "plain-folk Americanism" by historian James N. Gregory in his significant interpretation of "Okie" culture in California, *American Exodus: The Dust Bowl Migration and Okie Culture in California* (New York: Oxford University Press, 1989). See also Dan Morgan, *Rising in the West: The True Story of an "Okie" Family from the Great Depression through the Reagan Years* (New York: Knopf, 1992).

5. For more on regional political cultures, see Daniel J. Elazar, "Political Culture on the Plains," *Western Historical Quarterly* 11 (July 1980): 261–83; Daniel Elazar, ed., *American Federalism: A View from the States* (New York: Harper & Row, 1984).

6. In the 1920s, Frederick Jackson Turner's interpretation of the American part dominated American historiography. In his famous essay "The Significance of the Frontier in American History," Turner identified sequential stages of settlement along the American frontier: Indian traders, ranchers, farmers, and finally urban and industrial civilization. Frederick Jackson Turner, "The Significance of the Frontier in American History," reprinted in *History, Frontier, and Section: Three Essays*, ed. Martin Ridge (Albuquerque: University of New Mexico Press, 1993). See also Hattie Mabel Anderson, "A Study in Frontier Democracy: The Social and Economic Bases of the Rise of the Jackson Group in Missouri, 1815–1828," *Missouri Historical Review* 30 (April 1938 to April 1940).

7. Duane F. Guy, "The Panhandle-Plains Historical Society: The Formative Years, 1921–1940," *Panhandle-Plains Historical Review* 69 (1996): 1–24.

8. See John Bodnar, *Remaking America: Public Memory, Commemoration, and Patriotism in the Twentieth Century* (Princeton: Princeton University Press, 1992); Michael Kammen, *Mystic Chords of Memory: The Transformation of Tradition in American Culture* (New York: Knopf, 1991); and David Lowenthal, *The Heritage Crusade and the Spoils of History* (New York: Cambridge University Press, 1998).

9. Guy, "The Panhandle-Plains Historical Society," 5–7. Guy also notes the Turnerian influence on the early society.

10. Hattie Anderson to State Senator W. R. Bledsoe, in Guy, "The Panhandle-Plains Historical Society," 5–6.

11. *Canyon News,* 17 and 31 October 1929; David L. Nail, *One Short Sleep Past: A Profile of Amarillo in the Thirties* (Canyon, Tex.: Staked Plains Press, 1973), 13–14, 68; Gordon Ruthardt, interview by Darren G. Ruthardt, 18 April 1990, transcript, Panhandle Plains Historical Museum (PPHM). Feelings of superiority over easterners after the crash were not limited to the Texas Panhandle; Kansas newspaper editors echoed many of these themes. See Craig Miner, *Harvesting the High Plains: John Kriss and the Business of Wheat Farming, 1920–1950* (Lawrence: University Press of Kansas, 1998), 65; and Donald Worster, *Dust Bowl: The Southern Plains in the 1930s* (New York: Oxford University Press, 1979), 10, 119–20.

12. Garry Nall, "Dust Bowl Days: Panhandle Farming in the 1930's," *Panhandle-Plains Historical Review* 48 (1975): 42.

13. Nail, *One Short Sleep Past*, 50–51. See also Donald W. Whisenhunt, "The Texas Attitude toward Relief, 1929–1933," *Panhandle-Plains Historical Review* 46 (1973): 94–111.

14. Henry Ansley, *I Like the Depression* (Indianapolis: Bobbs-Merrill, 1932).

15. See, for example, Clyde Warwick's editorial praising Roosevelt's plans for local control for New York State. *Canyon News,* 5 February 1931.

16. *Amarillo Globe,* 26 February 1936; WPA Collection, PPHM; Ruby Winona Adams, "Social Behavior in a Drought-Stricken Texas Panhandle Community" (Master's Thesis, University of Texas, 1939), 56. I would like to thank Anna Summus for her help in compiling these WPA statistics. See also A. A. Meredith (WPA Administrator) to Judge C. C. Bishop, 25 March 1940, WPA Collection; A. A. Meredith to Clyde Warwick, 13 July 1942, Warwick Papers, PPHM; Nail, *One Short Sleep Past*, passim.

17. For an interesting interpretation of religion in the Dust Bowl, see Brad Lookingbill, "'A God-forsaken Place': Folk Eschatology and the Dust Bowl," *Great Plains Quarterly* 14 (Fall 1994): 273–86.

18. See *Ochiltree County Herald,* 13 September 1934, which provides a month-to-month, year-to-year chart of rainfall. For example, this northern Panhandle County received more than twenty inches of rain from 1926 to 1929. For the next four years, the county averaged only 17 inches of rain, most of which fell within a short period, limiting its agricultural benefits. See also Nall, "Dust Bowl Days," 42–63; Jerry T. Barton, "The Economic Development of the Texas Panhandle" (Master's Thesis, North Texas State College, 1950), 74–82; Charles E. Ritchie, interview by Kathryn Ritchie, 22 April 1933, transcript, PPHM; Mr. and Mrs. H. B. Urban, interview by Diane Urban, 15 June 1974, transcript, PPHM. See also Richard Ashby, "Town Farming in the Great Plains," *Rural Sociology* 4 (December 1941): 341–43. For more on the culture that spawned the Dust Bowl, see Worster, *Dust Bowl,* 164–77; John C. Hudson, "Who Was 'Forest Man'? Sources of Migration to the Plains," *Great Plains Quarterly* 6 (Spring 1986): 80–82; William Lockertz, "The Dust Bowl: Its Relevance to Contemporary Environmental Problems," in *The Great Plains: Perspectives and Prospects,* ed..

Marlin P. Lawson and Maurice E. Baker (Lincoln: University of Nebraska Press, 1981).

19. A 1936 WPA survey of Dust Bowl conditions described twenty-three of the twenty-six Panhandle counties as "very severe." Worster, *Dust Bowl*, 35; "Area Affected by Wind Erosion," Cowan Papers, file 3, PPHM.

20. For more on these arguments, see the penetrating analysis of New Deal frontier thought in David M. Wrobel, *The End of American Exceptionalism: Frontier Anxiety from the Old West to the New Deal* (Lawrence: University Press of Kansas, 1993), 122–36. See also Alan Brinkley, *Liberalism and Its Discontents* (Cambridge: Harvard University Press, 1999), 51.

21. These debates have continued in the historiography of the Dust Bowl. The three major schools of Dust Bowl historiography reflect the debates of the 1930s. Led by Donald Worster, the environmental/Marxist school stresses the undue demands that capitalist wheat farming placed on the arid Plains. Originally argued by James Malin in the 1930s and most recently by Paul Bonnifield, the cyclical/environmental school argues that the periodic drought is common on the Plains and that interference by the government only hinders farmers' normal agricultural adjustment learning curve. A third school, most recently led by R. Douglas Hurt, strives to remain neutral in the argument over capitalism and government involvement by emphasizing the unique conditions on the Plains and the ways that farmers have attempted to live within their environment. Brad D. Lookingbill has begun to expand our understanding of the Dust Bowl. In his *Dust Bowl U.S.A.: Depression America and the Ecological Imagination, 1929–1941* (Athens: Ohio University Press, 2001), he skillfully deconstructs the language used to describe the region and the era. For more on the historiography of the Dust Bowl, see Harry C. McDean, "Dust Bowl Historiography," *Great Plains Quarterly* 6 (Spring 1986): 117–26. Jay H. Buckley has carefully constructed an updated (1999) bibliography of Dust Bowl historiography in John R. Wunder, Frances W. Kaye, and Vernon Carstensen, eds., *Americans View Their Dust Bowl Experience* (Niwot: University Press of Colorado, 1999), 385–408.

22. For more on traditionalist challenges to New Deal thought, see Wrobel, *American Exceptionalism*, 136–42; Herbert Hoover, *The Challenge to Liberty* (New York: Charles Scribner's Sons, 1934); Twelve Southerners, *I'll Take My Stand: The South and the Agrarian Tradition* (New York: Harper and Brothers, 1930). See also Daniel Joseph Singal, *The War Within: From Victorian to Modernist Thought in the South, 1919–1945* (Chapel Hill: University of North Carolina Press, 1982), especially 198–231; George B. Tindall, *The Emergence of the New South, 1913–1945* (Baton Rouge: Louisiana State University Press, 1967), 576–649.

23. Working closely, but not always in agreement with Henry Wallace, Rexford Tugwell, Harold Ickes, and other reformers in the Roosevelt administration, Jones, between 1933 and 1941, helped draft and pass the Agricultural Adjustment Acts of 1933 and 1938. He also helped to create the Farm Credit

Administration and was instrumental in having cattle included as a basic commodity under the AAA. He penned legislation to provide loans so that farmers could save their farms and enabled tenants to borrow money and become landowners. He also helped establish federal soil conservation measures to rescue farmers in the Dust Bowl.

24. Marvin Jones, *Marvin Jones Memoirs*, ed. Joseph M. Ray (El Paso: Texas Western Press, 1973), 1–3, 22–30, 88–145. Irvin M. May, Jr., *Marvin Jones: The Public Life of an Agrarian Advocate* (College Station: Texas A & M University Press, 1980), 79–100, passim. See also David E. Hamilton, *From New Day to New Deal: American Farm Policy from Hoover to Roosevelt, 1928–1933* (Chapel Hill: University of North Carolina Press, 1991), 198, 221, 231–33; *Amarillo Globe,* 5 September 1971; Marvin Jones, interview by David Murrah, 1 August 1972, PPHM.

25. Jones, *Memoirs,* 92.

26. Congressional Record, 74th Congress, 1st Session, vol. 79, part 13, 14785; May, *Marvin Jones,* 144. Jones quoted in *Amarillo Globe,* 12 November 1933.

27. Adams, "Social Behavior," 34, 62, 64, 70–79. See also William W. Bremer, "Along the 'American Way': The New Deal's Work Relief for the Unemployed," *Journal of American History* 62 (December 1975): 636–52, for the psychological motivations behind many New Deal work programs.

28. Details about Haley's life and times are often obscured by myth and polemic—both in favor of Haley's political beliefs and against them. The only full-length biography of Haley is Bill Modisett, *J. Evetts Haley: A True Texas Legend* (Midland, Tex.: Staked Plains Press, 1996), a highly sympathetic account.

29. J. Evetts Haley, "Cow Business and Monkey Business," *Saturday Evening Post,* 8 December 1934; Haley, "Texas Control of Texas Soil," *West Texas Today* (July 1936): 14–16. See also Lookingbill, *Dust Bowl USA,* 119–20. In 1936, in the depths of the Depression, Haley had few public allies in the Panhandle. He made quite a few friends among the wealthier bankers, oil men, and other conservatives around Texas who despised Roosevelt and the New Deal. Historian George Norris Green has described these men and their rise to political power in his *The Establishment in Texas Politics.* Men like Haley, however, play a minor role in Green's work; he is primarily concerned with explaining how the movers and shakers in Dallas and Houston have manipulated the populace into supporting a conservative political agenda. It is precisely men like Haley that I would contend have played a monumental role in helping Texans, especially Panhandle Texans, articulate longstanding political beliefs. Green, *The Establishment in Texas Politics: The Primitive Years, 1938–1957* (Westport, Conn.: Greenwood Press, 1979), 30.

30. *Amarillo Globe,* 2 July 1936; "AAA Programs in Panhandle," Wilson Cowan Collection, PPHM; Worster, *Dust Bowl,* 40; John Temple Graves, "The South, Uneasy for Its Future, Picks Cotton," *New York Times Magazine,*

3 October 1937. *Dalhart Texan* quoted in John C. Dawson, *High Plains Yesterdays: From XIT Days through Drought and Depression* (Austin: Eakins Press, 1985), 243. See also C. Roger Lambert, "Dust, Farmers, and the Federal Government," in *Hard Times in Oklahoma: The Depression Years*, ed. Kenneth E. Hendrickson, Jr. (Oklahoma City: Oklahoma Historical Society, 1983), for an overview of New Deal programs in the Oklahoma Panhandle Dust Bowl.

31. *Amarillo Globe*, 19 May 1936.

32. *Canyon News*, 12 October 1944. For more on Pare Lorentz and *Plow*, see Vernon Carstensen, "'The Plow That Broke the Plains': Film Legacy of the Great Depression," in *Americans View Their Dust Bowl Experience*, ed. Wunder, Kaye, and Carstensen, 303–19.

33. This is largely the thesis of Michael Kazin's important book on conservatism and populist language. Kazin, *The Populist Persuasion: An American History* (Ithaca, N.Y.: Cornell University Press, 1998), especially 165–93, 222–66.

34. Richard Brooks, interview with author, 17 July 2000.

35. For a first-person account of the power of the John Birch Society, see Ben Ezzell, *The Editor's Ass and Other Tales from 50 Years behind the Desk of Editor* (Canadian, Tex.: The Canadian Record), 32–37; *The Canadian Record*, 9 March 1961. Panhandle editor Ben Ezzell attended the organizational meeting of the Amarillo JBS and was appalled by what he saw. His exposé of the JBS that appeared in the *Canadian Record* was circulated nationally, and he became known as one of the first to reveal the potential power of the organization.

36. *Tulia Herald*, 28 May 1964.

37. Seale turned out to be a controversial mayor; he turned down a federal grant that would have helped the city build a new waste sewage facility, and twice during his tenure he refused to recognize United Nations Day—a quasi-national holiday. Instead, he proclaimed United States Day. He also welcomed with official enthusiasm such Bircher heroes as Robert Welch, General Edwin Walker, Billy James Hargis, Clarence Manion, Dan Smoot, and Tom Anderson. He was defeated when he ran for Congress in 1962.

38. Kohler would only attend the special session. He was not reelected in 1962. As one of only two Republicans in the Legislature, Kohler was an object of some curiosity. He and the other Republican, from Houston and also elected solely for the special session, even posed for a photograph inside a telephone booth. The photo was syndicated and Kohler received international recognition when it was featured in *Stars and Stripes*. Richard Brooks interview; Ken Kohler interview with author; *Texas Observer*, 1 December 1961.

39. Paul Casdorph, *A History of the Republican Party in Texas, 1862–1965* (Austin: Pemberton Press, 1965), 220–24; Roger M. Olien, *From Token to Triumph: The Texas Republicans since 1920* (Dallas: Southern Methodist

University Press, 1982), 174–79; John R. Knaggs, *Two Party Texas: The John Tower Era, 1961–1984* (Austin: Eakin Press, 1986), 6–14; Mike Kingston, Sam Attlesey, and Mary G. Crawford, *The Texas Almanac's Political History of Texas* (Austin: Eakin Press, 1992), 154–57. The introduction of the potential for two-party elections in 1961 also had the curious effect of originating fundamental changes within the Democratic Party in Texas. Long dominated by conservatives, liberal Democrats (a relative term in Texas) urged conservatives to vote for Republican candidates. The liberal *Texas Observer* began to endorse Republican candidates and urge fellow liberals to do the same in an effort to create a viable two-party system in the state and to purge the Democratic Party of the conservatives who controlled it. See *Texas Observer*, 15 September 1961 and 19 January 1962; Knapp, *Two-Party Texas*; Olien, *From Token to Triumph*, 182.

40. Barry Goldwater and Jack Casserly, *Goldwater* (New York: Doubleday, 1988), 210.

41. Barry Goldwater, *The Conscience of a Conservative* (Sheperdsville, Ky. Victor Publishing Co., 1960). See also Goldberg, *Barry Goldwater*, 138–41; Goldwater and Casserly, *Goldwater*, 119–22; Richard Brooks interview.

42. David Farber points out the prescience of the Goldwater "values" campaign in his "The Silent Majority and Talk about Revolution," *The Sixties: From Memory to History*, ed. David Farber (Chapel Hill: University of North Carolina Press, 1994), 298–99. For more on bourgeoisie support of conservatism, see Perlstein, *Before the Storm*, and McGirr, *Suburban Warriors*.

43. For more on the emergence of the term *conservative* among Texans, see Knaggs, *Two-Party Texas*, 58–60. Belden's Texas Poll, October 1964, Belden's Texas Poll, June 1968, Roper Center, Storrs, Connecticut; Walter L. Shelly, "Political Profiles of the Nixon, Humphrey, and Wallace Voters in the Texas Panhandle, 1968: A Study in Voting Behavior" (Ph.D. dissertation, Texas Tech University, 1972), 49–56.

44. These projections are from the Population Estimates and Projections Program (PEPP), Texas State Data Center, Texas Agricultural Experiment Station, Texas A&M University System and the Center for Demographic and Socioeconomic Research and Education, Department of Rural Sociology, Texas Agricultural Experiment Station, Texas A&M University System, "Projections of the Population of Texas and Counties in Texas by Age, Sex and Race/Ethnicity for 1990–2030," May 2000. The PEPP ran several different scenarios basing their projections on past changes in the region. Each came to different conclusions, but all showed a dramatic increase in the Hispanic populations of major cities.

45. See Jan Blodgett, *Land of Bright Promise: Advertising the Texas Panhandle and South Plains, 1870–1917* (Austin: University of Texas Press, 1988).

46. Quote from Blodgett, *Land of Bright Promise*, 96–98. The racial demo-

graphics of the twenty-six Panhandle counties changed little from the 1930s to the 1970s. In 1930, the Panhandle was 97.6 percent white, 2.2 percent African American (most in Amarillo) and 1.1 percent Hispanic. Across the entire five northern counties there were only two African Americans, 1930 Census.

47. Jesus L. Solis, interview by John Solis, 30 April 1973, transcript, PPHM; Frances Powell, interview by Laurie Groman, 24 July 1987, transcript, PPHM; Winfred G. Steglich, "Population Trends," in *A History of Lubbock*, ed. Lawrence L. Graves (Lubbock: Texas Technological College Press, 1962), 440–45. In 1970, 94 percent of neighborhoods in Amarillo and Lubbock were segregated. A city map published by the Lubbock Chamber of Commerce in 1967 still labeled four schools as "Colored." *The Catalyst*, 10 February 1970. Sean-Shong Hwang and Steve H. Murdock, "Residential Segregation in Texas," *Social Science Quarterly* 63 (December 1982): 737–48. Ecumenical Council on Social Concerns, Papers, Southwest Collection, Texas Tech University, Lubbock, Texas (SWC).

48. William H. Jones, "The Status of Educational Desegregation in Texas," *The Journal of Negro Education* 25 (Summer 1956): 334. William H. Jones, "Desegregation of Public Education in Texas—One Year Afterward," *The Journal of Negro Education* 24 (Summer 1955): 350–52. See also Alan Scott, "Twenty-five Years of Opinion on Integration in Texas," *The Southwestern Social Science Quarterly* 48 (September 1967): 155–63. Both Jones and Scott, as well as most historians of twentieth-century Texas, agree that the racial demographics in West Texas in general and the Panhandle specifically engendered a more moderate stance on civil rights and desegregation than the rest of the state.

49. These feelings have not faded in the past thirty years. In 1992, the Pi Kappa Alpha fraternity at Texas Tech was suspended from campus after several of its member dressed in Ku Klux Klan regalia for a party and had photographs taken in which other members dressed in black face with outrageous Afro wigs or as Hispanic gang members cowered at the Klansmen's feet. *Amarillo News*, 23 October and 5 November 1992.

50. The best book on Wallace's impact on conservative politics is Dan T. Carter, *The Politics of Rage: George Wallace, The Origins of the New Conservatism, and the Transformation of American Politics* (New York: Simon and Schuster, 1995). See also Dan T. Carter, *From George Wallace to Newt Gingrich: Race in the Conservative Counterrevolution, 1963–1994* (Baton Rouge: Louisiana State University Press, 1996).

51. Belden's Texas Poll, 1972, Roper Center; Mahon Papers, Box 348. See also sample ballots from 1970–1974 for the remarkable uniformity of responses over time.

52. Mahon Papers, Box 348. *Plainview Herald*, 13 December 1974; Hazelwood to HWW, 3 March 1969, Hazelwood Collection, Drawer 19.

53. "Busing: The Other Side," *Accent West* 4 (January 1975): 20; Pam Guest, interview by Dwight Coffer, 23 April 1989, PPHM.

54. "Busing: The Other Side," 20; Betty Ramsey, interview with author, 13 July 2000.

55. V. P. Perry, "Guest Opinion," *Accent West* 4 (January 1975): 23.

56. Urban theorist Mike Davis makes a very similar argument in *Magical Urbanism: Latinos Reinvent the U.S. City* (London: Verso, 2000).

Hispanics on the Texas South Plains

YOLANDA ROMERO

Compared to other peoples who have traversed or inhabited the Southern Plains, Mexican Americans are recent players to the region.[1] Certainly, historians recognize the presence of Mexican *pobladores* (settlers) who, by the late nineteenth century, had searched out work opportunities in northwest Texas. For example, in Lubbock County Andrew Gonzales, a sheepshearer with one of the many migrant crews that worked the area seasonally, appeared in the 1880 Lubbock County census. Further north, in Oldham County, Casimiro Romero and his associates from New Mexico went into business as sheep raisers. Romero brought his family, as well as Agapito Sandoval and Henry Kimball, into the Canadian River Valley in 1876. Soon others, including the Borrego, Trujillo, Valdes, Ortega, Chávez, and Tecolote families, followed. In the Canadian River Valley, then, *ganaderos* (sheepmen) and their *pastores* (sheepherders) found the gateway to the High Plains and its endless pastures. For the next decade or so, ganaderos would prosper until cattlemen began challenging them for the land.

In this frontier area of northwest Texas, the settlers founded the town of Tascosa and strengthened its Catholic roots. By early 1881, Reverend

John C. Splinters was traveling to the Texas Panhandle to celebrate mass. In fact, *Sadlier's Catholic Directory* of 1883 indicates that Spanish Catholics could be found throughout various Panhandle counties. Romero himself contributed to the faith by permitting his home to serve as the chapel for Catholics of Tascosa for some twenty years. In 1892, the first Bishop of Dallas, Thomas F. Brennan, visited Romero's home to confer the sacrament of confirmation; this was probably the first Episcopal function held in the Texas Panhandle.[2]

For the most part, the Hispanic sheepmen returned to New Mexico following intense competition with cattlemen over the range. But many of these pastores stayed behind to work in developing farming and ranching industries. As late as 1912, *The Hereford Brand* (Hereford, Texas) reported that a "Mexican sheep herder had frozen to death thirty miles west of Hereford in sub-zero temperatures." It is interesting that the death records for Deaf Smith County make no mention of this death.[3]

Phases of Settlement

Notwithstanding these early activities, Mexican Americans as late as the 1920s had not arrived on the Texas Plains in great numbers. The kinds of stable and permanent settlements, such as the ones other Mexican-origin people established in southern Texas some two centuries earlier, came late to the Panhandle. That such a course lagged on the Southern Plains hardly represents an aberration in Mexican American history, however. Some historians argue, for instance, that modern Chicano history does not begin until the turn of the twentieth century. It revolves around massive migration from Mexico into the Southwest and the transplantation of Mexican American culture into northern U.S. regions after that. Further, until about World War II, the migration remained primarily a rural phenomenon. Southern Plains community building, then, appeared to conform to these patterns of delayed dispersal and settlement.[4]

Actually, the push into the Texas Plains during the early decades of the twentieth century unfolded tentatively, entailing alternating penetration of the area and then retreat toward the homeland: either southern Texas or Mexico. During the initial thrust that continued into the late 1920s, Mexican Americans and Mexicans joined the state's migrant labor force and gradually augmented the Hispanic population in northwest Texas. The first move north involved men who were hired onto railroad and highway gangs or employed by infant agricultural concerns. In November of 1912, for instance, 350 Hispanic laborers constituted part of the crews building a road between Paducah and Lubbock. Ten months later, 100 Hispanic men worked laying railroad track between Lubbock and Littlefield.[5]

Along the migrant route, Mexicans and Mexican Americans lived out in the open in housing provided by their employers. Although the living conditions were poor, such circumstances did not stop farmhands from moving northward to seek a living. In fact, as the years went on, informal means of communications developed among the farmworkers and more and more of them began to settle permanently. At first, family networks acted as contact points for farmworkers, but by the 1930s small barrios began emerging in several of the towns. Tirso Domínguez, who fought first with Pancho Villa and then became a Carranzista, helped start the barrio in Slaton, Texas. Other revolutionaries who aided in the establishment of barrios in northwest Texas included Rodolfo Ritz in Meadow and Dolores García in Lubbock.[6]

A second stage in this intermittent pattern of settlement into the Southern Plains occurred with the massive swing of cotton pickers into the region during the 1930s and the building of labor camps by the early 1940s to accommodate the migrants. Individuals as well as whole families found this peregrination north fairly easy. *Contratistas* (contractors) provided transportation for laborers, charging fees for their services. Other Mexican and Mexican American families often piled into an old car or truck and traveled the migrant trail alone or in caravans. Family members wrote home to tell others of money to be made and countless opportunities available. These family networks kept laborers informed of work openings as well as the addresses where their family and friends could be found.[7]

A significant factor in this second stage of settlement in northwest Texas was the appearance of labor camps. These government-subsidized or privately built way stations were intended to ameliorate the deplorable conditions that some migrant families faced on their travels. The first official labor camp was built in 1941 at Lamesa, with later camps erected in Hereford, Muleshoe, Dimmitt, Plainview, Lubbock, and other towns. Camps throughout the migrant circuit provided families with facilities such as those at the camp that W. G. McMillan constructed outside Lubbock at a cost of $5,975, and which became a contact point for farmers seeking laborers. Housing, regardless of family size, consisted of

Government subsidized or privately built labor camps helped ameliorate living conditions for migrant laborers who moved to northwest Texas. This photograph of Felipe Garcia was taken at the Ropesville, Texas, labor camp in 1956. Courtesy Yolanda Romero.

two rooms. Families carried their own makeshift stoves and bedding but often cooked and slept outside, especially during the hot summer months. Since there was no refrigeration, families kept their food in coolers and took a daily trip to the grocery store. Camp residents shared centrally located showers and toilets.[8] Labor camps offered more than just a temporary place to stay, however. They served as a link to keep contact throughout an expanding cultural zone taking shape in northwest Texas. For as more and more people from the southern sections of Texas and from Mexico entered the region, they altered the new frontier's social and demographic landscape.[9]

After coming and going, often for years, many migrants eventually decided to settle down and make a life for their families away from the competition in southern and central Texas and other more densely populated areas of the state. This cycle would be repeated by thousands of families heading north toward the Panhandle for the rest of the century and marks the third stage of migration. Starting in the 1940s, then, many Mexican families decided to move from the labor camps into northwest Texas barrios and become permanent settlers.[10] During this decade, Hispanic communities consequently transformed the Southern Plains into a region with a permanent and distinctive Hispanic influence. Farmers needed labor, and Hispanics filled the void. Although not always welcomed by Anglo-Americans, they continued arriving for the next two decades as new acreage came under cultivation.

Adaptation

The Mexican and Mexican American working people who entered the Texas Southern Plains from the early 1900s to the late 1940s settled in an area that even in the early twenty-first century remains isolated from the rest of the state. Indeed, northwest Texas was a drastic contrast to the ambient many of the migrants knew back in the homeland, whether Mexico or southern Texas. Differences included topography, climate, culture, and inhabitants. The Plains, for instance, lacked less familiar imprints of Spanish Mexican civilization. Cotton pickers on the farms of southern Texas worked under extremely hot conditions; in the Plains, people hit the cotton fields until just before winter set in. Population ratios on the Plains, furthermore, diverged sharply from what people saw back home. In the old point of origin, Mexicans predominated, but in the Panhandle, Anglos held the numbers edge by a large percentage. When Hispanic families chose to move permanently to northwest Texas, therefore, they certainly understood that this monumental decision meant they were leaving their roots behind and that they could not easily return to southern Texas or Mexico.

But this wave of late arrivals to the Southern Plains possessed the spirit and toughness demanded of anyone bent on sinking roots in a new place. They exhibited the endurance characteristic of nineteenth-century Anglo settlers moving west to live, work, and build a new beginning for their families. Mexican and Mexican American pioneers encountered hardships in any number of places they settled. Unemployment, deplorable housing and working conditions, no medical benefits, language difficulties, transportation, violence, limited pay, and discrimination stand out as the major problems that greeted the newcomers.[11] Most persevered.

The migrants found support for their determination to make the Southern Plains their home by turning to such traditional and familiar institutions as the Catholic Church, which extended to them spiritual, emotional, and even monetary assistance. The Catholic Church and the growth of the Amarillo Diocese became an important force in sustaining new Spanish-speaking communities in northwest Texas. The Diocese provided a cultural buffer that many Mexicans appreciated. The church as well as its parishioners faced prejudice and discrimination from Anglo Protestants throughout the Diocese, but together they resisted. A symbiotic relationship emerged between parishioners and the Diocese, so that the size of both groups grew with the support of the other.

Their ability to confront adversity and go on despite it also explains the migrants' success in restarting lives so far removed from the homeland. Southern Plains folks were not tolerant of racial minorities, especially those perceived as serving the laboring needs of the region. According to Pauline Kibbe of the Good Neighbor Commission, Anglo-Americans looked upon Mexicans thus:

> Generally speaking, the Latin American migratory worker going into West Texas is regarded as a necessary evil, nothing more nor less than an unavoidable adjunct to the harvest season. Judging by the treatment that has been accorded him in that section of the State, one might assume that he is not a human being at all, but a species of farm implement that comes mysteriously and spontaneously into being coincident with the maturing of the cotton, that requires no upkeep or special consideration during the period of its usefulness, needs no protection from the elements, and when the crop has been harvested, vanishes into the limbo of forgotten things—until the next harvest season rolls around. He has no past, no future, only a brief and anonymous present.[12]

Exploitation took its toll, but Hispanic communities endured to add cultural variety to a new corner of the Lone Star State.

The newcomers adapted to the "strange" setting by also taking stock of the immediate geography and environment. Certainly Southern Plains topography differed from the terrain back home, but northwest Texas was a farming region nonetheless, much like the other parts of the state that cotton pickers traversed on the "Big Swing." Seasonal agricultural work was no step upward on the occupational ladder, but in some cases field labor paid slightly better than did cleaning and picking in southern Texas. Living conditions in Southern Plains communities offered little or no improvement either, but some saw opportunities for social mobility there that they did not have in the homeland. Adapting, many stayed.[13]

A desire to retain in-group culture also served the newcomers well. Though isolated from large numbers of other Hispanics, the newcomers continued traditional practices. A "culture corridor," traceable to Hispanic activity in northwest Texas when Casimiro Romero and others had made the Panhandle their home, perceptively took form as a string of neighborhoods formed a familiar backdrop that assisted in the adjustment to the faraway land. The Spanish language, as well as special events and the Catholic Church, buttressed this expanding culture corridor. Traditional Mexican holidays and ceremonies celebrated within this ethnic zone included the Diez y Seis de Septiembre (16 September), Cinco de Mayo (5 May), *quinceañeras* (coming-out parties for fifteen-year-old girls), and *bailes caseros* (house dances). *Compadrazgo* (co-parenthood) was also an important institution to these Hispanics in northwest Texas.[14] Over time, Mexican Americans integrated the Plains ambient into aspects of their identity, for they gradually began associating themselves with the Llano Estacado. By the latter decades of the twentieth century, groups took names like the "Llano Estacado Farmworkers de Tejas," for instance. Since the 1970s, the weeklong 16 September commemoration in Lubbock has taken the name of the Llano Estacado celebrations.

Community on the Llano Estacado

That Mexican Americans in the Southern Plains opted for loyalty to old ways by no means indicated a rejection of the Anglo-American milieu. To the contrary, adaptation to the adopted land meant continued appreciation of the economic and political institutions that the native-born migrants (and even those of foreign birth) had previously accepted in Southern and Central Texas. Such adjustments were most evident in the communities of Amarillo and Lubbock, which grew into the two largest towns in Northwest Texas.

Lubbock attracted Hispanic-owned businesses because of its size and location in northwest Texas. The earliest Mexican American businesses in Lubbock appeared about thirteen years after Hispanics first settled there permanently in 1912. Anita García Lara remembered that during the early 1920s Juan Montoya operated a neighborhood store two houses down from where she grew up on Avenue M in the barrio.

By 1925, the *Lubbock City Directory* listed two businesses owned by Mexican Americans: a one-room barbershop belonging to Julio Flores and a grocery store owned by the Lucero family. Hispanics could also trade at Joe Baldrige's shop as well as the Boyd Brothers meat market.[15]

In the 1930s, Dr. Armando Durán came to Lubbock. At first, Durán and a relative, a Dr. Pescatello, rented a downtown office for the migrant season. Pescatello eventually stopped coming but Durán became a permanent Lubbock resident. The doctor built a lucrative practice administering medicine for over four decades to the Hispanic population, renting the same office on 13th street for thirty-five years. Mexicans and Mexican Americans learned that a Spanish-speaking doctor practiced in Lubbock and drove long miles to seek out Durán when afflicted by illness.[16]

By 1975 enough Mexican American–owned businesses existed so that Bidal Agüero, editor and owner of *El Editor*, could organize the Mexican American Chamber of Commerce. *Comerciantes Organizados Mexico Americanos* (COMA) incorporated under the Texas Non-Profit Corporation Act with Bidal Agüero, Roy Montelongo, and Ismael Hernández making up the Board of Directors. COMA met monthly, and approximately fifty professionals and businessmen and women attended meetings by March of 1975. At the March meeting, Mario Cadena, president of the Dallas Mexican American Chamber of Commerce, addressed the group on the origins and development of his own organization in Dallas. COMA continued to grow and eventually could be found in neighboring towns, including Plainview, where hairstylist Joe Alemán started a chapter in 1976.[17]

In the smaller towns of northwest Texas, the drive for money-making was as pronounced as it was in Lubbock. Of the several Hispanic-owned restaurants that existed throughout the years, two or three survived into the twenty-first century. In Hereford, the Ramírez family opened a *tortillería* next to the San José labor camp, and from it they distributed tortillas, tamales, hot sauce, and other Mexican dishes to grocers in the entire region. In Muleshoe during the 1950s, Noé Anzaldua opened El Jacalito and Aurelio Cuévas opened El San Francisco, a combination tortillería and restaurant; both establishments continue to thrive.[18] Muleshoe also became home to one of the wealthiest Mexican Americans in northwest Texas: Roberto Ruiz, who established a packing shed in that town.[19]

Still another type of businessperson to find a livelihood though creative entrepreneurship in northwest Texas was the *empresario* who supplied entertainment to the Hispanic population. Henry Rocha, Fermín Pérez, Cruz Alvarado, Carlos Pérez, Pepe Villegas, Willie Acosta, and dozens of other dance hall operators held numerous dances for Hispanic music fans. During the 1960s, they brought groups like Sonny and the Sunliners, Little Joe and the Latinaires, Cuco Sánchez, Shorty and the Corvettes, Flor Sylvestre, Antonio Aguilar, and others to play on Friday and Saturday nights on concrete platforms under the night sky or in rented dance halls. Late in that decade, a handful of these empresarios bought dance clubs and promoted dances regularly. The Paladium in Lubbock, El Fronterizo on the Tahoka highway outside of Lubbock, La Escondida (The Hideaway), and finally the Poor Boy in Ralls are examples of successful dance halls.

Bootlegging also became an attractive venture for the Mexican and Mexican American population in "dry" Lubbock. Prior to the 1970s, for example, at least eight bootleggers conducted business in Lubbock's Guadalupe barrio alone.[20] The bootlegger provided a safe place where barrio residents could either pick up a beer to take home or stay and share drinks with friends in the security of the Hispanic neighborhood.[21]

Entrepreneurs in the Southern Plains Mexican American communities served numerous functions. Many became role models and leaders, indicating by their example that financial success could still be derived from a capitalist system that generally exploited the laboring class. Hispanic businesses also acted as a bulwark to fledgling communities. Several made financial contributions to worthy barrio projects, while others promoted cultural awareness in their respective communities. Indeed, COMA served as a network of support for the community as a whole. Entrepreneurs and professionals not only offered services to the Hispanic community but also generally hired Spanish-speaking employees, and they therefore made it possible for many to earn a living without a good grasp of the English language. This, in turn, meant that they gave Spanish-speaking employees the opportunity to gain experience and skills that could lead to other jobs once workers mastered English. Although members of this class occasionally developed conflicts with their Spanish-speaking customers or employees, these men and women, for the most part, contributed positively to community-building in northwest Texas.[22]

Further evidence of adjustment to the Southern Plains was the willingness of Mexican Americans to engage in political struggles designed to accelerate their integration into American life. Just as their counterparts in southern and central Texas had launched campaigns for equal treatment of Mexican-descent citizens, so did the pioneers in the Panhandle want to become part of the political landscape, where they might discuss issues pertinent to their communities and make decisions for their well-being. Hispanic entrepreneurs and professionals were among the high-profile leaders promoting political change.

Inspired by south Texas civic groups that had organized to lead Mexican Americans in struggles against social and political injustices and to celebrate Hispanic cultural pride, political associations also surfaced in the Texas Southern Plains beginning in the 1940s. The League of United Latin American Citizens (LULAC) Councils, the American GI Forum, and Viva Kennedy Clubs increasingly popped up throughout northwest Texas in towns such as Dimmitt, Hereford, Post, and Levelland. By the 1960s, these organizations, which often shared the same membership, held "pay your poll tax" campaigns and also supported scholarship fund drives.

In an effort to change the Jim Crow status of Spanish-speaking residents in Slaton, Manuel Castro, acting for the Lubbock GI Forum, filed a discrimination complaint against the city. The 1961 case began when Slaton refused a Mexican American resident entrance into the town swimming pool. Publicity forced Slaton councilman Harry Stokes to acknowledge that Mexican American residents paid city taxes and therefore had a right to enter the tax-supported swimming grounds. Fear of being blacklisted by the Mexican government from participation in the bracero program finally convinced the Anglo-American residents of Slaton that they had no choice but to open the pool to Mexicans and Mexican Americans.[23]

Meanwhile, chapters of long-standing Texas organizations like LULAC and the GI Forum led Mexican American political activism in Lubbock. In June 1966, those organizations, with the help of the AFL-CIO, sponsored a "War on Poverty and Migrant Labor Conference" at Lubbock's St. Joseph's Catholic Church. The conference meant to aid "all people in West Texas interested in helping the poverty-stricken take advantage of various government programs." This activism continued in early 1967 when Manuel Garza, executive director of LULAC visited Lubbock to investigate charges of discrimination in the workplace. Garza maintained that Mexican Americans and African Americans received less pay as well as no promotions from Lubbock employers, although he never gave specific details.[24]

Because of the work of the AFL-CIO, LULAC, and the GI Forum, it should have come as no surprise when on 28 August 1972 Lubbock city sanitation workers walked off the job in "protest of poverty wages." Sanitation workers asked for a 15 percent pay raise that would increase their monthly salary from $357 to $410. The Construction and Municipal Workers Union, Local 1253, represented 75 percent of the employees in the city's public works departments.[25] Membership numbered 350, according to union business manager Robert Méndez. Over half of these members worked in the sanitation department. In the second week, employees from the street and water reclamation departments joined the sanitation workers, and the Lubbock Central Labor Council offered financial aid to the unionists. The city began to fill vacated positions, however, refusing to negotiate with the strikers. In the third week, the city council found replacements for all openings.

But the council's action generated an unexpected response from the Catholic clergy in the city. At a council hearing held on 15 September (which lasted approximately four hours), Lubbock priests promised to call on parishioners for a boycott against the municipal power service. Among those to address the council was Father Tom McGovern of Carlisle, representing the Priest Senate of the Amarillo Diocese, though he had little success in converting council members to an understanding of the strikers' cause. Then Father Henry Waldo of Our Lady of Grace spoke: "We came with the faith we would be heard, we have had our say but we're not sure you've been listening. We will go to our pulpits Sunday and press for economic sanctions and ask our people en masse to switch from Lubbock Power and Light to Southwestern Public Service and not to pay the garbage service charge." Father Waldo ended by declaring: "Lubbock Power and Light has said it is people power, let's see where the real power of the people lies." A crowd of at least three hundred, comprised of sanitation workers, families, clergymen, and friends attended the hearing of striking city employees.[26]

True to their word, Catholic priests on Sunday morning urged their parishioners to boycott Lubbock Power and Light and not pay the garbage duty unless the city council agreed to negotiate with the strikers. The priests outlined a five-point program distributed at all Lubbock churches. It called for a utility boycott, a refusal to pay the garbage fee, a rejection of replacement workers, and finally a request for contributions to the employee protest fund, care of American State Bank. At Our Lady of Grace alone, some five hundred of about fifteen hundred people attending mass signed "switchover" cards from Lubbock Power and Light to Southwestern Public Service.

That afternoon, door-to-door campaigns began in support of a utility boycott as the fourth week of the strike began. On Wednesday of that week, Gustavo Gaynett with the U.S. Justice Department arrived from the Dallas Office of Community Relations to act as a mediator. Gaynett maintained the Justice Department feared "outside agitators" might escalate the problems. He first spoke with city officials, then met with a delegation of priests. Meanwhile the boycott continued with a total of 250 actual customer changeovers and approximately 350 new requests. At the end of the week the city council invited the sanitation workers to resume their jobs. All strikers returned to work on 26 September 1972, with a 5 percent raise rather than the requested 15 percent increase. The strike demonstrated to the entire Lubbock community, however, that a nonviolent protest could be effective. Further, the strike energized a decade of protest and demonstration in the Lubbock barrios.[27]

The 1970s indeed proved to be a political watershed for the Hispanic population of northwest Texas.[28] The Chicano movement in California and Cesar Chavez's United Farm Workers' struggle, both rooted in the late 1960s, influenced activist participation in northwest Texas, as did the events that transpired in Crystal City, Texas, about the same time. In Lubbock and Amarillo, Mexican American students founded the Movimiento Estudiantil Chicano de Aztlán (MECHA). In Lubbock a *Teatro* Chicano formed as a means to deliver the *movimiento's* message to the community, and the Brown Berets set up chapters in various Hispanic communities. The many diverse groups in the region met in Lubbock in 1971, joining a March of Faith as a form of protest against city officials and against the treatment of Mexican Americans. The March of Faith ended at the courthouse steps. There, participants submitted twenty-three grievances and demands to the city. These complaints, compiled by "students, businessmen, ministers, priests, laborers, and housewives" from the Lubbock barrios, fell into five categories: justice, equal protection under the law, fair representation, equal employment, and education.[29]

The poorest and most needy of the Mexican American population in northwest Texas, meanwhile, received attention from the Texas Farm Workers Union (TFWU), which organized in 1975. Aided by Texas Rural Legal Aid and the various communities, the TFWU in 1978 began to address the problems haunting poverty-stricken farm workers and their families. In the mid-seventies, the TFWU became a force of

Hispanic social and political activism in northwest Texas took many forms in the 1970s, including the creation of a Teatro Chicano, which encouraged cultural pride. In this photo Lucas Trujillo examines a Teatro Chicano poster celebrating Chicano educators. Courtesy Yolanda Romero.

empowerment in communities like Cactus, where 97 percent of a population of about nine hundred was of Mexican descent.

The TFWU led by Jesús Moya continued its efforts in Hereford, Dimmitt, Plainview, Hale Center, and wherever Moya and his organizers could find farm workers. One of Moya's most active organizers, Don Manuel Medeles, happened to be seventy-six years old in 1980. At Hereford that year, the TFWU paralyzed the Howard-Gault Company with a six-week strike (the length of the onion season). At a time when minimum wage was $3.10, Howard-Gault workers received pay equivalent to $1.85 an hour, and at La Mantilla workers earned about the same. From Howard-Gault, the TFWU moved on to La Mantilla in the city of Dimmitt. During the strikes, two farmers in Castro County sprayed pickets with anhydrous ammonia gas, and another farmer exposed himself to female farmworkers. Field hands and organizers during the strikes received aid from the GI Forum, the Meat Cutters Union, LULAC, and churches in Houston, Austin, and San Antonio.[30]

Texas Rural Legal Aid represented workers in actions relating to organizational activities in Hereford.[31]

Almost simultaneous with the farmworkers movement in northwest Texas, the Southwest Voter Registration and Education Project (SWVREP) based in San Antonio began to take counties in northwest Texas into litigation in an effort to force the adjustment of precinct lines and to give the Mexican American population a voice in government. This initiative followed the contact various northwest Texas communities had made with SWVREP in 1982. The agenda for the first West Texas Regional Planning Committee meeting on 11 June 1983 included an opening statement from founder Willie Velásquez as well as a presentation by State Senator Lloyd Doggett. Mexican Americans from Abernathy, Crosbyton, Levelland, Littlefield, Lubbock, Plainview, Ralls, and other communities wished to challenge the at-large election method used to choose school board and city council members. In January 1983 Lubbock became the first in the area to receive a court order to adopt the use of single-member districts to assure minority representation. This is just one example of what historian Jeff Roche, in his essay in this volume, calls the challenge to the "politics of white supremacy" brought about by changing demographics.[32]

Diversity on the Southern Plains

Demographers today reckon that Hispanics comprise 32 percent of the total population of Texas, which is almost 21 million. In northwest Texas, they make up 46 percent of Dalhart and 97 percent of Cactus. Census takers predict that before 2010, Anglo-Americans will represent a minority in the state (outnumbered by Hispanics, African Americans, and Asian Americans) and that by 2030, Hispanics will account for almost half of the population in Texas.[33]

Northwest Texas is on a course to duplicate such forecasts. Though Mexican Americans were late arrivals on the Southern Plains of Texas, their numbers have increased exponentially since World War II. This remarkable population spurt has been evident during the last two decades of the twentieth century in cities such as Lubbock and Amarillo, as well as in counties and small communities. While residence in the Southern Plains has been fortuitous for many, for others things have not gone well. Such misfortune presents issues that city, county, state, and federal officials will have to address. Mexican American youths continue to drop out of school in high numbers, a calamity that affects their socioeconomic status. Early childhood education programs and more effective retention strategies with English as a Second Language (ESL) programs for immigrants, as well as outreach efforts, will be needed to avoid having to deal with a large undereducated and needier population that could be a drain to the region. On the other hand, a growing population could mean better representation and opportunities for Hispanics. If this becomes the case, Mexican Americans will have a positive outlook for the future. But that involves taking advantage of available programs, continuing to achieve higher levels of education, and increasing their political voice.

The stability of Mexican American communities in the Texas Southern Plains today (despite attendant problems of poverty, racism, political under-representation, and the like) underscores the historic capability of Mexican-origin individuals to be pioneers. Just as others had settled southern Texas in earlier times, Mexican-descent migrants came north in increasing numbers during the twentieth century and laid stake to a new beginning on the Plains. They superimposed a new way of life on the region, implanting old customs, celebrations, a different language, and broadened the base of the Catholic Church. They came to live in semi-autonomous communities that resembled those they had left behind either in southern Texas or Mexico. Catering to their cultural needs were other Hispanics belonging to a rising middle class. But few Mexican Americans desired to live apart from mainstream society; all wished recognition as loyal "Americans," and sought fuller participation in all realms of the American mainstream. Such patterns of adjustment and participation in community life could well be extended into places beyond the Panhandle, as certainly Hispanics are duplicating them in contemporary "frontiers" in Arkansas, Tennessee, and other southern states.

Wherever Hispanics go, the ideal for many has been a bicultural world of their own making. Maintaining such an "ideal" has never been difficult. It arises, on the one hand, from a desire to re-establish a comfort zone consisting of familiar traditions and institutions, and on the other, from an inevitable clash with Anglo-Americans whose response to different peoples (especially those of color) often includes suspicion and intolerance. The Southern Plains experience for Mexican Americans has hardly deviated from such a standard. Conflict arising from attempts to co-exist on each groups' terms will probably not disappear in the near future, but neither will the diversity that Mexican-descent people bring to frontiers, such as the Texas Southern Plains.

Notes

1. The boundaries of the area under discussion are as follows: south at approximately 33 degrees along State Highway 180 to modern-day Seminole, Lamesa, and Snyder. The northern, western, and eastern demarcations would be the state's contemporary borders, except that the eastern boundary extends south to State Highway 80.

2. Sister Nellie Rooney, O.S.F., "A History of the Catholic Church in the Panhandle-Plains Area of Texas from 1874–1916" (M.A. Thesis, Catholic University of America, 1954), 28–46; *Hereford Reporter*, 10 July 1901; John M. Harter, "The Creation and Foundation of the Roman Catholic Diocese of Amarillo, 1917–1934" (M.A. Thesis, West Texas State University, 1975), 10; Paul Carlson, *Texas Woolybacks: The Range Sheep and Goat Industry* (College Station: Texas A&M University Press, 1982), 73, 96–97, 102–103, 112, 140, 157–58, 163–86, 187–98, 213.

3. Hispanics came to northwest Texas in the early twentieth century because the area provided the opportunity for social improvement. For Mexicans fleeing the Mexican Revolution, bigotry and discrimination seemed better than facing violence, chaos, and poverty. See Arthur Corwin, ed., *Immigrants and Immigrants: Perspectives on Mexican Labor Migration to the United States* (Westport, Conn.: Greenwood Press, 1978), 53. In Mexico, George Coalson maintains, the worker needed an "eight fold increase in his wages just to survive. Life expectancy during the Porfiriato was about thirty years with an infant mortality rate of thirty percent." See George O. Coalson, *The Development of the Migratory Farm Labor System in Texas: 1900–1954* (San Francisco: R and E Research Associates, 1988), 14. See also Michael C. Meyer and William L. Sherman, *The Course of Mexican History* (New York: Oxford University Press, 1983), 470.

4. Gilbert G. González and Raúl Fernández, "Chicano History: Transcending Cultural Models," *Pacific Historical Review* 63 (November 1994): 469–97.

5. In 1913, the *Lubbock Avalanche* reported construction workers had sent over $1,400.00 through the post office money order route to Mexico. *Lubbock Avalanche*, Lubbock, Texas, October 1913.

6. Tirso Domínguez interview with Yolanda Romero, Slaton, Texas, 1 July 1985, Southwest Collection, Texas Tech University, Lubbock, Texas (hereafter SWCTTU); Frances Ritz interview with Yolanda Romero, Meadow, Texas, 3 July 1985; Anita García Lara interview with Yolanda Romero, Lubbock, Texas, 1 August 1989, all SWCTTU.

7. Ramón Beteta, *Pensamiento y Dinámica de la Revolución Mexicana, Antología de Documentos Politicosociales* (México: Editorial México Nuevo, 1950), 90–91; Coalson, *The Development of the Migratory Farm Labor System,* 13; Corwin, ed., *Immigrants and Immigrants,* 34–35; Andrés Tijerina, *History of Mexican Americans in Lubbock County* (Lubbock: Texas Tech University Press, 1979), 15–16.

8. United States Department of Agriculture, *Cotton and Manpower: Texas High Plains,* Bulletin 762 (College Station: Texas A & M College, 1952), 20–44; Lamesa Chamber of Commerce Records, Lamesa, Texas, 1919–1974, SWCTTU, 21–52; Farmer Placement Service, *Origins and Problems of Texas Migratory Farm Labor* (Austin, Texas: Texas State Employment Services, 1940), 13–17; Clay L. Cochran, Assistant Labor Relations Adviser, Amarillo, Texas, to Jesses B. Gilmer, Assistant Regional Director in Charge of Resettlement Projects concerning "Light Construction" Camps, December 4, 1941, Farmers Home Administration, Entry 106, Folder 028, Migratory Labor, Records of Resettlement Division, Record Group 96, National Archives; Fort Worth, Texas; Community Planning Council, Lubbock, Texas, Report of the Committee on Migrant Workers, October 1959, SWCTTU.

9. Such a process as applied to other frontiers is discussed in David J. Weber and Jane M. Rausch, *Where Cultures Meet: Frontiers in Latin American History* (Wilmington, Del.: Scholarly Resources, 1994).

10. United States Department of Agriculture, *Cotton and Manpower: Texas High Plains,* Bulletin 762 (College Station: Texas A&M College, 1952), 2–44; *West Texas Catholic,* Golden Jubilee (Diocese of Amarillo, 1976), 1–15; M. C. Lindsey, "The Trail of Years in Dawson County, Texas" (unpublished manuscript), 3–95. This study is not for circulation and is housed at the Texas State Archives. J. H. Bond, Director of Texas State Employment Services, Austin, Texas, to Wilson Cowen, Regional Director, Farm Security Administration, Amarillo, Texas, 9 December 1941, Records of the Farm Home Administration, Entry 106, Folder 028, Record Group 96, National Archives, Fort Worth, Texas; Deah Barela interview with Yolanda Romero, 11 and 13 June 1985, Lubbock, Texas; Senorina Pérez interview with Yolanda Romero, 8 July 1985, Meadow, Texas; and Catarina García Ovalle interview with Yolanda Romero, 28 July 1988, Los Yvañez, all SWCTTU.

11. Amarillo Dioceses, Church Records, Archives, Amarillo, Texas. *Coyotes* were also called *enganchadores* (the term translates into *hookers*), who not only recruited but transported workers to areas of the Southwest. Victor Clark, *Mexican Labor* (Washington, D.C.: Government Printing Office, 1908), 476. The head tax of eight dollars and the literacy test required of immigrants served as a deterrent to legal Mexican immigration. U.S. *Statutes at Large,* "Immigration Act," 39 (1917): 875, 877.

12. Pauline Kibbe, *Latin Americans in Texas* (Albuquerque: University of New Mexico Press, 1974), 176.

13. Tirso Domínguez interview with Yolanda Romero, 1 July 1985, Slaton Texas; Frances Ritz interview with Yolanda Romero, 3 July 1985, Meadow, Texas; Mary Rodríguez interview with Yolanda Romero, 8 September 1985, Lubbock, Texas, all SWCTTU; President's Commission on Migratory Labor, *Migratory Labor in American Agriculture* (Washington, D.C.: Government Printing Office, 1951); Wayne D. Rasmussen, *A History of the Farm Labor Supply Program, 1943–47* (Washington, D.C.: Department of Agriculture, 1951); Baptismal Records, 1914, Books 6, 7, 8, Diocese of Amarillo.

14. Alfredo Albídrez interview with Yolanda Romero, 11 January 1987, Lubbock, Texas; Tirso Domínguez interview; Telesforo Lara interview with Yolanda Romero, n.d., at Lubbock, Texas, all SWCTTU; Armando Ayala Anguiano, *La Independencia*, Extra 8, México de Carne y Hueso (Contenido, Octubre, 1978); Dirk Raat, *Mexico: From Independence to Revolution, 1810–1910* (Lincoln: University of Nebraska Press, 1982), 3–50; Matt S. Meier and Feliciano Rivera, *The Chicanos: A History of Mexican Americans* (New York: Hill and Wang, 1972), 22–37; "Fiestas Patrias," *Fort Concho Report* (Fall 1987).

15. Anita García Lara interview with Yolanda Romero, 17 August 1989, at Lubbock, Texas; Antonio Urtado interview with Andrés Tijerina, 26 March 1973, in Lubbock; Abran Flores interview with Andrés Tijerina, 28 March 1973, Lubbock, all SWCTTU; Tijerina, *History of Mexican Americans in Lubbock County*, 27.

16. In an interview Francis Ritz recalled that she often took her daughters to Lauf Clinic because it was cheaper even though there was a problem communicating with the English-speaking nurses. On the other hand, Trini Gámez preferred to drive the distance from Plainview and pay more money to see Dr. Durán. Francis Ritz interview; Trini Gámez interview with Yolanda Romero, 28 July 1989, Plainview, Texas; Justa Cruz interview with Yolanda Romero, 12 March 1989, Lubbock, Texas; Belén Velásquez interview with Yolanda Romero, 19 April 1989, Lubbock; Alfredo Velásquez interview with Yolanda Romero, 19 April 1989, Lubbock; Bidal Agüero interview with Yolanda Romero, 26 July 1985, Lubbock; Telesforo Lara interview; Olga Riojas interview with Yolanda Romero, July 24, 1985, Lubbock, all SWCTTU.

17. COMA Reference File, SWCTTU; Articles of Incorporation of *Comerciantes Organizados Mexico Americanos*; Bidal Agüero interview with David Zepeda, 7 September 1976, Lubbock, Texas; all in Bidal Aguero Papers, SWCTTU.

18. Bertha García interview with Yolanda Romero, 7 July 1987, Lubbock, Texas; Trini Gámez interview; Roberto Ruiz interview with Yolanda Romero, 21 August 1989, Muleshoe, Texas; Lucía Ruiz interview with Yolanda Romero, 21 August 1989, Muleshoe; Cecilia Garza interview with Yolanda Romero, 8 August 1989, Plainview, Texas, all SWCTTU.

19. The Ruiz Industries became a focus of the Texas Farm Workers Union and Jesús Moya because of the wages and working conditions in the packing sheds and Ruiz fields. Moya and the TFWU with the help of Texas Rural

Legal Aid would strike and go to court. Lucía M. Ruiz interview; Roberto Ruiz interview.

20. The 1970 tornado that hit on 11 May served to displace many of the residents in the Guadalupe barrio. Three of the bootleggers working the barrio moved to other areas of Lubbock in the wake of the tornado.

21. Edward Ochoa, Jr., remembered that by the age of six he peddled pints of Old Crow whiskey for $2.50 to dance goers throughout the fifties. He hid the bottles on the inside of his coat pockets. Ochoa attended dances at a warehouse on Texas Avenue and later the Latin Center on Broadway and Ave. F. He also sold bootlegged whiskey at the *plataforma* (concrete slab for dancing) in the barrio. Edward Ochoa, Jr., interview with Yolanda Romero, 5 January 1987, Lubbock, Texas; Alfredo Albídrez interview; Edward Ochoa, Sr. interview with Yolanda Romero, 14 January 1987, Lubbock, all SWCTTU.

22. Dr. Durán was notorious for charging his Spanish-speaking patients too much; yet many overlooked this policy because he spoke Spanish. Trini Gámez interview, Francis Ritz interview, Justa Cruz interview.

23. Lubbock, *El Noticiero*, 29 June 1956; 1 February 1957; and 22 August 1958, all 1; Lubbock, *La Prensa del Suroeste*, 24 January 1960, 1–3; Lubbock, *El Semanario*, 29 October 1960, 1 and 22 July 1960, 1; Tijerina, *History of Mexican Americans in Lubbock County*, 46–57; Agustin Estrada interview with Andrés Tijerina, 17 May 1973, Lubbock, Texas; Jorge Moreno interview with Andrés A. Tijerina, 16 May 1973, Lubbock, both SWCTTU; Ignacio M. García, *Viva Kennedy: Mexican Americans in Search of Camelot* (College Station: Texas A&M University Press, 2000), 83–97.

24. *La Voz del Mexicano*, Dimmitt, 4 November 1981, 1, 3, 8; *Chicano Accent*, Lubbock, 25 February 1981, 1, 8; *La Voz De Texas*, Lubbock, 29 December 1972, 1–3; "Community Action" folder, Bidal Agüero Papers; "Raza Unida" folder, Eliseo Solis Papers; and "Texas Farm Workers" folder, Luis Ordóñez Papers, all SWCTTU.

25. "Community Action" folder, Bidal Agüero Papers; "Community Action Board" folder, Nephtalí De León Papers, both SWCTTU; Nephtalí De León, *Chicanos: Our Background and Our Pride* (Lubbock, Tex.: Trucha Publications, 1972), 70–74; Tijerina *History of Mexican Americans in Lubbock County*, 66; *La Voz de Texas*, Lubbock, 11 August 1972.

26. Lubbock, Texas City Council Records, August 1968–1972; *Lubbock Avalanche Journal*, August 29–September 2, 5–9, 14, 15, 18–23, 1972.

27. Lubbock, Texas City Council Records, August 1968–1972; *Lubbock Avalanche Journal*, August 29–September 2, 5–9, 14, 15, 18–23, 1972.

28. *La Voz del Mexicano*, 4 November 1981, Dimmitt, Hereford, Earth, Hart, and Muleshoe, Texas, 1, 3, 8; *Chicano Accent*, 25 February 1981, Lubbock, Texas, 1, 8; *La Voz De Texas*, 29 December 1972, Lubbock, 1–3; "Chicanos Unidos" folder, Bidal Agüero Papers; "Farm Workers Activity" folder, Eliseo Solis Papers; and "Texas Farm Workers" folder, Luis Ordóñez Papers, all SWCTTU.

29. Groups present at the demonstration were the Young Socialist Alliance, the Student Organization for Black Unity, Young Democrats of Texas Tech University, Jewish Student Organization, Muslim Student Organization, Student Mobilization Committee to End the War in Vietnam, Women's Liberation, India Student Organization, and Vietnam Veterans Against the War. *State of Texas vs. Tim McGovern, et al.* (1972), No. 69455, 137th District Court of Lubbock County, Texas; Lucas Trujillo interview with Yolanda Romero, 24 March 1987, Plano, Texas, SWCTTU; *La Voz de Texas*, Lubbock, 8 November 1971; 25 August and 28 July 1972.

30. Jesús Moya interview with Yolanda Romero, 25 July 1989, Hidalgo, Texas, SWCTTU; *Howard Gault Co. vs. Texas Rural Legal Aid* (1985), United States District Court, Northern District Texas, Amarillo Division; Rod Davis, "The Onion Revolt," *The Texas Observer*, 8 August 1980, 2–8; Jane A. Grandolfo, "Migrant Housing Comes to Hereford," *The Texas Observer*, 20 November 1987, 14–15; *Amarillo Daily News*, October 25, 1985; November 23, 1985; February 7, 1986; November 2, 1987; Mark Seal, "High Noon in Hereford," *Dallas Morning News*, March 9, 1980; *The Hereford Brand*, Hereford, Texas, 27 January, 9 July, 9 August, 1985; *The Monitor*, McAllen, Texas, 11 August 1985.

31. *Howard Gault Co. vs. Texas Rural Legal Aid et al.* (1985); Geoffrey Rips, "The Possibility of Democracy," *The Texas Observer*, 24 January 1986, 2–4; Louis Dubose, "Hispanic Power in the Panhandle," *The Texas Observer*, 15 January 1988, 10–12; Louis Dubose, "Gramm Strikes Out," *The Texas Observer*, 20 November 1988, 2–3; *The Hereford Brand*, 6 March, 20 December 1985; *The Odessa American*, 24 December 1985. Texas Rural Legal Aid lawyers made from $14,000 to $18,000 a year. Geoffrey Rips, "Political Intelligence," *The Texas Observer*, 15 August 1986, 16; Geoffrey Rips, "The Possibility of Democracy," *The Texas Observer*, 24 January 1986, 2–4; letter from Bidal Agüero to Congressman Kent Hance, 22 January 1980, concerning critical comments made by the congressman about Texas Rural Legal Aid "Correspondence" folder, Bidal Agüero Papers; *Amarillo Daily News*, 10 December 1985; *Amarillo Daily News*, 26 December 1985; *Dallas Times Herald*, 17 December 1985; *Lubbock Avalanche Journal*, 21 February , 27 February , 1985, 10 March , 18 July , 1986; San Antonio *Times Herald*, 2 December 1986; *West Texas Hispanic News*, Lubbock, Texas, 13 November 1985.

32. Jeff Roche, "Water, Race, and Republicanism: The Political Future of the Southern Plains," paper in possession of author, 6; "Farm Worker Activity" folder, Eliseo Solis Papers.

33. *Houston Chronicle*, 13 March 2001.

CHAPTER EIGHT

Loving the Plains, Hating the Plains, Restoring the Plains

DAN FLORES

I know almost nothing useful about W. H. Auden, the twentieth-century British poet-critic, except that once he wrote these lines, which I committed to memory: "I cannot see a plain without a shudder; 'Oh God, please, please don't ever make me live there!'" There's an exclamation point at the end of that sentence. Auden's sentiment, I think—and most modern Americans would surely agree—captures the early twenty-first century view of the matter nicely. The Great Plains is not, by any standard measure of aesthetics, an admired part of America these days, a loved landscape of our contemporary times the way the Rockies or Sierra Nevadas or the southwestern deserts are loved. As even Deborah Epstein Popper, of Buffalo Commons fame (or infamy, depending on your politics) is reported to have remarked during a tour of the Southern Plains of Oklahoma and Texas in the early 1990s: "This is terrible country! . . . There is *nothing here*. It is un-country. It shouldn't be allowed to exist!"[1]

Anyone who has driven an automobile across the country Popper is describing recognizes her feeling. Through the car windows a vast emptiness of space assaults the senses. The horizon encircles the world like the rim of some immense plate, and no matter how fast you drive, it recedes in front of you, eventually placing you in a kind of Twilight Zone of suspended forward motion. The wind buffets and rocks your car. There are stretches where, if you roll down the windows, the country smells like a dustier Iowa, with more than a hint of ammonia, feedlots, and hog farms. Other than the frequent sight, oddly in these sere expanses, of thousands of waterfowl threading the blue bowl overhead, there is no visible wildlife—maybe a few pronghorns if you look really hard, a coyote if you are lucky. More than likely you do not see a single prairie dog. Throughout much of the day, the harsh light is almost too bright to look at, at least when there is no brown pall created by agriculture gone airborne. Tiny burgs memorable for the amount of windblown waste snagged on chain mesh fences loom and recede along the laser-straight highway. Billboards unintentionally advertising the Plains social order—Jesus, cowboys, pesticides, cowboy boots, farm machinery, banking loans, the Dallas Cowboys—become welcome breaks in the monotony. A pervading notion characterizes such drives: "I wish to God I'd have flown."

So we react to the modern world of the Great Plains. But it was not always so. A century or two ago, the reactions were very different. To stoke our sense of wonder at the variability of human response to place, let me quote a few of them. They are quite remarkable.

The first is from Sir William Dunbar, the Natchez, Mississippi, scientist whom Thomas Jefferson engaged to help him lead what would have been the first American exploration into the heart of the Southern Plains. Situated as he was on the forested edges of fascination with the country farther west, Dunbar assembled for Jefferson a sense of the Southern Plains two centuries ago:

> By the expression plains, or prairies . . . it is not to be understood a dead flat without any eminences. . . . The western prairies are very different; the expression signifies only a country without timber. These prairies are neither flat nor hilly, but undulating in gently swelling lawns, and expanding into spacious valleys, in the center of which is always found a little timber, growing on the banks of brooks and rivulets of the clearest water. . . . Those who

have viewed only a skirt of these prairies speak of them with a degree of enthusiasm, as if it were only there that nature was to be found truly perfect; they declare that the fertility and beauty of the vegetation, the extreme richness of the valleys, the coolness and excellent quality of the water found everywhere, the salubrity of the atmosphere, and above all, the grandeur of the enchanting landscape which this country presents inspires the soul with sensations not to be felt in any other region of the globe.[2]

There were, Dunbar told Jefferson, "wonderful stories of wonderful productions," among them mountains of pure or partial salt and silver ore lying about in chunks on the prairie. And there were unfathomed wildlife riches—bears, "tygers," wolves, and buffalo and other grazers beyond imagination, even great herds of feral horses that had already become the focus of a thriving market. There were stories of giant water serpents, and some said there were unicorns out on the Southern Plains.[3]

William Dunbar never got to see the region of those wonderful productions that at least one contemporary American map was already calling the "Great Plains."[4] But plenty of his contemporaries did. Among scores of such passages from the Lewis and Clark ascent of the Missouri River through the Northern Plains, this one, from Meriwether Lewis in what is now South Dakota, serves as well as any:

> Monday Sept. 17 1804 this plane . . . is intirely occupied by the burrows of the *barking squiril* heretofore described; this anamal appears here in infinite numbers. . . . the shortness and virdue of the grass gave the plains the appearance throughout it's whole extent of beatifull bowling-green in fine order. . . . a great number of wolves of the small kind, halks [hawks] and some pole-cats were to be seen. . . . this senery already rich pleasing and beatiful was still farther heightened by immence herds of Buffaloe, deer Elk and Antelopes which we saw in every direction feeding on the hills and plains.[5]

Zebulon Montgomery Pike, in 1806, famously found the Arkansas River country a match for the "sandy deserts of Africa." And of course the Stephen Long Expedition pronounced—many of us are tempted to think with some savvy—the Southern High Plains "unfit for agriculture" after their trek along the Canadian and Arkansas during what we now know, according to Connie Woodhouse's essay in this volume, was the very dry year of 1820. With equal insight, though, they noted that "travelling over a dusty plain of sand and gravel, barren as the deserts of Arabia" was never tedious because of the thrilling Plains wildlife spectacle, whose closest analogue was (once again) Africa. On the Arkansas River, Captain John Bell wrote that there were "thousands of buffalo on both sides of the river." Naturalist Thomas Say, no Plains Romantic, added that the vast herds were never without a roiling accompaniment of "famine-pinched wolves and flights of obscene and ravenous birds."[6]

These descriptions could continue without end, for those in the last century who were amazed and startled by the Plains—or smitten with admiration—are virtually too numerous to list. Washington Irving was enthralled with the Plains. So were James Fenimore Cooper, George Catlin, Prince Maximilian, John James Audubon. A favorite Plains quote of mine, whose inversion of the modern reaction is endlessly pleasing to me, is from a little-known but gifted writer who, remarkably, was a New Mexico mountain man. In 1831, Albert Pike and a troop of colorful trappers, having stripped the Sangre de Cristo and Jemez and San Juan ranges of beaver, looped out across the High Plains, hoping vainly for undiscovered beaver streams. After months out on the great horizontal sweeps, this is how the landscape struck him.

> The sea, the woods, the mountains, all suffer in comparison with the prairie. . . . The prairie has a stronger hold upon the senses. Its sublimity arises from its unbounded extent, its barren monotony and desolation, its still, unmoved, calm, stern, almost self-confident grandeur, its strange power of deception, its want of echo, and, in fine, its power of throwing a man back upon himself.[7]

Even in the twentieth century, after the Plains wildlife extermination war but before modern agriculture ripped the grass off much of the Plains, the region entranced with the same magic that had moved Albert Pike. Young Georgia O'Keeffe, seemingly sentenced to a career as an art teacher in High Plains Texas during World War I, marveled at how you could just drive or walk "off into space." Writing her friend Daniel Catton Rich as late as 1949, O'Keeffe told him that "crossing the Panhandle of Texas is always a very special event for me . . . driving in the early morning toward the dawn and rising sun—The plains are not like anything else and I always wonder why I go other places." [8]

Yet another twentieth-century woman artist, Willa Cather, reacted similarly. As she told a back-home newspaper in 1921:

> I go everywhere. I admire all kinds of country. . . . But when I strike the open plains, something happens. I'm home. I breathe differently. That love of great spaces, of rolling open country like the sea—it's the grand passion of my life. I tried for years to get over it. I've stopped trying. It's incurable.[9]

I could go on. But to progress to my point, let me finally cite that ultimate American lover of being in the world, Walt Whitman. Whitman saw the Plains for the first time after the Civil War, when the animals and native inhabitants of the Old West held sway and the greatest dramas of the so-called frontier were being played out. This was his reaction:

> I am not so sure but that the prairies and plains, while less stunning at first sight, last longer, fill the esthetic sense fuller, precede all the rest, and make North America's characteristic landscape.[10]

There's an obvious question to pose from this exercise: What has happened to make the modern reaction to the Great Plains so different now? How, in other words, do you get from Albert Pike and Willa Cather to the "un-country" of Deborah Popper?

The Great Transformation

The answer to the change in reaction probably does have at least some gender nuances, but primarily it has to do with the extraordinary transformation the Great Plains underwent in the late nineteenth and early twentieth centuries. In effect, we dismantled a ten-thousand-year-old ecology, very likely one of the most exciting natural spectacles in the world (and world-famous because of it), in the space of a half-century. For many male observers of the Plains who made careers out of the loss—among them people like Charlie Russell, Frederic Remington, and Zane Grey—it was a perceived life in "wilderness," among Native people and thronging wildlife, that they mourned. Even so experienced a naturalist as John James Audubon, on the Missouri River in 1843, was beside himself out on the "wild" nineteenth-century Plains. He was, he wrote, in "the very midst of the game country." "My head is actually swimming with excitement," he closed a letter that summer, "and I cannot write any more."[11]

For women especially attuned to the Plains—painters and novelists like O'Keeffe and Cather—it was not the wildlife spectacle but a sense of freedom derived from a vast, uncluttered space of grasslands that appealed so strongly. "Space" and expanses like "the sea" serve as code-words for the spirit-stirring freedom available to independent women on the open grasslands of the West in the early twentieth century. The novelist Mari Sandoz, although she, too, mourned the world of American Plains Indians and thronging wildlife, in the twentieth century thrilled to the same effect O'Keeffe and Cather mentioned.

But historical forces that mounted in intensity a century and more ago destroyed *that* Great Plains, seemingly forever. At a time when government had not progressed to the point of protecting species from eradication and science had not grasped the values and balances inherent in ecological diversity, hunters blessed by the free market devastated the most singular wildlife species of the Plains. Anglo—and yes, Hispanic, Métis, and American Indian—hunters slaughtered thirty million buffalo, perhaps in excess of fifty million pronghorns, tens of thousands of wild sheep, untold numbers of elk, for robes, hides, pelts, meat, and tongues in demand by the global market. Hunters and stockmen pursued and shot down grizzly bears, which had once ranged as far out on the Plains as North Dakota, Kansas, and West Texas, until they drove the few that remained into exile in the mountains of the West. It was partly the market for pelts and a kind of war against the wild on behalf of Christianity and civilization, but mostly it was the livestock industry's capture of the federal government's Animal Damage Control Department that resulted in every last Plains lobo wolf getting hunted down or trapped or poisoned. The very last wolf on the Texas Plains ended up gutshot with a .22 by picnickers near Amarillo in 1924.[12] In Montana, a livestock-controlled state legislature even passed a law requiring veterinarians to infect captured wolves with sarcoptic mange and release them to spread the disease among wild canids.[13]

Then came the campaign against such seemingly inoffensive Plains creatures as prairie dogs, ground squirrels, magpies, and ravens, which had the unintended (although evidently welcome) effect of also vanquishing many of the 160-odd species that had evolved to the particular ecologies of vast prairie-dog towns on the Plains. Some of the most notable of these now endangered species were black-footed ferrets, swift foxes, and mountain plovers, the latter one of the most common High Plains birds a century ago and of which fewer than 5,500 remain today.

The big, charismatic Plains species that had defined the region in world imagination in the nineteenth century fled to refuges deep in the Rockies. And now out on the great sweeps, a century after the assault on Plains wildlife commenced in earnest, there are 55 threatened or endangered grassland species in the United States, and an astonishing 728 candidates (including black-tailed prairie dogs, which once may have comprised the single largest living biomass on the Plains) considered as possible or likely listings. The one Great Plains fauna that still seems abundant to modern travelers, its birds, declined 25 to 65 percent in the 1980s, the largest population loss of any species group on the continent.[14]

The war on Plains wildlife was one of the biggest steps in the creation of "un-country," but it was only the beginning. Act Two was the agricultural assault. Because level, grassy plains did not appear to present the kind of obstacles to agriculture that other landscapes did, between the 1850s and 1930s—as John Opie's and John Miller Morris's essays in this book describe—homesteading policies privatized the overwhelming bulk of the American Great Plains. In Southern Plains locales like western Kansas/eastern Colorado, the big breakout took place under the nineteenth-century homestead laws, and mostly in the decades on either side of the twentieth century. In Oklahoma, the land rushes resulting from American Indian allotment and sale of "excess" acreage was the trigger. Settlers broke out Eastern New Mexico mostly after the passage of the Enlarged Homestead Act of 1909. And in Texas, with its anomalous lands history and long devotion to privatization, the sale and breakup of the XIT Ranch in 1915, along with disposed railroad tracts, brought farmers by the trainload to the Llano Estacado and Rolling Plains.

I am far from an agricultural historian and will leave it to Opie, Morris, and others to address the regional details of how Plains agriculture played out, and will play out, in history. The point I want to address has to do with the resulting environmental history, which saw a landscape already de-buffaloed and de-wolved now almost de-grassed, too. The Southern Plains became almost all privately held, with all the property rights implications of such ownership, including an almost overnight, wholesale replacement of the evolved Plains ecology with a new one consisting of introduced Old World animals and plants.

The losses, in any case, were staggering. Conservation biology now points to plowing up the tallgrass prairie, whose extent on the Southern Plains has been reduced by agriculture to less than 1 percent of its original coverage, as the greatest disaster perpetrated against nature in modern continental history. Even on the mid-grass and shortgrass plains, from Texas to Canada, the losses have been mind-boggling. By 2001, Saskatchewan had only 19 percent of its native prairie left. North Dakota had only 28 percent. Texas has an average of 20 percent of its prairie today, although the part of the High Plains I know best, the central Llano Estacado, is in far worse shape. Lubbock County by the 1980s had lost 97 percent of its native grasslands. Literally all that remained was in Yellow House Canyon, country too rugged to plow up and to plant cotton.[15]

The contrast between the Great Plains and Rocky Mountains in Lewis and Clark's day was clear in the party's longing to escape the wildlife-poor mountains and return to the Plains. In our time, following two centuries of history we have accomplished an entire reversal: the federally managed Rockies are now home to most of the West's wildlife, while the privately owned Great Plains has become a monument to the American sacrifice of nature.[16] "Un-country," it would seem, is the only Southern Plains future within the scope of our imagining.

Preserving the Plains

But this is a three-act story. Once we thrilled to the Great Plains. Then we wreaked havoc on its ecology, and many Americans came to despise the result. For the past three-quarters of a century, a third phase—undoubtedly not the last—has been building momentum. As a result of some tragic historical misses, to an extent, stage three is still a vision. But there have been some successes, too.

In our time, environmentalism and conservation biology seem finally to have recognized natural grasslands and prairie ecosystems as among the most undervalued natural regions around the world. Despite acclaimed examples of grassland parks like the Serengeti and Kruger Parks in Africa and the Elmas in Brazil, in United States environmental history we have famously overlooked or bypassed plains and prairies in the federal preservation agenda.[17] The irony that the first visionary call for an American national park (George Catlin's in 1832) was for a park on the Great Plains, while National Park Service (NPS) history is in fact a study in apathy towards plains parks and monuments, has finally begun to influence the American conservation community.[18] But it was not always so.

A century ago, concerns for watershed protection directed the major American conservation initiative of the time—national forest designa-

Eroded spires of the canyon country at the head of the Red River represent the part of the Southern Plains that conservationists have most often looked to in preserving natural areas in the region. Photograph courtesy Dan Flores.

tions—toward the mountain ranges of the public lands in the West. Except for a scattering of island mountain ranges on the Plains, most on the Northern Plains, the national forest initiative ignored the Great Plains. Similarly, although for different reasons, during the initial phase of national park history (the 1870s to the 1930s), the scenic ideals of the Romantic Age, which centered on sublime scenery, dominated American landscape preservation. Yellowstone and Rocky Mountain National Parks, along with the great canyons like Yosemite, Zion, and the Grand Canyon, were the ne plus ultra examples of American parks —not monumental merely, but monumentally *vertical*.[19] No landscapes on the Plains seemed very interesting to a park service with this kind of value system. Although early on the NPS did accept three Great Plains parks—Sullys Hill in Nebraska, Platt in Oklahoma, and Wind Cave in South Dakota—the three totaled fewer than thirty thousand acres altogether (compared to 2.2 million acres for Yellowstone alone). Eventually, the NPS downlisted all but Wind Cave. The result was that almost the only Great Plains nature preservation in the early twentieth century occurred with the creation of national wildlife refuges such as the Wichita Mountains Wildlife Refuge in southwestern Oklahoma, established in 1906.

In the twentieth century, as the park service moved slowly from monumentalism (what Robert Sterling Yard liked to call the "Scenic Supremacy of the United States") toward some incorporation of ecosystem protection in its criteria for parks, a new problem emerged. Until passage of the Land and Water Conservation Fund Act in 1964, the park service had no acquisition budget, which became an almost insurmountable obstacle on parts of the Plains, where privatization had proceeded to the point that literally every potential site for a park was outside NPS reach. In the 1920s, the pioneering ecologist Victor Shelford and the Committee of Ecology of the Grasslands began to press for large Great Plains preserves based on ecology rather than monumentalism. They studied eleven sites, found four more than acceptable, and eventually submitted one (spanning three-fourths of a million acres in Nebraska and South Dakota) to the park service and Congress. But the NPS fumbled the ball.[20]

Historians of the American park system generally accept that the philosophical direction the service took in its early years was the result of first director Stephen Mather's personal vision. According to his biographer, Mather developed a set of evaluative criteria for new additions to the park/monument system that were essentially followed by his successor and protege, Horace Albright. The Mather criteria centered around the requirement of a large, preferably contiguous area with natural features so extraordinary as to be of national interest—namely, scenery, and of a particularly unusual and impressive quality.[21] To take care of the "low-grade" sites with only regional or local interest, Mather used the NPS (and especially its regional officers) to promote a state parks movement.

Thus, while scientists like Victor Shelford were already thinking in terms of preserving representative ecosystems, the park service had the Mather scenery inertia to overcome. This is undoubtedly why, as service personnel began to look beyond the mountains and remembered the role of the Great Plains in Western history, they concentrated their efforts not on the rolling, grassy uplands most typical of the region but on the more dramatic badlands and canyonlands country, the erosional equivalents of the Colorado Plateau, where parks like Bryce and Zion were already gestating.

A classic southwestern slot canyon in the erosional maze of the Palo Duro Canyon system was, at various times in the 1930s, considered both for national park and national monument status. Photograph courtesy Dan Flores.

The problem was that no landscapes on the Great Plains measured up when compared to the scale of these places. So in the 1920s and 1930s, the NPS disappointed the ecologists by turning down one Plains proposal after another. South Dakota had first proposed its yellow-cream-and-buff Badlands as a park in 1909, and since much of its acreage consisted of "excess" American Indian lands and parcels never selected in the homesteading process, it was a prime candidate for a High Plains park. Yet sentiments against the lack of vertical relief in the proposed "Teton National Park" prevailed against it. Roger Toll, chief investigator for the NPS, examined the Badlands in July 1928 and decided that "it is not a supreme scenic feature of national importance." The Badlands, Toll reported, "are surpassed in grandeur, beauty and interest by the Grand Canyon National Park and by Bryce National Park."[22] However, because 60 percent of the Badlands was still public domain and because South Dakota promised to acquire and transfer to the NPS 90 percent of the private holdings, Toll recommended that Congress invoke the Antiquities Act (which targeted landscapes of unusual archeological or geologic interest) to proclaim 68,000 acres of the Badlands a national monument. Congress approved Badlands National Monument in 1929. Enlarged to some 250,000 acres, it became reality with President Roosevelt's proclamation in 1939.[23]

Something similar happened with North Dakota's Little Missouri Badlands, which the NPS initially found "too barren" for a national park. Local ranchers also opposed the idea vociferously. But rancher opposition swirled away with the Dust Bowl and the Depression, and the NPS finally acquired the area in 1947—but as a historical/memorial park based on President Theodore Roosevelt's presence in the area, not the ecosystem park Shelford was calling for.[24]

Interesting to ponder, during the 1930s when scientists were gradually pulling the NPS in the direction of ecosystem thinking, it was the Southern Plains where—at least briefly—park personnel toyed with the idea of a large ecosystem Great Plains park that would have gone far toward preserving the old magic of the Plains. What makes this all the more intriguing is that while the NPS upgraded Badlands and Theodore Roosevelt to full national park status with the Omnibus Parks Bill of 1978, and (added to Wind Cave and Saskatchewan's Grassland National Park, created in 1981) thus gave the Northern Plains a fine start in plains restoration, today the Southern Plains entirely lacks large-scale preserved federal lands. The Southern Plains does possess a scattering of national wildlife refuges and small national monuments, notably Alibates Flint Quarry in the Texas Panhandle and Capulin Volcano on the New Mexico Plains. But early in the twenty-first century, agriculturally remade "un-country" prevails on much of the Texas, Oklahoma, Kansas, Colorado, and New Mexico plains.

A Historic Missed Opportunity: Palo Duro Canyon

In the 1930s, with the exception of the Black Hills, Palo Duro Canyon in the Texas Panhandle was probably the most famous Great Plains landscape. The Texas congressional delegation had mentioned it several times, beginning in 1908, as worthy of national park consideration. But Palo Duro had long since gone under private fence and the owner's jealously guarded access; only a handful of people had ever seen it. Yet it was widely known not only for its reputedly dramatic and colorful scenery (painted by a young Georgia O'Keeffe around the time of the Great War), but also because it had been the site of the last major engagement of the American Indian wars on the Southern Plains, and the location of rancher Charles Goodnight's famous JA Ranch.

A sixty-mile-long, eight-hundred-foot-deep roar of color formed where the headwaters of the Red River sliced and diced through the Llano Estacado tableland, Palo Duro not only had historic and scenic values, but it exposed 250 million years of North American geology going back to the Triassic. As elsewhere on the Plains, by the twentieth century its large fauna had been decimated, and there had been botanical deterioration wrought by overgrazing. But Goodnight and his wife, Mary, were known to have preserved a small herd of Southern Plains bison on the JA. And the canyon continued to harbor a splendid floral and small faunal mix, a unique combination of eastern and western species including several relict and endemic species.[25] Acquisition of a small (fifteen-thousand-acre) state park was already under way in the early 1930s.[26] And Palo Duro had some champions. Among them were historian J. Evetts Haley; newspaper columnist Phebe Warner, who wrote numerous articles on behalf of a national park in the canyon; and architect Guy Carlander, who headed a local national park association. Even Enos Mills, "the John Muir of the Rockies," went on record as supporting a national park in Palo Duro.[27] But it seems to have been Albright's unplanned layover in Amarillo in 1932—and the consequent chance to peruse photographs of Palo Duro—that led the director to

The Narrows of Tule Canyon, a stunning tributary gorge of Palo Duro Canyon, was a spot that impressed Roger Toll of the National Park Service in the 1930s. Photograph courtesy Dan Flores.

decide to add Palo Duro to an upcoming investigative tour of possible Texas park sites by Roger Toll.[28]

I have argued in print—to general consternation in Texas I am pretty sure—that over the long term Roger Toll will be a more significant figure in Texas, for more people, than Davy Crockett. Toll was a one-man-make-it-or-break-it whirlwind for the NPS whose opinion basically gave the West most of the national parks that the NPS targeted during the early 1930s, including Texas's Big Bend, Guadalupe Mountains, and Padre Island. At the time of his Texas tour (the winter of 1933–34), Toll was still a Mather-style scenery advocate. But at park service offices in Washington, the ecologists evidently regarded his upcoming examination of Palo Duro Canyon as the masterstroke of Plains preservation they longed for. While Toll journeyed to Texas, the scientists were assembling maps and materials for the creation of a "National Park of the Plains" around Palo Duro, a huge swath of territory half the size of Yellowstone. This park would have included not just the canyonated sections but adjacent High Plains grasslands so that restoration biologists could return bison and pronghorns to their old home.[29]

Toll spent four days in Palo Duro in January 1934 in the company of writer and historian J. Evetts Haley. Together they traversed much of its sixty-mile length from Dreamland Falls (where the Red River cuts through Triassic sandstones) to the stunning Tule Canyon Narrows, which Randolph Marcy described during his exploration of 1852 as the most dramatic scene he had ever witnessed.[30] Toll was impressed: he regarded Palo Duro as scenically superior to the Badlands, which he had recommended for monument status six years earlier. But whereas Big Bend was monumental, like the Dakota Badlands, Palo Duro was merely "interesting and picturesque." In sum, as Toll put it in his report, on a scale of sublimity, Palo Duro was "not well qualified for a national park as its scenery is not of outstanding national importance." He wrote new NPS director Arno Cammerer, "It would rate below the present scenic national parks." Herbert Maier, NPS regional chief based in Oklahoma City, agreed, adding the clinching argument: "Since its general characteristics are so much like those of the Grand Canyon in Arizona, the Palo Duro as a national park would be a 'tail to a kite.'" [31] The NPS also had concerns about land prices. Palo Duro lands were not quite as "worthless" as those in Big Bend, and the state had somehow ended up paying twenty-five dollars an acre for lands that normally sold for five dollars, when it created the state park.[32]

Despite Toll's report, ecosystem values continued to gain ground in the NPS. And Palo Duro had now caught the eye of the agency. Both the Washington and regional offices now had files on the Southern Plains canyon, which included several black-and-white photographs of the area taken by J. Evetts Haley. Just two ranches owned the bulk of the canyon below the state park, a great advantage in acquisition negotiations. One, the JA, seemed seriously intent on unloading its holdings, at one point offering the ranch to the newly oil-wealthy Osage Nation of Oklahoma and at another proposing that the Defense Department acquire the canyon as a bombing range! The service's new Everglades National Park in Florida, established for its ecological values instead of classic scenery reasons, demonstrated that NPS interest in ecosystems was to be taken seriously. And new parks like Acadia (Maine), Shenandoah (Virginia), and Great Smoky Mountains (Tennessee/North Carolina) were demonstrating that citizen initiatives could create national parks in states lacking a public domain.

The individual who emerged as champion of large-scale Southern Plains nature preservation after 1935 was Texas Senator Morris Sheppard, and he tried a different tack. As High Plains farming fell apart in the Dust Bowl of the 1930s, the federal government re-acquired thousands of acres of homesteaded lands on the Southern Plains, creating the nucleus of the present National Grasslands. Senator Sheppard began to press for a different form of federal economic salvation for the region by having President Roosevelt make Palo Duro into a national monument by proclamation. Dr. Herman Bumpas, noted geologist and advisor to the NPS, became an inside supporter of the idea. As Bumpas told Planning Chief Ben Thompson, a Palo Duro Canyon National Monument seemed almost a necessity in another of the service's new themes: public education about the natural world. Located just south of Route 66 (now Interstate 40), one of the principal routes across the country, Palo Duro could play the geological role of "First Chapter of Genesis" for tourists heading west, since its bottom-most geological strata ended exactly where those at the rim of the Grand Canyon began.[33]

Thus in October 1938, Wendell Little, NPS planning coordinator, initiated a second review of Palo Duro Canyon, this time as a candidate for a rather more modest 134,658-acre national monument. By this point in NPS evolution, evaluation strategy was much more systematic than when Roger Toll's visual impression could decide a landscape's fate. From the Santa Fe regional NPS offices, eight experts in as many fields, ranging from archeology to recreation, descended on Palo Duro during March and April 1939. The result was an eighty-nine-page document assessing everything from the botany and wildlife of the canyon to its geological and historical significance. It included a detailed estimate of the cost of federal acquisition of the land, a figure that ran to $294,000, plus $264,000 for the fifteen-hundred-acre state park. The proposed boundaries extended from Dreamland Falls 35 miles down-canyon to Paradise Valley, owned by the JA Ranch. The plan omitted the wide, bottom end of Palo Duro, which features Tule Canyon and its spectacular gorge. Nor did the report include any significant description of bison and pronghorn restoration; needless to say, it did not broach the subject of recovering Southern Plains wolf populations at all.[34] The idea five years earlier of a large, restored Southern Plains landscape seems mostly to have evaporated by 1939.

This "Investigative Report on Proposed Palo Duro National Monument, Texas," which has long lain forgotten in the NPS papers in Washington, did recommend national monument status for Palo Duro. But flipping through its pages now, it is hard not to think that its arguments could have been far stronger. True enough, geologist Charles Gould made an eloquent plea. "From the standpoint of Geology and scenery," he wrote, "Palo Duro is well worthy of being made into a national monument. It is the most spectacular canyon, carved by erosion, anywhere on the Great Plains of North America." While the majority of the members of the investigative team echoed those sentiments, they missed many opportunities to point up ecological or historical uniqueness. Confronted with a long stretch of heavily timbered canyon above the state park, the forester failed to recognize it as a relict forest of Rocky Mountain junipers. While the wildlife biologist noted the unusual mixing of eastern and western species, he missed specially evolved endemics like the Palo Duro mouse. The most glaring omission was the historian's failure to even mention the Battle of Palo Duro Canyon, 1874, as much a finale for American Indians on the Southern Plains as the Little Big Horn was on the Northern.

In Washington, the recommendation in favor of monument status met with mixed reviews. Those who had actually seen Palo Duro were uniformly in favor of national monument status. Others, like NPS Chief of Engineering Ben Thompson, who saw only black and white photos, thought the scenery not "particularly outstanding" and wrote a rebuttal

South Prong Canyon of Caprock Canyons State Park is part of Texas' efforts on behalf of wildlands preservation on the Southern Plains. The state parks preserve only small fragments of the far larger region the National Park Service was interested in protecting during the 1930s, however. Photograph courtesy Dan Flores.

to the recommendation.[35] But again, in a nonpublic lands state, the most important element was cost. In the 1930s, the NPS entirely lacked acquisition funds except when a government or private individuals provided them. And whereas public support for the idea of a large Southern Plains national monument poured in from places like Denver, Albuquerque, and even Oklahoma City, Texans seemed strikingly ambivalent to the prospect.[36] Its cultural identity based on the aggressive, free-wheeling, speculative strains of the American personality, Texas in the 1930s and 1940s appeared largely uninterested in preservation of the natural world of the Plains—or environmental preservation in general.[37] So lacking a commitment from Texas or one of its philanthropists, that $558,000 cost for the 135,000 acres seemed insurmountable. Nor was the matter helped when one of the landowners, an absentee owner from Chicago who had title to a much admired scenic area above the state park, wrote the NPS that he was willing to sell his 3,000 acres "NOW . . . in a spirit of cooperation" for a mere $475,000.[38]

That was the swan song for Palo Duro National Monument. As Interior Secretary Harold Ickes told Senator Sheppard in 1940, "The Department probably would be willing to recommend the establishment as a national monument of approximately 135,000 acres of land . . . if the necessary area could be acquired. . . . No funds are available to this Department for the purchase of these lands."[39] It is at that point that the documents trail in the NPS papers ends.

Restoring the Magic of the Plains

Of course, the story of Southern Plains restoration, let alone the visionary project of returning to the Great Plains some of the magic that compelled so many travelers and observers in the nineteenth century, does not end there. Missing out on an expansive Southern Plains national monument—to say nothing of the early 1930s vision of a million-acre ecosystem Plains park—in hindsight was a huge, shortsighted miss for both nature *and* civilization. But in our time the Great Plains finally has champions again. As Frank and Deborah Popper are given to arguing these days with respect to their Buffalo Commons idea, Plains outmigration, the emergence of American Indians as major environmental players, and a new excitement about ecological restoration are making their *idea* reality, just on a smaller and more decentralized scale than they had originally envisioned.[40]

Undoubtedly, there is reason for excitement. There is every evidence of state, private, and grassroots activity across the Plains: groups like the Southern Plains Land Trust in southeastern Colorado, which is seeking to acquire High Plains acreage for restoration; the recent establishment of a Nature Conservancy office in Amarillo; Texas Parks and Wildlife's persistent, if so far unsuccessful, search for a large High Plains state park where buffalo and elk might roam at large again; and groups like the Great Plains Restoration Council in Denver, which presently acts as an information clearinghouse for hopes to create a million-acre Buffalo Commons. The Bob Scott/Institute for the Rockies vision for a "Big Open" in Montana has been around for more than a decade, and a number of nonprofit groups like the American Buffalo Foundation and the High Plains Ecosystem Restoration Council are attempting to advance that cause, too, if a bit vaguely. In the summer of 1999, the journal *Wild Earth* published a proposal for a biological corridor around the Caprock of the Llano Estacado into which biologists might release

One of dozens of waterfalls and pools located in the recess of the Caprock Canyonlands of the Southern Plains. Photograph courtesy Dan Flores.

wolves and other native charismatic fauna. And the *Great Plains Natural Resources Journal* has published a proposal on a "Greater Black Hills Wildlife Protection Area."[41] Even the Sierra Club, for decades interested only in mountains until it discovered the Colorado Plateau in the 1950s, is now a prairie advocate, with an evolving proposal for High Plains biological corridors linking preserved "core" areas, modeled on the Yellowstone-to-Yukon idea for the Northern Rockies.[42]

So far, aside from Ted Turner's several buffalo ranches, the most successful small-scale efforts have been those of the Nature Conservancy, whose thirty-thousand-plus-acre prairie acquisition near Tulsa in northeastern Oklahoma may finally serve as the core area around which a tallgrass prairie national park will get established.[43] But American Indian peoples, especially on the Northern Plains reservations where tribal land bases still exist, have become major players in prairie restoration. The Inter-Tribal Bison Cooperative has been an unexpectedly successful project, managing to place bison herds—some of them thousands of animals—with nearly forty tribes over the past decade. And tribes like the Blackfeet, the Gros Ventres/Assiniboines, and the Cheyenne River Sioux have been able to pursue prairie-threatened and endangered species recovery programs (for Swift foxes and ferrets, for example) more adroitly than any federal land managers.[44]

As has been the case in American environmental history for more than a century, though, it is, after all, the federal initiatives that give prairie advocates the most hope. The park service has long known that what it needs is both tallgrass and High Plains ecosystem parks.[45] And pressure has been mounting for a decade now for a large park that would quite literally restore the Plains that excited Audubon to speechlessness: tens-of-thousands of wild bison, elk back out on the undulating sweeps, prairie dog towns as far as the eye can reach, and the predators—wolves and grizzlies—right in there with the ferrets and foxes. Conservation biologists say that for such a Catlinesque park to work it should at least cover 2.5 million acres, about the size of Yellowstone, although ten to twenty million acres (!) would be a more effective size.[46] This would be an act of conservation statecraft at the level of a Yellowstone or a Wilderness Act, a worthy goal for a new century.

There is nothing so ambitious in the real-life works. But a smaller version might emerge from the Clinton administration's proclamation in 2000 of a Missouri Breaks National Monument centered on the

White Cliffs section of the Wild and Scenic Missouri River. Merge this 377,346-acre monument with the 150,000-acre Charlie Russell National Wildlife Refuge just downriver, as prairie advocates are hoping, and federal managers would have a sizeable chunk of the last *sanctum sanctorum* of the bison plains, handily located in a state that already has wolves and grizzlies in its mountains and a buffalo source available on nearby American Indian reservations. On the Southern Plains, restoration of that old world of grass, animals, and the magic of space is a little harder to see. More than fifteen years ago, Oklahoma geographer Bret Wallach called on us at least to consider preserving the river corridors on the Southern Plains.[47] And using Palo Duro's history, I have tried to rescue the idea of a national ecosystem park on the upper Red River that would not only restore the Southern Plains world of nature but would confer the Comanches, Kiowas, and Southern Cheyennes special privileges of use.[48] In large part (you have to suspect) because of the political and ideological obstacles in a conservative and anti-federal region, whose roots Jeff Roche describes elsewhere in this volume, no serious plans for implementing these ideas exist. Yet.

Ecologists Fred Samson and Fritz Knopf, writing in *Bioscience,* have argued that for preserving biological diversity in North America, the Great Plains has now become "a priority, perhaps the highest priority."[49] I could see where such a statement might strike many Americans, utterly bored by the Great Plains in its present skinned form, as preposterous, perhaps a joke perpetrated by geeky scientists who don't quite get that it's not funny. But among those of us who know some history, who have read Lewis and Clark, Albert Pike, Audubon, Cather, Sandoz, and O'Keeffe, nobody is laughing.

Notes

1. Quoted in Anne Matthews, *Where the Buffalo Roam: The Storm over the Revolutionary Plan to Restore America's Great Plains* (New York: Grove Press, 1992), 122–23. See also Neil Evernden, "Beauty and Nothingness: Prairie As Failed Resource," *Landscape* 27 (1983): 3–6.

I need to express my heartfelt thanks to my long-time friend and one-time graduate student, Blake Morris, whose graduate school career consisted almost solely of flying off to Washington, D.C., to collect the National Park Service documents on Palo Duro (cited in this essay for the first time) for me. To Blake and to Eric Bolen, another old friend who was then a dean in the graduate school at Texas Tech and who gave us the research money: Southern Plains conservation history is indebted to you.

2. William Dunbar to Thomas Jefferson, Natchez, 9 June 1804, and "Journal of a Voyage, 10 December 1804," in *Life, Letters, and Papers of William Dunbar*, ed. Erin Dunbar Rowland (Jackson: University Press of Mississippi for the Mississippi Historical Society, 1930), 133–35, 307–308.

3. Dan Flores, "A Very Different Story: Exploring the Southwest from Monticello . . .," *Montana, the Magazine of Western History* 50 (Spring 2000): 8–9.

4. "Great Plains" was laid in boldface across the country up the Red River in an untitled map compiled by American General James Wilkinson in 1804. The original is owned by the Houghton Library at Harvard University.

5. Meriwether Lewis, *The Journals of Lewis and Clark*, ed. Bernard DeVoto (Boston: Houghton Mifflin, 1953), 28.

6. Zebulon Montgomery Pike, *The Journals of Zebulon Montgomery Pike*, vol. 1, ed. Donald Jackson (Norman: University of Oklahoma Press, 1966); Edwin James, "Account of an Expedition from Pittsburgh to the Rocky Mountains Performed in the Years 1819, 1820," in *Early Western Travels, 1748–1846*, vol. 17, ed. Reuben Gold Thwaites (Cleveland: Arthur H. Clark, 1906). The "Arabia" and Arkansas River quotes: John Bell, "The Journal of Captain John R. Bell, Official Journalist for the Stephen H. Long Expedition to the Rocky Mountains, 1820," in *The Far West and the Rockies Historical Series, 1820–1875*, vol. 6, ed. Harlin Fuller and Leroy Hafen (Glendale, Calif.: Arthur H. Clark, 1957), 178, 215. Say's remark is quoted in Patricia Tyson Stroud, *Thomas Say: New World Naturalist* (Philadelphia: University of Pennsylvania Press, 1992), 113.

7. Albert Pike, *Albert Pike's Journeys in the Prairie, 1831–1832*, ed. J. Evetts Haley (Canyon, Tex.: Panhandle-Plains Historical Society, 1969), 23.

8. Georgia O'Keeffe to Daniel Catton Rich, Abiquiu, 13 November 1949, in *Georgia O'Keeffe: Art and Letters*, ed. Jack Cowart, Juan Hamilton, and Sarah Greenough (Washington, D.C.: National Gallery of Art, 1987), 249.

9. *Lincoln State Journal*, 2 November 1921.

10. Walt Whitman, *The Uncollected Poetry and Prose of Walt Whitman*, 2 vols., ed. Emory Holloway (New York: Garden City Publishing, 1921), 2:35.

11. First quote in Robert McCracken Peck, "Audubon and Bachman: A Collaboration in Science," in *John James Audubon in the West: The Last Expedition, Mammals of North America*, ed. Sarah Boehme (New York: Harry Abrams, 2000), 84; second quote in Robert McCracken Peck, "Audubon, Bachman, and the Quadrupeds of North America," *Antiques* (November 2000), 749.

12. Oral history tape, "The Last Wolf Killed in the Panhandle," Harrell Family Papers, Panhandle-Plains Historical Museum Archives, Canyon, Texas.

13. Dan Flores, *Horizontal Yellow: Nature and History in the Near Southwest* (Albuquerque: University of New Mexico Press, 1999), 270.

14. Fred Samson and Fritz Knopf, "Prairie Conservation in North America," *Bioscience* 44 (1994): 418–19; Mark Matthews, "Saving the Hated Prairie Dog," *Washington Post*, 16 August 1999.

15. Samson and Knopf, "Prairie Conservation"; Peter Lesica, "Endless Sea of Grass—No Longer," *Kelseya* 8 (1995): 1–9; Dan Flores, *Caprock Canyonlands: Journeys into the Heart of the Southern Plains* (Austin: University of Texas Press, 1990), 45.

16. For a discussion of the different conservation histories of the two regions, see Dan Flores, *The Natural West: Environmental History in the Great Plains and Rocky Mountains* (Norman: University of Oklahoma Press, 2001), chapters 7–9.

17. Kenton Miller, "The Natural Protected Areas of the World," and Claude Mondor and Steve Kun, "The Lone Prairie: Protecting Natural Grasslands in Canada," in *National Parks, Conservation, and Development: The Role of Protected Areas in Sustaining Society,* ed. Jeffrey A. McNeely and Kenton R. Miller (Washington, D.C.: Smithsonian Institution Press, 1984), 21, 508–17.

18. Catlin's "call" was a very public one. From George Catlin, *Letters and Notes on the Manners, Customs, and Traditions of the North American Indian,* 2 vols. (New York: Dover Edition, 1973), 1:332.

19. See, particularly, Barbara Novak, *Nature and Culture: American Landscape Painting, 1825–1875* (Cambridge: Oxford University Press, 1979), and Alfred Runte, *National Parks: The American Experience,* 2d ed. (Lincoln: University of Nebraska Press, 1987).

20. Victor Shelford, "Preservation of Natural Biotic Communities," *Ecology* 14 (1933): 240–45; Jerry Shepard, "Singing Out of Tune: Historical Perceptions and National Parks on the Great Plains" (Ph.D. dissertation, Texas Tech University, 1995).

21. Robert Shankland, *Steve Mather of the National Parks,* 3d ed. (New York: Alfred A. Knopf, 1970), 210–15. Richard Sellars has shown how difficult it was for the ecologists to bring the park service around to their way of thinking. Richard West Sellars, *Preserving Nature in the National Parks: A History* (New Haven: Yale University Press, 1997).

22. Roger Toll to Horace Albright, 23 November 1928. Proposed National Parks, File 0–32, Box 2948, Record Group 79, National Archives (hereafter NARG 79).

23. Hal Rothman, *Preserving Different Pasts: The American National Monuments* (Urbana: University of Illinois Press, 1989), 89–118; John Ise, *Our National Park Policy: A Critical History* (Baltimore: Johns Hopkins University Press, 1961), 339–40, 411; Robert Righter, "National Monuments to National Parks: The Use of the Antiquities Act of 1906," *Western Historical Quarterly* 13 (August 1989): 281–301.

24. Newton Drury, Memorandum, August 1946, File 0–32, Box 2954, NARG 79; Elise Broach, "Angels, Architecture, and Erosion: The Dakota Badlands as Cultural Symbol," *North Dakota History* 59 (Spring 1992): 2–15.

25. See Duane F. Guy, ed., *The Story of Palo Duro Canyon* (Canyon, Tex.: Panhandle-Plains Historical Society, 1979); and David Adams, "Vegetation-Environment Relationships in Palo Duro Canyon, West Texas" (Ph.D. dissertation, University of Oklahoma, 1979).

26. Peter Petersen, "A Park for the Panhandle: The Acquisition and Development of Palo Duro Canyon State Park," in Guy, *Palo Duro Canyon,* 145–46; John Jameson, "The Quest for a National Park in Texas," *West Texas Historical Association Year Book* 20 (1974): 47–60.

27. See, especially, Phebe Warner, "Palo Duro—as a National Park," *Southwest Plainsman,* 16 November 1930, and "The Mission of Our Palo Duro Canyon," *Southwest Plainsman,* 21 November 1930. Enos Mills's support is in Enos Mills, "Address to Amarillo Kiwanis Club on Palo Duro as a Park," *Amarillo Daily News,* 20 October 1921.

28. *Canyon News,* 23 June 1932; Horace Albright to Dr. R. P. Jarrett, File 0–32, Box 2948, NARG 79.

29. See Regional Form and Map, National Park of the Plains, Proposed National Parks and Monuments, File 0–32, Box 2948, NARG 79.

30. Randolph Marcy, *A Report on the Exploration of the Red River, in Louisiana* (Washington, D.C.: Government Printing Office, 1854). Eugene Hollon had speculated that Marcy's romantic descriptions ("gigantic escarpments . . . giddy heights . . . unreclaimed sublimity and wilderness") were of Tule Canyon. I believe I laid the matter to rest in *Caprock Canyonlands,* 106–108, 114–15.

J. Evetts Haley was an interesting selection as a guide. He undoubtedly knew the country marvelously, and in the 1930s evidently was a national park advocate. But he became a notorious conservative critic of New Deal and later Great Society federal programs, penning a scathing critique (*A Texan Looks at Lyndon*) of liberal politics.

31. Roger Toll to Arno Cammerer, 7 March 1934, File 0–32, Box 9, NARG 79; Herbert Maier to State Park Division, 8 June 1935, File 0–32, Box 2948, NARG 79.

32. Petersen, "A Park for the Panhandle," 150.

33. Memorandum, Ben Thompson to Charles Wirth, 1 December 1938, File 0–32J, Box 2948, NARG 79.

34. "Investigative Report on Proposed Palo Duro National Monument, Texas, May 1939, File 0–32J, Box 2948, NARG 79. The team consisted of Charles Gould and Ross Maxwell, geologists; Aubrey Neasham, historian; Erik Reed, archeologist; Ward Yeager, forester; John Kell, landscape architect; and Milo Christianson, recreation. Daniel Brand later provided a wildlife report.

35. The report recommending monument status is in Hilory Tolson to Arno Cammerer, 10 May 1939, File 0–32, Box 2948, NARG 79. Thompson's rebuttal is in Ben Thompson, "Comments on Proposed Palo Duro National Monument."

36. See Palo Duro Files, Panhandle-Plains Historical Museum Archives, Canyon, Texas.

37. During this same era, as the NPS was similarly searching for funds in Texas to transfer Big Bend lands to the service, the sort of public campaigns that in states like Maine, Virginia, and Tennessee were significantly aiding national park creations in those states, in Texas netted the total sum of

$8,346.88 for Big Bend National Park. The sentiment went all the way back to the Forest Reserve Act of 1891 (which created the national forest system); Texans were the major voices against it. See Flores, *Horizontal Yellow,* 148.

38. Fred Emery to Marvin Jones, 6 December 1939; Jones to Emery, 8 December 1939. Emery's offer priced his parcel at $150 an acre, roughly thirty times the prevailing market value of Palo Duro land.

39. Acting Under Secretary Underhall, on behalf of Secretary Ickes, to Senator Sheppard, 19 January 1940.

40. Frank Popper, keynote address for the Inter-Tribal Bison Cooperative, Polson, Montana, November 1999; interview with Frank Popper, Lincoln, Nebraska, April 2000, notes in possession of the author.

41. Andrew Kroll and Dwight Berry, "Carnivores in the Caprock: Re-Wilding the High Plains of Texas," *Wild Earth* 9 (Summer 1999): 35–40.

42. See the Sierra Club website: *http://www.sierraclub.org/ecoregions/prairie/html.*

43. E. Raymond Hall first recommended a tallgrass prairie park (along with a High Plains park) in "The Prairie National Park," *National Parks Magazine* 44 (February 1962): 5. A competitor site for a Tallgrass Prairie Park is near Strong City, Kansas, in the Flint Hills.

44. Flores, *The Natural West,* chapter 9. Also see the ITBC web site: *http://www.intertribalbison.org.crst.htm.* The Nez Perce Tribe provided an example by famously taking responsibility for wolf recovery under the Endangered Species Act in the state of Idaho. On the Plains, Defenders of Wildlife has worked with the tribes mentioned in the text in Swift fox releases in advance of U.S. Fish and Wildlife Service programs. See Michelle Nijhuis, "Return of the Natives," *High Country News* 33 (26 February 2001): 1, 8–12; Steve Pavlik, "Will Big Trotter Reclaim His Place? The Role of the Wolf in Navajo Tradition," *American Indian Culture and Research Journal* 24 (Fall 2000): 1–19.

45. Jerry Shepard, "Singing Out of Tune," 140–72; Victor Shelford, "The Preservation of Natural Biotic Communities," *Ecology* 14 (April 1933): 240–45.

46. Ernest Callenbach, *Bring Back the Buffalo! A Sustainable Future for America's Great Plains* (Washington, D.C.: Island Press, 1996), 154–55.

47. Bret Wallach, "The Return of the Prairie," *Landscape* 28 (1985): 1–5.

48. Flores, *Caprock Canyonlands,* chap. 8.

49. Samson and Knopf, "Prairie Conservation," 418. See also their book, Fred Samson and Fritz Knopf, eds., *Prairie Conservation: Preserving North America's Most Endangered Ecosystem* (Washington, D.C.: Island Press, 1996).

Select Bibliography

Anderson, Gary. *The Indian Southwest, 1580–1830: Ethnogenesis and Reinvention*. Norman: University of Oklahoma Press, 1999.

Bamforth, Douglas. *Ecology and Human Organization on the Great Plains*. New York: Plenum Press, 1988.

Berry, Wendell. *The Unsettling of America: Culture and Agriculture*. San Francisco: Sierra Club Books, 1986.

Bloemink, Barbara. *Georgia O'Keeffe: Canyon Suite*. New York: George Braziller, 1995.

Blodgett, Jan. *Land of Bright Promise: Advertising the Texas Panhandle and South Plains, 1870–1917*. Austin: University of Texas Press, 1988.

Blouet, Brian, and Merlin Lawson. *Images of the Plains: The Role of Human Nature in Settlement*. Lincoln: University of Nebraska Press, 1975.

Bolton, Herbert Eugene. *Coronado: Knight of Pueblos and Plains*. Albuquerque: University of New Mexico Press, 1964.

Bonnifield, Paul. *The Dust Bowl: Men, Dirt, and Depression*. Albuquerque: University of New Mexico Press, 1979.

Bowden, Charles. *Killing the Hidden Waters*. Austin: University of Texas Press, 1977.

Bowden, Martyn L. "The Great American Desert and the American Frontier, 1800–1822: Popular Images of the Plains." In *Anonymous Americans: Explorations in Nineteenth-Century Social History*, ed. Tamara Hareven. Englewood Cliffs, N.J.: Prentice-Hall, 1971.

_____. "The Perception of the Western Interior of the United States, 1800–1870: A Problem in Historical Geography." *Proceedings of the Association of American Geographers* I (1969): 16–21.

Brennan, Mary C. *Turning Right in the Sixties: The Conservative Capture of the GOP*. Chapel Hill: University of North Carolina Press, 1995.

Briggs, Charles, and John Van Ness, eds., *Land, Water, and Culture: New Perspectives on Hispanic Land Grants*. Albuquerque: University of New Mexico Press, 1987.

Brooks, Elizabeth, and Jaque Emel, with Brad Jokisch and Paul Robbins. *The Llano Estacado of the U.S. Southern High Plains: Environmental Transformation and the Prospect for Sustainability*. New York: United Nations University Press, 2000.

Burroughs, Jean M. "Homesteading the Llano Estacado." *New Mexico Magazine* 56 (April 1978): 17–23.

Callenbach, Ernest. *Bring Back the Buffalo! A Sustainable Future for America's Great Plains*. Washington, D.C.: Island Press, 1996.

Canonge, Elliott. *Comanche Texts*. Norman: University of Oklahoma Press, 1958.

Carlson, Paul H. "Panhandle Pastures: Early Sheepherding in the Texas Panhandle." *Panhandle-Plains Historical Review* 53 (1980): 1–16.

Carter, Dan T. *From George Wallace to Newt Gingrich: Race in the Conservative Counterrevolution, 1963–1994.* Baton Rouge: Louisiana State University Press, 1996.

_____. *The Politics of Rage: George Wallace, the Origins of the New Conservatism, and the Transformation of American Politics.* New York: Simon and Schuster, 1995.

Castañeda, Carlos. *Our Catholic Heritage in Texas, 1519–1936*, vol. 5. Austin: Von Boeckmann-Jones, 1958.

Coalson, George O. *The Development of the Migratory Farm Labor System in Texas: 1900–1954.* San Francisco: R and E Research Associates, 1977.

Comstock, Gary, ed. *Is There a Moral Obligation to Save the Family Farm?* Ames: Iowa State University Press, 1988.

Cordell, Linda. *Prehistory of the Southwest.* Orlando: Academic Press, 1984.

Corwin, Arthur, ed. *Immigrants and Immigrants: Perspectives on Mexican Labor Migration to the United States.* Westport, Conn.: Greenwood Press, 1978.

Cowart, Jack, Juan Hamilton, and Sarah Greenough. *Georgia O'Keeffe: Art and Letters.* Boston: Bullfinch Press, 1987.

Culley, John J., and Peter L. Petersen, "Hard Times on the High Plains: FSA Photography during the 1930s." *Panhandle-Plains Historical Review* 52 (1979): 15–38.

Davis, Michael. *Magical Urbanism: Latinos Reinvent the U.S. City.* London: Verso, 2000.

Dillehay, Tom. "Late Quarternary Bison Population Changes on the Southern Plains." *Plains Anthropologist* 19 (August 1974): 180–96.

Dobie, J. Frank. *The Mustangs.* New York: Bramhill House, 1934.

Doughty, Robin. "Settlement and Environmental Change in Texas, 1820–1900." *Southwestern Historical Quarterly* 89 (April 1986): 423–42.

Eaves, Charles Dudley, and C. A. Hutchinson. *Post City, Texas: C. W. Post's Colonizing Activities in West Texas.* Austin: Texas State Historical Association, 1952.

Elazar, Daniel J. "Political Culture on the Plains." *Western Historical Quarterly* 11 (July 1980): 261–83.

Flores, Dan. "Bison Ecology and Bison Diplomacy: The Southern Plains from 1800 to 1850." *Journal of American History* 78 (September 1991): 465–85.

_____. *Caprock Canyonlands: Journeys into the Heart of the Southern Plains.* Austin: The University of Texas Press, 1990.

_____. *Horizontal Yellow: Nature and History in the Near Southwest.* Albuquerque: University of New Mexico Press, 1999.

_____. *The Natural West: Environmental History in the Great Plains and Rocky Mountains.* Norman: University of Oklahoma Press, 2001.

_____. "Place: An Argument for Bioregional History." *Environmental History Review* 18 (Winter 1994): 1–18.

_____. "The Plains and the Painters: Two Centuries of Landscape Art from the Llano Estacado." *Journal of American Culture* 14 (1991): 19–28.

Flores, Dan, and Amy Winton. *Canyon Visions: Photographs and Pastels of the Texas Plains*. Lubbock: Texas Tech University Press, 1989.

Gonzalez, Gilbert G., and Raul Fernandez. "Chicano History: Transcending Cultural Models." *Pacific Historical Review* 63 (November 1994): 469–97.

Green, E. Donald. *Land of Underground Rain: Irrigation on the Texas High Plains, 1910–1970*. Austin: University of Texas Press, 1973

Green, George Norris. *The Establishment in Texas Politics: The Primitive Years, 1938–1957*. Westport, Conn.: Greenwood Press, 1979.

Guy, Duane F., ed. *The Story of Palo Duro Canyon*. Canyon, Tex.: Panhandle-Plains Historical Society, 1979.

Haley, J. Evetts. *Charles Goodnight: Cowman and Plainsman*. 1936. Reprint, Norman: University of Oklahoma Press, 1949.

_____. *George L. Littlefield, Texan*. Norman: University of Oklahoma Press, 1943.

_____. "Lore of the Llano Estacado." In *Texas and Southwestern Lore*, ed. J. Frank Dobie. Austin: Texas Folklore Society 6 (1927): 72–89.

_____. *The XIT Ranch of Texas, and the Early Days of the Llano Estacado*. 1936. Reprint, Norman: University of Oklahoma Press, 1953.

Hamilton, David E. *From New Day to New Deal: American Farm Policy from Hoover to Roosevelt, 1928–1933*. Chapel Hill: University of North Carolina Press, 1991.

Hendrickson, Kenneth E. *Hard Times in Oklahoma: The Depression Years*. Oklahoma City: Oklahoma Historical Society, 1983.

Himmelstein, Jerome. *To the Right: The Transformation of American Conservatism*. Berkeley: University of California Press, 1990.

Hodgson, Godfrey. *The World Turned Right Side Up: A History of the Conservative Ascendancy In America*. Boston: Houghton Mifflin, 1996.

Hollon, W. Eugene. *The Great American Desert, Then and Now*. New York: Oxford University Press, 1966.

_____. *The Southwest: Old and New*. New York: Alfred A. Knopf, 1967.

Hurt, Douglas. *The Dust Bowl: An Agricultural and Social History*. Chicago: Nelson-Hall, 1981.

Hyde, George E. *Indians of the High Plains: From the Prehistoric Periods to the Coming of Europeans*. Norman: University of Oklahoma Press, 1981.

Isenberg, Andrew. *The Destruction of the Bison: An Environmental History, 1750–1920*. New York: Cambridge University Press, 2000.

Jackson, Berenice. *Man and the Oklahoma Panhandle*. North Newton, Kans.: Mennonite Press, 1982.

Jackson, Wes, Wendell Berry, and Bruce Colman, eds. *Meeting the Expectations of the Land: Essays in Sustainable Agriculture and Stewardship*. San Francisco: North Point Press, 1984.

Jordan, Terry. *Environment and Environmental Perceptions in Texas*. Boston: American Press, 1981.

_____. *North American Cattle-Ranching Frontiers: Origins, Diffusions, and Differentiation.* Albuquerque: University of New Mexico Press, 1993.

_____. "Perceptual Regions in Texas." *The Geographical Review* 68 (July 1978): 293–307.

Kavanagh, Thomas. *Comanche Political History: An Ethnohistorical Perspective, 1706–1875.* Lincoln: University of Nebraska Press, 1996.

Kazin, Michael. "The Grass-Roots Right: New Histories of U.S. Conservatism in the Twentieth Century." *American Historical Review* 97 (February 1992): 136–55.

_____. *The Populist Persuasion: An American History.* Ithaca: Cornell University Press, 1998.

Kemmis, Dan. *Community and the Politics of Place.* Norman: University of Oklahoma Press, 1990.

Kenner, Charles. *A History of New Mexican–Plains Indian Relations.* Norman: University of Oklahoma Press, 1969.

Kibbe, Pauline. *Latin Americans in Texas.* Albuquerque: University of New Mexico Press, 1974.

Klatch, Rebecca E. *A Generation Divided: The New Left, the New Right, and the 1960s.* Berkeley: University of California Press, 1999.

Knobloch, Frieda. *The Culture of Wilderness: Agriculture as Colonization in the American West.* Chapel Hill: University of North Carolina Press, 1999.

Kromm, David, and Stephen White. *Conserving the Ogallala: What Next?* Manhattan: Kansas State University Press, 1985.

_____. eds. *Groundwater Exploitation in the Great Plains.* Lawrence: University Press of Kansas, 1994.

Lawson, Marlin P., and Maurice E. Bakers, eds. *The Great Plains: Perspectives and Prospects.* Lincoln: University of Nebraska Press, 1981.

Leckie, William. *Military Conquest of the Southern Plains.* Norman: University of Oklahoma Press, 1963.

Levy, Jerold. "Ecology of the South Plains." In *Symposium: Patterns of Land Use and Other Papers,* ed. Viola Garfield, 18–25. Seattle: University of Washington Press, 1961.

Licht, Daniel S. "The Great Plains: America's Best Chance for Ecosystem Restoration, Part 1." *Wild Earth* 4 (Summer 1994): 47–53.

_____. "The Great Plains: America's Best Chance for Ecosystem Restoration, Part 2," *Wild Earth* 4 (Fall 1994): 31–36.

Lisle, Laurie. *Portrait of an Artist: A Biography of Georgia O'Keeffe.* Albuquerque: University of New Mexico Press, 1986.

Lookingbill, Brad. "A God-forsaken Place: Folk Eschatology and the Dust Bowl." *Great Plains Quarterly* 14 (Fall 1994): 273–86.

_____. *Dust Bowl, USA: Depression America and the Ecological Imagination, 1929–1941.* Athens, Ohio: Ohio University Press, 2001.

Lowitt, Richard. *The New Deal and the West.* Bloomington: Indiana University Press, 1984.

Maass, A., and R. L. Anderson. *And the Desert Shall Rejoice: Conflict, Growth and Justice in Arid Environments.* Cambridge: The MIT Press, 1978.

Malin, James C. *The Grassland of North America: Prolegomena to Its History, with Addenda and Postscript.* Gloucester, Mass.: Peter Smith, 1967.

_____. *History and Ecology: Studies of the Grasslands.* Ed. Robert Swierenga. Lincoln: University of Nebraska Press, 1984.

Matthews, Anne. *Where the Buffalo Roam: The Storm over the Revolutionary Plan to Restore America's Great Plains.* New York: Grove Press, 1992.

McCarty, John L. "Literature of the Plains." *Panhandle-Plains Historical Review* 13 (1940): 80–90.

Meinig, Donald W. *Imperial Texas: An Interpretive Essay in Cultural Geography.* Austin: University of Texas Press, 1969.

_____. *The Interpretation of Ordinary Landscapes: Geographical Essays.* New York: Oxford University Press, 1979.

Miller, Thomas Lloyd. *The Public Lands of Texas, 1519–1970.* Norman: University of Oklahoma Press, 1972.

Moore, John. *The Cheyenne Nation: A Social and Demographic History.* Lincoln: University of Nebraska Press, 1987.

Morris, John Miller. *From Coronado to Escalante: The Explorers of the Spanish Southwest.* New York: Chelsea House, 1992.

_____. *El Llano Estacado: Exploration and Imagination on the High Plains of Texas and New Mexico, 1536–1860.* Austin: Texas State Historical Association, 1997.

Myres, Samuel D. *The Permian Basin: Petroleum Empire of the Southwest.* Vol. 1, *Era of Discovery, From the Beginning to the Depression.* El Paso: Permian Press, 1973.

Nash, Gerald. *The American West Transformed: The Impact of the Second World War.* Bloomington: Indiana University Press, 1985.

Newcomb, William. W. *The Indians of Texas: From Prehistoric to Modern Times.* Austin: University of Texas Press, 1978.

Norman, Mary Anne. "Childhood on the Southern Plains Frontier." *The Museum Journal* 18 (1979): 49–142.

Nostrand, Richard. *The Hispano Homeland.* Norman: University of Oklahoma Press, 1992.

Olien , Roger M., and Diana Davids Olien. *Easy Money: Oil Promoters and Investors in the Jazz Age.* Chapel Hill: University of North Carolina Press, 1990.

_____. *Life in the Oil Fields.* Austin: Texas Monthly Press, 1986.

_____. *Oil and Ideology: The Cultural Creation of the American Petroleum Industry.* Chapel Hill: University of North Carolina Press, 2000.

_____. *Oil Booms: Social Change in Five Texas Towns.* Lincoln: University of Nebraska Press, 1982.

_____. *Oil in Texas: The Gusher Age, 1895–1945.* Austin: University of Texas Press, 2002.

_____. *Wildcatters:Texas Independent Oilmen.* Austin:Texas Monthly Press, 1984.

Opie, John. *The Law of the Land:Two HundredYears of American Farmland Policy.* Lincoln: University of Nebraska Press, 1987.

_____. *Ogallala:Water for a Dry Land.* Lincoln: University of Nebraska Press, 2000.

Owen, Edgar Wesley. *Trek of the Oil Finders:A History of Exploration for Petroleum.* Tulsa: American Association of Petroleum Geologists, 1975.

Paehlke, Robert. *Environmentalism and the Future of Progressive Politics.* New Haven:Yale University Press, 1989.

Peña, Devon, ed. *Chicano Culture, Ecology, Politics: Subversive Kin.*Tucson: University of Arizona Press, 1998.

Popper, Deborah Epstein, and Frank Popper. "A Daring Proposal for Dealing with an Inevitable Disaster," *Planning* 53 (December 1987): 12–18.

_____. "The Fate of the Plains." *High Country News* 20 (1988): 15–19.

_____. "The Reinvention of the American Frontier." *Wild Earth* 2 (Spring 1992): 16–18.

Prindle, David. *Petroleum Politics and the Texas Railroad Commission.* Austin: University of Texas Press, 1981.

Rathjen, Frederick W. *The Texas Panhandle Frontier.* Austin: University of Texas Press, 1973.

Riebsame, William. "The Dust Bowl: Historical Image, Psychological Anchor, and EcologicalTaboo." *Great Plains Quarterly* 6 (1986): 127–36.

_____. "Sustainability of the Great Plains in an Uncertain Climate." *Great Plains Research* 1 (1991): 133–51.

_____. "The United States Great Plains." In *The Earth as Transformed by Human Action,* edited by B. L.Turner II et. al. Cambridge: Cambridge University Press, 1990.

Riley, Carroll L. *The Frontier People:The Greater Southwest in the Protohistoric Period.* Albuquerque: University of New Mexico Press, 1987.

Robbins, Roy. *Our Landed Heritage:The Public Domain, 1776–1970.* Lincoln: University of Nebraska Press, 1976.

Robinson, Roxana. *Georgia O'Keeffe,A Life.* New York: Harper and Row, 1989.

Runte. Alfred. *National Parks:The American Experience.* Lincoln: University of Nebraska Press, 1987.

Samson, Fred B., and Fritz L. Knopf. *Prairie Conservation: Preserving North America's Most Endangered Ecosystem.*Washington, D.C.: Island Press, 1996.

Sauer, Carl O. *Seventeenth Century North America.* Berkeley:Turtle Island, 1980.

Scarborough, Dorothy. *The Wind.* Austin: University of Texas Press, 1988.

Schulman, Edmund. *Dendroclimatic Change in Semiarid America.*Tucson: University of Arizona Press, 1956.

Shepard, John, Colleen Boggs, Louis Higgs, and Phil Burgess. *A New Vision of the Heartland: The Great Plains in Transition*. Denver, Colo.: Center for the New West, 1994.

Sherow, James Earl. *Watering the Valley: Development Along the High Plains Arkansas River, 1870–1950*. Lawrence: University Press of Kansas, 1990.

Shields, Rob. *Places on the Margin: Alternative Geographies of Modernity*. London: Routledge, 1991.

Sinise, Jerry. *Black Gold and Red Lights*. Burnet, Tex.: Eakin Press, 1982.

Snider, L. C. *Oil and Gas in the Mid-Continent Fields*. Oklahoma City: Harlow Publishing Co., 1920.

Spielmann, Katherine A., ed. *Farmers, Hunters, and Colonists: Interaction between the Southwest and Southern Plains*. Tucson: University of Arizona Press, 1991.

Spratt, John Stricklin. *The Road to Spindletop: Economic Change in Texas, 1875–1901*. Dallas: Southern Methodist University Press, 1955.

Stegner, Wallace. *The American West as Living Space*. Ann Arbor: University of Michigan Press, 1987.

Thomas, Alfred Barnaby. *After Coronado: Spanish Exploration Northeast of New Mexico, 1696–1727*. Norman: University of Oklahoma Press, 1935.

Thompson, Paul B. *The Spirit of the Soil: Agriculture and Environmental Ethics*. London: Routledge, 1995.

Tuan, Yi-Fu. *Topophilia: A Study of Environmental Perception, Attitudes, and Values*. Englewood Cliffs, N.J.: Prentice-Hall, 1974.

Turner, Frederick. *Beyond Geography: The Western Spirit against the Wilderness*. New York: Viking, 1980.

Wallace, Ernest, and E. Adamson Hoebel. *The Comanches: Lords of the South Plains*. Norman: University of Oklahoma Press, 1951.

Webb, Walter Prescott. *The Great Plains: A Study in Institutions and Environment*. Boston: Ginn, 1931.

Weber, David. *The Spanish Frontier in North America*. New Haven, Conn.: Yale University Press, 1992.

Weber, David, and Jane M. Rausch. *Where Cultures Meet: Frontiers in Latin American History*. Wilmington, Del.: Scholarly Resources, 1994.

Weaver, Bobby D., ed. *Panhandle Petroleum*. Canyon, Texas: Panhandle-Plains Historical Society, 1982.

West, Elliott. "Called out People: The Cheyennes and the Southern Plains." *Montana: The Magazine of Western History* 48 (Summer 1996): 2–15.

_____. *The Contested Plains: Indians, Goldseekers, and the Rush to Colorado*. Lawrence: University Press of Kansas, 1998.

_____. *The Way to the West: Essays on the Central Plains*. Albuquerque: University of New Mexico Press, 1995.

Worster, Donald. *Dust Bowl: The Southern Plains in the 1930s*. New York: Oxford University Press, 1979.

_____. "Grassland Follies: Agricultural Capitalism on the Plains." In *Under Western Skies: Nature and History in the American West*, ed. Donald Worster. New York: Oxford University Press, 1992.

_____. *Nature's Economy: A History of Ecological Ideas*. New York: Cambridge University Press, 1977.

_____. *Rivers of Empire*. New York: Oxford University Press, 1984.

_____. *An Unsettled Country: Changing Landscapes of the American West*. Albuquerque: University of New Mexico Press, 1994.

Wrobel, David, and Michael Steiner, eds. *Many Wests: Place, Culture, and Regional Identity*. Lawrence: University Press of Kansas, 1997.

Wunder, John, ed. *Law and the Great Plains: Essays on the Legal History of the Heartland*. Westport, Conn.: Greenwood Press, 1996.

Wunder, John, Frances W. Kaye, and Vernon Carstensen. *Americans View Their Dust Bowl Experience*. Niwot, Colo.: University Press of Colorado, 1999.

Contributors

DAN FLORES is the A. B. Hammond Professor of History at the University of Montana, Missoula. He is the author of numerous books and articles, including *The Natural West: Environmental History in the Great Plains and Rocky Mountains, Horizontal Yellow: Nature and History in the Near Southwest,* and *Caprock Canyonlands: Journeys into the Heart of the Southern Plains.*

JOHN MILLER MORRIS, a native son of the Texas Panhandle, is the author of *El Llano Estacado: Exploration and Imagination on the High Plains of Texas and New Mexico* and *A Private in the Texas Rangers.* He is Associate Professor of Political Science and Geography at the University of Texas at San Antonio.

DIANA DAVIDS OLIEN, Senior Lecturer in History at the University of Texas-Permian Basin, has coauthored with her husband, Roger M. Olien, six books on the American petroleum industry. The most recent are *Oil in Texas: The Gusher Age, 1895–1945* and *Oil and Ideology: The Cultural Construction of the American Petroleum Industry.*

JOHN OPIE is author of *Nature's Nation: An Environmental History of the United States, Ogallala: Water for a Dry Land, The Law of the Land: Two Hundred Years of American Farmland Policy,* and the forthcoming *Virtual America: Sleepwalking through Paradise.* He is Distinguished Professor, Emeritus, at New Jersey Institute of Technology, and a lecturer in the Environmental Studies Program at the University of Chicago. He lives on the Indiana Dunes of Lake Michigan.

JEFF ROCHE, Assistant Professor of History at the College of Wooster, is a native of the Southern Plains. He is the author of *Restructured Resistance: The Sibley Commission and the Politics of Desegregation in Georgia,* the forthcoming *Cowboy Conservatism: The Emergence of Western Political Culture, 1933–1984,* and several articles and essays on the history of conservative politics. He received his Ph.D. from the University of New Mexico in 2001.

YOLANDA ROMERO grew up in Lubbock, Texas, and teaches at North Lake Community College in Dallas, Texas. When she earned her Ph.D. from Texas Tech University in 1993, she became the first Mexican American woman to receive a doctorate in history from a Texas institution. Her research interests include the northwest Texas area, as well as the role of Tejanos in the Vietnam War.

SHERRY L. SMITH is Professor of History and Associate Director of the William B. Clements Center for Southwest Studies at Southern Methodist University in Dallas, Texas. Her most recent book, *Reimagining Indians: Anglo Views of Native Americans, 1880–1940*, blends her research interests in the American West, American Indian, and U.S. cultural history.

ELLIOTT WEST is Distinguished Professor of History at the University of Arkansas, Fayetteville, and author of many books and articles, including the acclaimed *The Contested Plains: Indians, Goldseekers, and the Road to Colorado*. West is a social and cultural historian whose primary research fields are the American West and American Indian history.

CONNIE WOODHOUSE is a research scientist at the NOAA paleoclimatology program and the University of Colorado's Institute of Arctic and Alpine Research, both in Boulder, Colorado. She received her Ph.D. from the University of Arizona in 1996. Her research interests focus on the reconstruction of past climate variability from tree rings, and include climatology, paleoclimatology, and the applications of hydroclimatic reconstructions from tree rings to water resource management.

Index